A Historical
around
Mynyddislwyn
Mountain

by
Len Burland

Old Bakehouse Publications

Abertillery

© Len Burland

First published in November 2002

The rights of the author to this work has
been asserted by him in accordance with the Copyright,
Designs and Patents Act, 1993.

ISBN 1 874538 84 0

Published in the U.K. by
Old Bakehouse Publications
Church Street,
Abertillery, Gwent NP13 1EA
Telephone: 01495 212600 Fax: 01495 216222
http:/www.mediamaster.co.uk/oldbakebooks

Made and printed in the UK
by J.R. Davies (Printers) Ltd.

British Library Cataloguing in Publication Data: a catalogue
record for this book is available from the British Library.

Introduction

The author has long been interested in Mynyddislwyn Mountain and over the years he has walked it in every possible direction. As such, historical and other interesting information began to be collected, but not put to any use.

The book came about as a suggestion to the author to put pen to paper as a project in readiness for Millennium Year. Research has involved many miles of travelling to search out accurate information, including numerous visits to the National Library of Wales and the Royal Commission of Historic and Ancient Monuments, both in Aberystwyth, the Public Records Office in London and the Gwent Record Office. That research, along with countless hours visiting and talking to people who have connections with The Mountain, has resulted in this publication being a little late for the new millennium, for which I offer my apologies.

The author was involved with the costly Millennium Project to hang bells in the tower of St. Tudor's Church, Mynyddislwyn. All profits from the sale of this book will go towards that bell fund, to help in some small way towards their cost, and towards their future upkeep.

Throughout this book, the name Mynyddislwyn has many difficult spellings. They are not spelling mistakes, but as recorded in old documents. Similarly, the name Abercarne has an 'e' at the end, which was its correct spelling from earliest times until the late 1800s.

Contents

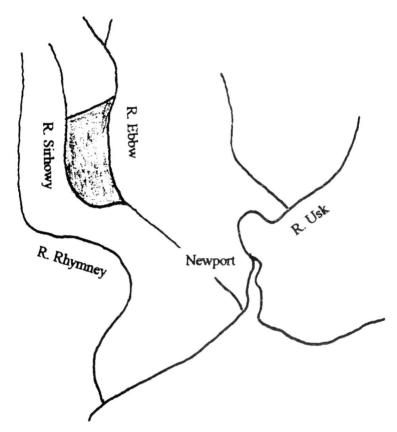

Mynyddislwyn Mountain, a valleys ridge in north west Gwent.

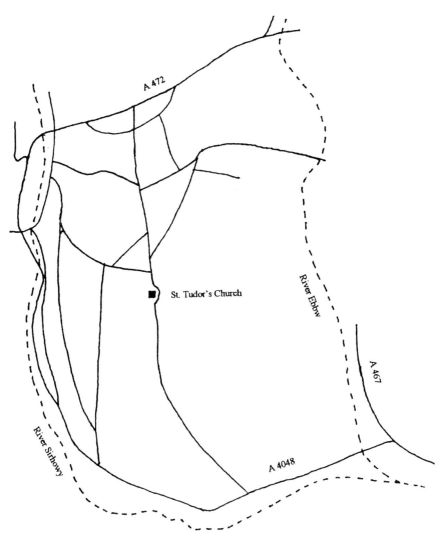

Mynyddislwyn Mountain, surrounded by the Ebbw and Sirhowy Valleys, with the A472 road as its northern edge.

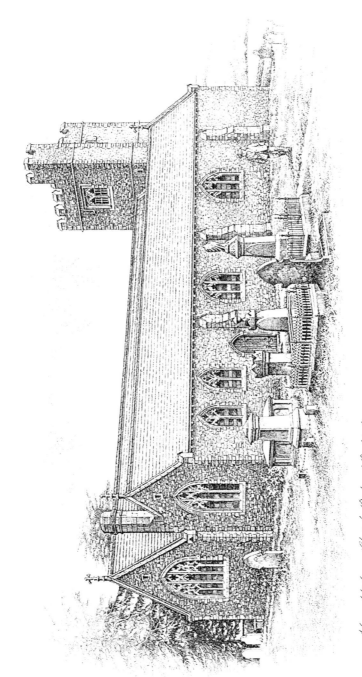

Aberystwyth Church Proposed Restoration 1907

Long Ago - A Background

The area covered by this book is an upland area in north-west Gwent. It is a ridge that lies between the Sirhowy and Ebbw Valleys. Most of our South Wales ridges run down to the coastal lowlands, but because the Sirhowy and Ebbw rivers join at Risca to become one, Mynyddislwyn Mountain is cut off from those lowlands.

The steep climb onto the southern spur of Mynyddislwyn Mountain did not stop the early advance of man. On the open common of Mynydd y Lan is a burial cairn from the Bronze Age period. Other similar cairns along neighbouring ridges have been dated to the Early Bronze Age, from 2,000 to 1,400 years B.C. At about 4,000 years old, this cairn is the oldest man-made structure on The Mountain.

Unfortunately, at some unknown time in the past, the cairn has been dug into, and no record survives today with any professional body of any find from that dig. The body interred within was probably laid to rest in a coffin-shaped stone lined cist, similar to one visible on the next ridge to the west (Mynydd y Grug) or the cist visible on the Gelligaer ridge. But the Bronze Age people sometimes cremated their dead and buried the remains in an earthenware pot, so a cremation pot could have been under this cairn.

The author's two dogs on the low mounded burial cairn on Mynydd y Lan.

Chronologically speaking the next remains that have been found on The Mountain are from Roman times. Two finds have turned up from almost 2,000 years ago. The portion of a base and sides of a mortarium of cream-coloured ware was found at Cwmnantyrodyn about 1950. The National Museum of Wales has dated it as Romano-British, possibly from the second century A.D.

1

During its manufacture, coarse grit was pressed into clay on the inside of the mortarium. Certain foods could be rubbed around the inside of the mortarium using a hand, with the coarse grit helping to grind down that food. It was a sort of mortar and pestle with the pestle replaced by the hand.

The remains of a Roman mortarium. The flat base and gently sloping sides can be seen.

This find was first reported in the Bulletin of Celtic Studies, published in 1952.

The other Roman find is a small copper-alloy figurine of a horse, only three inches (75mm) long. It was found along the northern edge of the Mountain, near Pentwynmawr, in 1949. The National Museum of Wales was again involved, and they have identified it as La Tene style from the Roman period. The large eye sockets probably held decorative objects, now missing. The four legs have been broken off above the knees.

Are the two finds indicative of a possible Roman or Romano British settlement in the area covered by this book?

The small figurine of a horse of the Roman period, found in 1949.

St. Tudor's Church is almost certainly a pre-Norman foundation. It is dedicated to the sixth-century Celtic St. Tudor. It is in a typical position for an early church, on a major ridge route but sheltered by higher ground.

Before the Normans reached South Wales our area was part of the Kingdom of Gwynllwg, and belonged to the great Welsh Church at Bassaleg.

By the early 1100s the Norman Lord, Robert FitzHamon had conquered much of Gwent and Glamorgan. One of his lieutenants was Robert de la Hay, who came into our upland area. The Benedictine Priory of Bassaleg, a few miles to the south, was founded by Robert de la Hay and his wife Gundreda between 1101 and 1120 on the site of the great Welsh Church. Soon afterwards, de la Hay conferred on the Abbey of Glastonbury (Somerset) Bassaleg and its subordinate 'churches', of which Mynyddislwyn was one, for the good of their souls and the souls of their ancestors. 'Monitistlon' was referred to in 1107. Its value to Glastonbury Abbey was the land that formed the parish, which was liable to the collection of taxes in the form of Tithes each year.

One clue to the venerable age of St. Tudor's lies in the ancient yew trees that almost surround it. Five such trees are to the south of the church with the dead stumps of one to the east, and one to the north. Originally there could have been more that may have died over the years. Add to this the roughly circular wall, or enclosure, around the burial ground to the east of the church, with the road running around it, and we can see an ancient site.

Very close to St. Tudor's church lie the remains of a castle mound or motte, almost certainly from that early Norman period, which would have pre-dated the stone church building that we see today. The motte (Twyn Tudur) was probably built as part of a campaign to extend Norman influence in the hills, possibly in defence of Glastonbury's claim to the church and its lands. On top of the motte there would have been a wooden stockade to protect the small number of troops stationed there. No evidence exists today of an enclosed Bailey attached to the motte, but excavation could reveal one.

The Cistercian Abbey of St. Mary of Caerleon, better known as Llantarnam, owned much of Gwent, of which our Mountain was part. In 1179 there was a charter drawn up by Howell ap Iorwerth, Welsh Lord of Caerleon, which lists 'Menet Eslin'. The whole of Mynyddislwyn Mountain became one of a number of Granges for Llantarnam Abbey, and parts of it were probably brought into cultivation by the monks and lay brothers to provide food, wool and leather for the Abbey. Those monks stationed away from the mother Abbey needed a place for worship. That grange was granted to Llantarnam at some time between its foundation by Hywel ap Iorwerth in 1179, and the Great Survey of church property in 1291.

'Menet Eslin' was mentioned in Pope Nicholas's Taxation of 1291 stating that taxes were fully collected by the monks of Llantarnam Abbey. The Survey mentions that there was a priest at 'Menedusteley'. The Bishop allowed him only a 'paltry stipend' of £4 a year. That meagre stipend was afterwards augmented by the grant of what we now call a Vicarage Farm. At that time Bedwellty Chapel had fallen into decay, a situation that appears not to have altered by the year 1441 when the parishioners in the Chapelry of 'Bedwelltie' forwarded a petition to the

Pope - *'The said parishioners of Bedwelltie are want to hear mass in the Chapel of Menetheslyn and now they cannot go by reason of floods breaking the bridges nor can the chaplain of Menetheslyn go to them'.*

The existence of an early church may imply a small settlement around it, which could have shrunk or disappeared at the time of climate deterioration in the early 1300s, and could have been replaced by the present pattern of dispersed farms.

Although on high ground, much of Mynyddislwyn Mountain is good farm land. During the 12th and 13th centuries when the climate was known to have been better, our area would have been suitable for arable farming. The area around the church was presumably cleared and under cultivation at the time the church was being developed in Norman times.

With climate deterioration in the 1300s the monks were probably forced to give up growing crops on The Mountain. The poor weather led to a decline in population and the monks would have found it increasingly difficult to recruit lay brothers. They probably had tenants on much of the land, paying a small fine at the start of their tenancy, then a fixed rent annually, plus a tithe. But they were peasant farmers.

By the mid 1300s the Bishops of Llandaff were claiming the tithes of Mynyddislwyn, along with Bedwellty, Bassaleg and Henllys.

The lands of north west Gwent were eventually absorbed into the Lordship of Newport and formed a part of the great upland Marcher Manor of Machen. That was subdivided, and our area fell into the Manor of Abercarne, centred around the Grange farm of Abercarne. This was the emergence of the Manor of Abercarne.

Up until 1536 when Henry VIII changed things, Mynyddislwyn Church, like every other church in the United Kingdom, was Catholic. After that date it became Church of England, and remained so until the formation of The Church in Wales in 1921.

Henry VIII seized the Lordship of Newport (including Mynyddislwyn) for the Crown. Most of the Lordship of Newport and great Manor of Machen was given by the King to William Herbert, future Earl of Pembroke, in 1547, and in 1560 Herbert bought from Queen Elizabeth what parts of our area that he did not own, including *'the town of Mynyddislwyn within the Lordship of Abercarne'*. So Mynyddislwyn Mountain became Pembroke lands. Llantarnam Abbey was rented out to John Parker. The first rent collected by Parker included £35-16-11$^{1}/_{2}$ (£35.85) for Mynyddislwyn.

William Herbert was succeeded by his son Henry in 1570, and the Second Earl of Pembroke had a detailed survey drawn up in that year, the earliest detailed survey to include Mynyddislwyn. It suggests that the area was being intensively farmed at that date and that the area under cultivation was expanding.

The survey tells us that most of the farms, or tenements, were small, ranging from half an acre to 6 acres. Half an acre and cottage was not much to live on, but there would have been animals pastured on 'the waste'.

Most of the properties listed in the survey are under the name of the tenant, with the properties not named, making identification impossible. However, there are a few exceptions - *'Lewis ap Rosser holds by indenture dated on the Feast of St. Andrews A.D. 1489 for term of 99 years, a water mill called Melin Brynau and one acre belonging to the same, paying yearly at the Feast of St. Andrew the sum of 6 shillings and 8 pence'.*

The above mill was Brynar Mill, mentioned later in this book as being in the Welfare Ground at Springfield.

In another survey of Abercarne Manor in 1631 is listed *'Brook called Nant Brynau'*, and also *'The Lord's waste lands called Monithe y Llan'*. It lists that there were no freeholders within the Manor of Abercarne, so all land at that time was held in lease from the Lord of the Manor (Earl of Pembroke). Among those tenants (who sub-leased out) in Mynyddislwyn were Henry Morgan, Esquire, Arnold Morgan, Gentleman, and Mathew Morgan. No doubt, their descendants eventually gained the freeholds to be part of Tredegar Estate. William Harry was listed as encroaching a parcel of the Lord's land called Craig y Mirion, containing 6 acres of Welsh measure, value 8 pence, in 'Monithusloyne'.

Another survey of Abercarne Manor was carried out in 1653, for the Lord of the Manor, Phillip, Earl of Pembroke. Again, there were no freeholders in the Manor, and the Commissioners stated that *'we do not know of any Bastard that do hold any lands belonging to this Manor'*. They stated that there was no peculiar fishing or fowling within the Manor. An interesting addition is that the Lord of the Manor had Mines of Coal and Quarries of Slate and Tile Stone upon his lands. There was no fair or market kept at any time of the year within this Lordship. Thomas David was the Lord's Bailiff, and he was paid £13 6s 6d a year.

After Civil War broke out in 1642, the period until 1660 saw Mynyddislwyn under Puritan rule. In 1645 Commissioners removed the bells from St. Tudor's church, possibly because they saw those bells as marring the simplicity of religious worship. There was a strong undercurrent of opposition to the new Puritanism. The curate in charge at Mynyddislwyn was a lay man called Henry Rees. He was reported to be *'not Godly enough'* and the Puritans ejected him.

The balance sheet of the Requestrators Accounts for Monmouthshire for 1650-51 show that £368 8s 10d was divided between seventeen Godly Gospellers of the Churches of Monithisloyn and Llanvaches, who went forth to promote the word of God.

The Pistyll MSS tells us that *'in the church was a stately statue gilded, a staff lying by it and a letter sealed up. The letters fair but fell to pieces when the air came to it. It was supposed to be an effigy of Sir Theodore Powell, patron on the Church'*. Nothing is known of that effigy.

A document of 1703 stated that the Right Honourable Thomas, Lord Viscount Windsor was the Lord of the Manor of Abercarne, while another document dated 1733 states that John Burgh of Troy, near Monmouth, was then the Lord. Burgh was succeeded by his son Rev. Henry Burgh before 1750, and he was succeeded by his daughter Maria and her husband Thomas Johnes, who sold the Manor to Samuel Glover in 1787. Glover sold the Manor to Richard Crawshay of Cyfarthfa Ironworks in 1808, and he in turn 'sold' it to his son-in-law Benjamin Hall for 5 shillings. In truth, he gave the Manor to Hall, but not as a wedding present as other writers have stated, because the gift was nearly eight years after

Hall's wedding to Crawshay's daughter Charlotte. The actual document stated that *'For the great esteem, regard, love and affection which Richard Crawshay had to his son-in-law Benjamin Hall, Richard Crawshay was desirous to give Hall the full benefit and advantage of the purchase, and to supply Hall with the purchase money'.*

So Abercarne Manor, and in particular Mynyddislwyn Mountain, came into the ownership of Hall. Under Hall's son, who became Lord Llanover, the Manor was absorbed into Hall's Llanover Estate, and although Manorial law has been abolished, Llanover Estate has been the landlord of many, and remains the landlord of many in our area.

Throughout most of its history, the Lord of the Manor of Abercarne personally owned all the land and buildings with his manor (except the church). Every person living here was subject to a lease granted by the Lord, to annual rents, and to a death duty in the form of best beast or chattel. Many rich people held land under lease and sub-leased it to tenant farmers, taking a percentage of the annual rent themselves. Since the mid 1700s freeholds were beginning to be sold off, to those rich enough to afford them. But those freeholders were still subject to Manorial laws, which were finally abolished in the 1930s. Much of the Manor of Abercarne was not sold, and was retained by the Lord. Such land became known as Abercarne Estate.

St. Tudor's Church

The parish church is dedicated to Saint Tudur, or Tudor, and is believed to date from the sixth century, the age of the Celtic Saints. He was reputedly a Welsh prince who came to this peaceful area and lived as a hermit above the nearby Nant Hafod Tudur. He was a celebrated preacher and missionary. He is credited with converting the district to Christianity, and was reputedly buried under the nearby Twyn Tudur mound (but there is a discrepancy of about five hundred years between the two structures, the mound probably being of late 11th early 12th century origin.)

In the oldest extant list of Welsh parishes, there is mention of Bedwas, Bedwellty and Llanhiddel. Adjoining Bedwellty is Plwyf Tudur ab Hywel (the parish of Tudur, son of Hywel), which must be the original name for our parish. That list is from a document said to have been compiled in the thirteenth century during the reign of Llewelyn ab Gruffydd, the last independent Prince of South Wales.

Another legend links the founding of the first religious settlement here with Yddon (or Iddon) the son of Ynyr, the Welsh Lord of Gwent in the sixth century. Yddon is said to have won a great battle against the Saxons, who attempted to invade Gwent. By way of a thanksgiving offer for that victory, he gave his lands near Llanarth to the Church *'in exchange for an eternal country'*. He became a hermit and dwelt in a cell on Mynyddislwyn Mountain. His name survives at Ton Iddon, one of the oldest surviving buildings on the Mountain.

Another tradition exists that takes us back even further in time, where Saint Paul preached here when he went on a pilgrimage to the Isles of the West.

Another tradition is that Caractacus (Caradoc) introduced Christianity to Gwent on our mountain on his return from Rome.

It was the legend of the founding of the Church that has given its name to our area. The original sixth century crude wattle and daub structure was started to be built on a piece of ground overlooking a grove where pagan ceremonies had once been practised. However, the new structure mysteriously collapsed on two occasions at night. Eventually the builders kept a night vigil and heard a celestial voice saying to them *'Myned is y llwyn'* meaning *'Go below the bush or grove'*. They abandoned the unhallowed site and moved a short distance down the hillside to begin building at the site that the present church building occupies. Over the centuries *'Myned is y llwyn'* could have been altered to Mynyddislwyn.

Mr. Col Cook told the author that many years ago, with other members of his family, he was ploughing the then rough ground in the 'Nineteen Acre Field' across the road and up-hill from the Church, when they hit stones which appeared to be the base of a structure. They knew of no record of a barn ever having been there. Could this have been the stone foundations on which the wattle and daub hermit's cell from the legend was built?

Another version of the Church's present position is that the Church was to have been built higher up the hillside, but that one of the priests in charge of the construction did not want to haul the building stones that far, and that where he rested was considered far enough up the hillside. He shouted to his comrades '*I'r llwyn, I'r llwyn*' (to the grove) which is where they started building.

Having read about Robert de la Hay and the Normans in the previous chapter, it appears that in the very early 1100s there was a church of sorts and valuable church lands at Mynyddislwyn. But there can be little doubt that the Church in question looked nothing like the grand structure that we see today. It would have been a small wooden building, like the castles in the area at that time. It would have been at least another hundred years before it was rebuilt out of local stone. Probably the first part to be built in stone was the tower, which could have been used as a place of defence in those unruly times, when the church as it then was would have been viewed by the local Welsh as a piece of Norman oppression. The nave and chancel would have been built of stone in the 1200s.

St. Tudor's Church, surrounded by its ancient and mighty yew trees, flanked by Twyn Tudor to the right and the Church Inn to the left.

In 1774 a resident clergyman (Edward Hyett) was appointed to Mynyddislwyn Church with a stipend of £40 a year. The tithes were not paid to the Vicar at that time.

Some time just before 1800 St. Tudor's Church was badly damaged by fire and many of the church records were lost. For some years the parishioners would have attended services at Bedwellty Church. When Archdeacon Coxe toured the area in 1799 and published his book about the tour in 1801, he made no mention of Mynyddislwyn Church. As his book mentions every other parish church in Gwent, it seems odd that he did not come here. The probable answer is that the church was in such a bad state of repair that it wasn't worth a visit.

About the year 1820 St. Tudor's Church underwent major rebuilding work, a fact that was recorded on a stone plaque, which unfortunately has become lost in recent years. Work must have been completed by 1822, because in July of that year twelve year old Henry Grant Hall died and was buried inside the church (he was a younger brother of Benjamin Hall of Abercarne House, Lord of the Manor of Abercarne, later Lord Llanover). A plaque on the vestry wall remembers that event.

Unfortunately, no record survives of that rebuilding programme, and there is no known description of St. Tudor's before that event. It seems likely that in the 1820 rebuild, the north wall was removed, to be replaced by the arches and pillars that survive today, and that the North Aisle was then built from new, almost doubling the size of the church. The whole structure was then covered by an enormous single span roof. Certain architectural features have disappeared from the church, namely the stone Chancel arch, possibly a wooden Rood Screen and Rood Loft above it, and spiral stairs up to that loft. Did these go with the 1820 re-build or were they desecrated by the Puritans 160 years earlier? We will never know.

After the rebuilding programme, the following extract from an affidavit sworn by John Llewellin in December 1829, Agent to Benjamin Hall, shows that accommodation for worship in the parish was still inadequate -

'... and this deponent further saith that the said Abercarne Estate comprizes the greater part of the said parish of Mynyddysllwyn, otherwise Monythusloyne... and that the present accommodation for the Celebration of Divine Service within the said parish is very inadequate to the wants of the existing population, amounting to 5,000 persons, or thereabouts, there being only one Church at the southern extremity of the said parish which affords very insufficient accommodation, and it would be for the convenience and advantage of the parishioners and inhabitants if additional accommodation for the celebration of divine service was provided. And this deponent further saith that it is therefore proposed to appropriate a piece of land, not exceeding one acre, situate in the central part of the said Abercarne Estate and of the said parish of Mynyddyslliwyn, otherwise Monythusloyne, for the erection of a Church for the celebration of Divine Service according to the rites of the Church of England, and that the said Benjamin Hall intends, at his own expense, to endow such Church when built'.

In 1907 St. Tudor's applied to the Bishop of Llandaff for permission to carry out a major rebuilding programme. Some of that work was carried out, much was not. The 'Faculty' as seen on page 14 outlines those plans. Part of the work involved lowering the floor inside the church so that the nave would be lower than the chancel. Over the centuries burials had taken place inside the church, some barely below the floor surface. Lowering the floor meant removing human remains. It was intended that bones from those graves should be kept at the base of the tower until the job was completed, when they would be reburied in the graveyard. The soil from that excavation was to be put on farm land near the church. The entire project outlined in the 'Faculty' was to be paid for by a lady patron, but it was reported to her that there were human bones in the soil being thrown on the field. In disgust, she withdrew all support and many of the grand alterations to St. Tudor's were never carried out.

Until the floor level was lowered the church had underfloor heating, run from a boiler at the bottom of the tower.

9

In 1946 the lead was stolen from the roof of the church. At that time lead was in short supply, making it very expensive. The lead was not missed until the caretaker entered the church after a downpour of rain and found a dreadful mess. The church itself was not in a financial position to replace the lead, so it fell to the good deeds of a few locals. Mr. Frank Withers (of the Howells and Withers bus company) was a local councillor with Mynyddislwyn Urban District Council, and a member of the church. He sought the voluntary help of men from the council workshop, and they worked weekends using metal panels from buses. They were Bert Williams, Herbert Jones, Keith Ferrier, and Les Jones. Councillor Withers paid for the materials.

The stained glass window over the altar is handpainted. It was donated by the Pritchard family of Crumlin, who ran a brewery there. It was in memory of their daughter. They asked the vicar if they could have their pet dog painted into the window, and the poodle is there now looking out over the congregation.

The modern stained glass window was given to the church by Jones the Builders, Bryn, in the early 1960s. The artist was John Petts of the Abergavenny area, famous for his window designs all over the world.

The large painting at the base of the tower was by Mr. Armitage, an Englishman who studied in France. All his works were large, either religious or of battle scenes. Some of his works were commissioned to hang in the Guildhall, London. His painting in St. Tudor's is from about 1856 and was one of his earliest works. It has no great monetary value, but is of interest to art historians.

There are two graveyards at St. Tudor's, the Old and the New. The new graveyard, part of the Old Waun, was bought in about 1975 when the old churchyard surrounding St. Tudor's became full. Some of the oldest gravestones are to be found near the south porch, where they were re-sited after being removed from within the church in about 1907. They originally formed the church floor. The original burial ground was to the south of the church, as in all old parish churches. In more superstitious and less crowded times, the north side of the church was not used for burials, but for festivals and games. Cock fighting was a popular pastime on this dark side of the church.

The font is not original, but was put in as part of the 1907 rebuilding work. Before that date there was a Baptismal Pool in the floor of the church, at the back of the nave in front of the tower arch. Originally people would have been Baptised in a nearby pool, filled from the stream running down between the Blacksmiths pub and the new graveyard.

In 1951 a Tortoise Stove was put into the church in the north aisle to help with heating. In the same year gas lighting was installed using bottled gas, taking over from oil lamps. Also during that year the War Memorial Plaque was fitted on to the south wall.

In the early 1900s the church had a choir, a flourishing Sunday School and a Youth Club. By the 1950s there was no choir, and the Sunday School closed in June 1961 as there were too few children living on the Mountain.

In the 1980s St. Tudor's Church was under threat of closure with St. Augustines at Pontllanfraith being preferred. The people gathered around and many who had not attended for some years voted with their feet and went back to St. Tudor's. The church is now in a very good state of repair having had financial support from CADW, Lottery Funding, and a very generous gift by Phineas James of Glebe Farm.

There were bells at St. Tudor's prior to the Civil War, but no details of them have survived. Records state that the bells of Mynyddislwyn and Gelligaer were removed during the period of the Commonwealth.

In 1752 two bells for Mynyddislwyn were cast at the bell foundry of William Evans of Chepstow.

In 1844 another two bells were cast at the Jefferies and Price bell foundry in Bristol (making a total of four), but at the beginning of the twentieth century there were only three bells in the church, prompting the speculation that one of 1752 had been damaged and was recast in 1844.

In 1917 there were three bells hanging in the tower, but the floor collapsed on a Sunday afternoon and the bells crashed to the floor of the tower. Two were damaged. When St. Mary's Church, Penllwyn, was built in the 1950s it received a bell from St. Tudor's, but when it was hung it made an awful noise and was found to be cracked. It was taken down and another bell was hung there in the 1980s. In 1999 the bell from Holy Trinity Church, Pentwynmawr was hung there, and the St. Tudor's bell was returned home. Holy Trinity was a Mission Church built in 1919 but was closed in 1987.

St. Tudor's three bells existed until 1999 when two of them were sent to Taylor's bell foundry at Loughborough to be melted down and recast, in preparation for the Millennium bell project. One was sent off in June and the other in December. The third bell was sent to Taylor's in January 2000 for the clanger to be replaced and the head stock altered. This third bell was one of the pair cast in 1844 and had been chimed until Millennium Eve as a Service Bell. It has now been re-hung at St. Tudor's as the Service Bell.

The above mentioned three bells were William Thomas and William Thomas, Church Wardens. Cast by William Evans 1752. 30^1/2 inch diameter.
John Davies, Hannah Morgan and John Jones. Cast by Jefferies and Price 1844. 31^1/2 inch diameter.
Jefferies and Price 1844. 26^1/2 inch diameter.

To mark the new Millennium it was decided to install a new peal of eight bells in the tower. Work actually began on Millennium Eve, and then a small group of volunteers worked every Saturday for 2^1/2 months in preparing the tower to take the vast amount of steel girder work needed to hang the bells. All of this steel work, and the bells, were delivered to the church on Monday 13th March 2000, and had to be man handled into the church. Unbelievably, the bells were hung after two very hard week's work, by the small group of volunteers and one professional bell hanger from Taylor's Foundry.

In 1947 eight bells were cast at the Whitechapel bell foundry in London and hung at Saint Luke's Church, Abercarn, to mark the twenty first anniversary of that church. They were hung for chiming only and not for full circle ringing, due to limited space in the tower.

11

Those bells were -

	DIAMETER			WEIGHT				
1.	2 feet	0 ins	3 tons	0 cwt	4lbs	F sharp	Treble
2.	2 "	1 "	3 "	1 "	5 "	E sharp	
3.	2 "	3 "	4 "	0 "	12 "	D sharp	
4.	2 "	5 "	4 "	2 "	17 "	C sharp	
5.	2 "	7 "	5 "	2 "	10 "	B natural	
6.	2 "	9 "	6 "	2 "	25 "	A sharp	
7.	3 "	1 "	9 "	1 "	12 "	G sharp	
8.	3 "	5 "	12 "	1 "	13 "	F sharp	Tenor

After Saint Luke's Church closed, three of those bells, numbers 3, 5, and 6 were stolen. The other five were rescued and were safely stored waiting to be re-hung at Mynyddislwyn when the bell project got under way. This project began in 1997 with an application for a Faculty and application for Millennium funding. The five Abercarn bells were to be used with the two damaged St. Tudor's bells (which were melted down and recast by Taylor's bell foundry at Loughborough in February 2000) and one completely new bell, making a total of eight bells for full circle ringing. In addition, the old 1844 bell has been re-hung to be chimed only as the service bell, making a total of nine bells in St. Tudor's tower. The total cost of the project has been estimated at over £45,000. No Millennium funding was obtained as the application was two weeks too late. A substantial part of the money has been raised through grants, donations and sponsorships.

St. Tudor's Bells in place in the tower.

12

While work was progressing on the bell project, other very important work was being undertaken. The roof needed attention and was re-felted and tiled. The walls were letting in damp in places so they were completely re-pointed using lime mortar. Windows were removed and sent off to a specialist firm for shot blasting to remove two hundred years of rust and paint, and now look like new, and when set back in place new sills were fitted. New doors and frame were added to the south porch, whilst inside the church it had become increasingly more dangerous to climb the spiral stairs of the tower with over 800 years of erosion. The most badly damaged stone stairs and newel post were removed and replaced with new. The massive pillars separating the nave from the north aisle were found to be sitting on rubble, so that was stabilised and encased in blocks of dressed sandstone. Finally, to show off all the new work, greatly improved lighting was fitted.

Over the years the many vicars of Mynyddislwyn have had different homes, some of which were farms on the mountain - Pentre, Cwmcaesyngrug, Glebe Farm, Pembrey House Pontllanfraith, Gilwern House (for a short time), and now the Rectory, Pontllanfraith.

Faculty

Early in the twentieth century it was proposed to carry out restoration and enlargement work to Saint Tudor's Church, Mynyddislwyn, which would have altered the outside appearance of the Church. Some of the intended work was carried out, much of it was not. The original plans for those intended alterations survive, together with the below printed Faculty.

Dated 22 April, 1907

Consistorial Court of Llandaff

Parish Church of Mynyddislwyn
County of Monmouth

FACULTY

JOSEPH EARLE OLLIVANT, Master of Arts, Vicar General and official Principal of the Right Reverend Father in God Joshua Pritchard, by Divine Permission Lord Bishop of Llandaff, lawfully constituted.

To all Christian People to whom these presents shall come or may or shall in any wise concern, and more especially to The Reverend Hugh Price James, Clerk, Vicar of the Parish of Mynyddislwyn in the County of Monmouth and in our Diocese of Llandaff; and to Trevor Coleridge Griffiths and Catherine Lewis, Churchwardens of the Parish aforesaid.

Greetings:-

- - - - - - - - - - -

Whereas it hath been represented and alleged unto us, by and on behalf of you the said Vicar and Churchwardens, in a Petition accompanied by plans and particulars, now deposited in the Registry of the Consistorial Court of Llandaff at 13 Castle Street, Cardiff and duly signed, and dated the 26th day of February, 1907:-

1. That the above Parish Church consists of a Tower 19 feet square, rising to a height of 48 feet to the top of the parapet coping from the present level of the Churchyard; Nave (including the portion used as a Sanctuary) 78 feet by 22 feet 6 inches; North Aisle, 51 feet by 16 feet 3 inches; Vestry at the West End of the North Aisle 15 feet by 19 feet, together with a modern South Porch and a small doorway in the South Wall, near the Sanctuary.

That it is proposed to restore and enlarge the above Church and in addition to general repairs the following work will be executed:-

To make good the floors and roof of the Tower, and to lower the level of the present floor of the Church to a depth of 2 feet 6 inches so as to use the original floor level, and to excavate a trench around the Church to a depth of about 9 inches below the floor level.

The Nave and South Aisle Roofs will be removed and the Nave and Aisle roofed in with trussed rafters, boarded and panelled on the underside, as shown by the new plans; the lines of the Nave Roof to correspond with the old drip stones now existing on the East Face of the Tower Wall. To open out the one ancient Arch of Arcade at the West End of the North Nave Wall. To remove the fireplace in present Vestry and its unsightly chimney-stack. To pull down the division Wall at the West End of the North Aisle, now forming the Vestry. To lower the Nave and Aisle Floors to the old level, and to lay them with Wood block flooring. To insert new Windows, of the design shown on the plans, of Doulting Stone, in the Walls of Nave and North Aisle. To build a New South Porch, and to pull down the part of present Nave Wall which is out of plumb, to rebuild this Wall, and to extend the Nave Eastwards by 12 feet so as to provide a Chancel, and to extend the North Aisle. Also to provide an Organ Chamber, Choir, and Priest's Vestry, and to construct a heating-chamber under the Vestry, all of which is shown upon the plans.

The restored Church will then consist of a <u>Nave</u> 60 feet long by 22 feet 6 inches wide; <u>Chancel</u> 29 feet long by 22 feet 6 inches wide; <u>North Aisle</u> 61 feet by 16 feet 3 inches; <u>Organ Chamber and Choir Vestry</u> 16 feet 3 inches by 10 feet; <u>Vestry</u> 16 feet 3 inches by 15 feet and <u>New South Porch</u> 8 feet by 7 feet. The Church will be heated by High Pressure hot water system, with radiators placed in the Window Recesses, with fresh air passing over them.

The Chancel will be furnished with Oak Seats, and the remainder of the Church will be seated with chairs to replace the old High Backed Pews constructed of yellow pine, stained and varnished.

The plans and specifications have been prepared by Mr. E.M. Bruce Vaughan, F.R.I.B.A. of Cardiff, under whose supervision the work will be carried into effect.

2. That save as appears by paragraph 6, no further private rights will be affected so far as can be ascertained.

3. That at a Vestry Meeting of the Parishioners duly convened and held on the 16th day of April 1906, and at a subsequent Church Meeting held on the 4th August 1906, the proposals were considered and resolutions adopted approving of the work. A copy of these resolutions is annexed thereto marked 'A'.

That it is proposed as funds permit to execute the work in the following sections, viz:-

1.	Stripping roof of Nave and Aisle, lowering floor to old level, putting in four new Windows, new Roof, flooring, etc. and the provision of 300 chairs.	£1,500
2.	Building new Chancel and Vestry.	£1,450
3.	Restoration of Tower.	£ 265
4.	New steps to Turret.	£ 50
5.	Building new Porch.	£ 50
		- - - - -
	Estimated Total Cost	£3,315

4. That owing to the very dangerous state of the Roofs of the Church, which were out of plumb to the extent of two feet, leave was, on the 20th day of July 1906, given by the Deputy Chancellor of the Diocese (with the concurrence of the Bishop), to proceed with the work of re-roofing the Church, which has since been completed. The late Incumbent of the Parish, Rev. John Jones Lewis, who had the matter of the proposed Restoration and Enlargement under consideration, died on the 19th day of October, 1906, and the Petitioner, the said Hugh Price James, was Instituted to the Benefice on the 22nd Day of January, 1907.

It is now intended to complete the work included in the first section. Towards the amount required there is a sum of £505 in hand, and an additional £200 promised. The balance required for completing this section will be raised by voluntary contributions, and in the meantime the deficit will be guaranteed by the Vicar and Churchwardens.

5. That the accommodation provided in the existing Church is for 177, but by the proposed enlargement seating accommodation will be secured for 327 Worshippers.

6. That in excavating a trench around the Church to a depth of 9 inches below the floor level it will be necessary to interfere with 24 Graves, the headstones of which are now lying flat, and of which a Schedule, marked 'B' is annexed to the Petition.

The Headstones of those numbered 1 to 7 near the Porch on the south side of the Church will be relaid *in situ*. Those numbered 8, 9, 10, and 11 which come within the line of the proposed Trench, will be taken up and affixed against the south wall of the Church as nearly as possible to their respective Graves. The Memorial Stones covering the Graves numbered 12 to 18, which will come within the proposed extended Chancel, it is intended to take up and affix against the east end wall, outside the Church. A Special Schedule of these Graves (to be deposited in the Parish Chest for future reference) will be prepared on Parchment, recording the original positions of such Graves, and of the removal of the Memorial Stones to the east end wall, as aforesaid. The Stones covering the Graves 19 to 24 will be relaid *in situ*. In no case will there be any interference with Coffins or Human Remains.

That for the purposes of the extension of the Chancel it will be necessary to take down from the East Wall (left of Chancel Window) a Memorial Tablet erected to the memory of William Edmunds (died 1850) and Sarah his wife (died 1857). This Tablet will, however, be affixed to the North Wall of the extended Chancel. That by reason of the proposed interference with Graves, as hereinbefore mentioned, and with a view to safeguarding as far as possible the rights of the Parishioners and others who may be legally interested therein, the Petitioner the said Hugh Price James as Vicar of the said Parish, has caused a notice to be inserted in the 'Western Mail' and 'South Wales Daily News' (both newspapers having a very large circulation in the County of Monmouth) in the words and form following :-

'Mynyddislwyn Parish Church

Notice is hereby given that it is intended to apply forthwith to the Consistorial Court of Llandaff for a Faculty for restoring and enlarging the above Parish Church. In carrying out the proposed work it will be necessary to interfere with certain Graves, a Schedule of which has been prepared, and, together with the plans, is in the possession of Trevor C. Griffiths, Solicitor, Pembrey House, Pontllanfraith (one of the Churchwardens) where they may be inspected and full information obtained as to the proposals. Any objection by the owners of such Graves should be sent in writing forthwith to The Rev. Hugh Price James, Vicar of Mynyddislwyn, Abercarn, Mon.'

The said Notice was advertised in the 'Western Mail' on 12th, 13th, and 15th, February, and in the 'South Wales Daily News' on the 12th, 14th, and 15th, February, and copies of the respective papers containing the said Notice are filed in the Diocesan Registry.

7. That subject to a Faculty the Plans have been approved by the Lord Bishop of Llandaff.

And whereas it being desired that a Faculty should be granted for the purposes aforesaid, We, the said Vicar General, did decree all persons having or pretending to have any right or interest in the said premises, and having any objections to allege, that they forward the same in writing to the Diocesan Registry, 13 Castle Street, Cardiff, on or before the Twenty sixth day of March, 1907, so that a day might be fixed thereafter for such persons to appear before Us, our Surrogate, or other competent Judge in this behalf in the Consistory Court to be holden at the Consistory Court within the Cathedral Church of Llandaff, then and there to show sufficient cause why our Faculty should not be granted to the said Petitioners for the purposes aforesaid, and further to do and to receive, as unto Law and Justice should appertain, under pain of the Law and contempt thereof, and further intimating or causing to be intimated to all persons so cited, that in default of such written objections, We the said Vicar General, our Surrogate, or other competent Judge in this behalf, would proceed to consider and decree a Faculty or Licence for the purposes aforesaid, or such of the same as might seem to us fit.

And whereas We have been duly certified by the Registrar of the said Consistory Court that no written objection or objections have been lodged as directed by the said citation, and no intimation has been received of any opposition to the work aforesaid.

And whereas it hath been further represented unto us that on the first day of April 1907, a Bond was duly entered into by the said Hugh Price James and Trevor Coleridge Griffiths, together with William Jones, Outfitter, and Albert Harries, Builder, both of Abercarn in the said Parish of Mynyddislwyn, for securing to Henry Rees of Pontllanfraith, in the same Parish, Builder, the sum of £1,130 10s 0d, being the amount of the Contract for executing the first portion of the work, as set out in paragraph 3 of the hereinbefore written Petition, and a copy of the said Bond is now filed with the proceedings in the Diocesan Registry.

THEREFORE WE, the said JOSEPH EARLE OLLIVANT, Master of Arts, Vicar General and Official Principal of the Right Reverend Father in God Joshua Pritchard, by Divine Permission, Lord Bishop of Llandaff, lawfully constituted, do by these presents give and grant unto you the said Petitioners our FACULTY for the purposes hereinbefore mentioned, and according to the representations made to us which are hereinbefore expressed and set forth, and subject to the following express conditions, that is to say

1. That a schedule of all the Graves with which it will be necessary to interfere, be prepared on Parchment (for deposit in the Parish Chest for future reference) setting out clearly the destination of the Headstones and particularly those belonging to the Graves numbered 8, 9, 10, and 11 on the Plan, which it is proposed to affix to the South Wall outside the said Church, and of the Graves numbered 12 to 18 which will come within the proposed extended Chancel, and the Headstones of which will be taken up and affixed against the East End Wall outside the said Church.

2. That all sanitary precautions be duly observed in dealing with the said Graves, such as the use of disinfectant and powdered charcoal, and the earth taken from such Graves be properly screened, and any remains be reverently reinterred under the supervision of the Vicar of the Parish, and that the Memorial Tablet referred to in paragraph 6 of the Petition be reaffixed on the North Wall of the extended Chancel.

3. That before proceeding with any of the work contemplated in sections 2, 3, 4, and 5, as set out in paragraph 3, satisfactory evidence shall be produced to the Diocesan Registrar that the necessary Funds are duly secured.

And provided always and upon condition that you take special care that the said works be carried out as soon as practicable, and so as to interrupt or interfere with the performance of Divine Service as little as possible, and be careful to fulfil with due diligence all other the conditions hereinbefore expressed or implied, the right and jurisdiction of the Ordinary in the premises being reserved.

Dated at Llandaff under our Seal of Office, the twenty Second day of April in the year of our Lord one thousand nine hundred and seven.

Work that was done on the church included -

Lowering the floor level of the nave by 2 feet 6 inches (750 mm) to the original floor level. This has meant stepping down into the nave after entering the south porch. It has also meant that the chancel is raised above the nave. The new floor level was laid with a wood block floor.

The south-east wall of the chancel was out of plumb by 2 feet (600 mm). It was taken down and re-built, and the join can be seen from inside the church. The old Priest's Door was removed, and a buttress added to strengthen the join in the wall. The huge single span roof was removed and replaced by two roofs, one over the nave/chancel, and another over the north aisle, totalling much less weight.

The old High Back Pews were removed to be replaced with chairs. The Three Tier pulpit was probably removed at this time, but is not mentioned in the Faculty.

A new barrel-vault ceiling was put over the north aisle in place of the lower flat ceiling that had existed.

The organ was removed from the north wall of the north aisle, and the fireplace and chimney stack were removed from the vestry.

Work that was intended to be carried out, but was not, included -

Extending the nave and chancel by 12 feet, and extending the north aisle by about 20 feet to square off the east wall.

The organ chamber, Priest's Vestry and heating chamber under the vestry in the extended north aisle, and outside steps down into that chamber were not built.

Removing the outside door into the vestry from near the north-west corner, and replacing it near the north-east corner of the north aisle.

The dividing wall between the vestry and north aisle was not removed, leaving the vestry where it had been. Seats were not added in the vestry area for the congregation.

Beautiful new windows were not added in place of the cast iron ones, and the three buttresses were not added outside the north wall.

The south porch remains as it had been, and was not replaced, and the worn stairs in the tower turret were finally replaced in the Millennium improvements in year 2000.

St. Tudor's Church, before the early 1900's alterations.

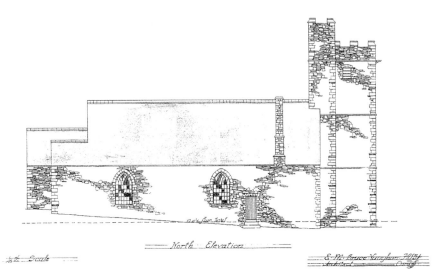

Mynyddislwyn Parish Church as it was before restoration.

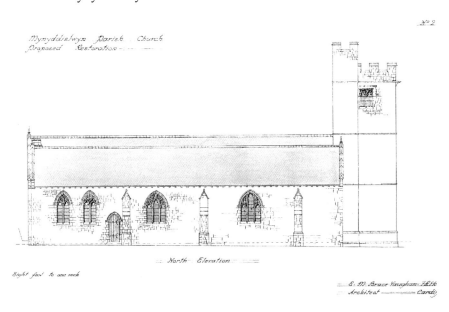

Mynyddislwyn Parish Church proposed restoration.

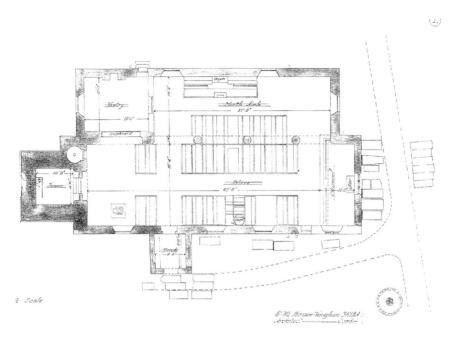

Mynyddislwyn Parish Church as it was before the restoration of 1907.

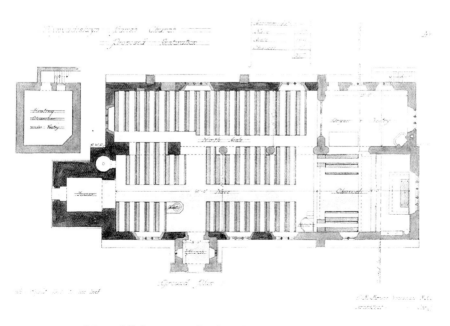

Mynyddislwyn Parish Church proposed restoration.

21

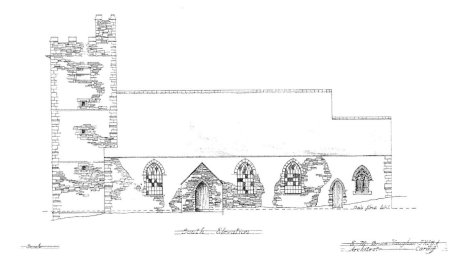

Mynyddislwyn Parish Church as it was before the proposed restoration.

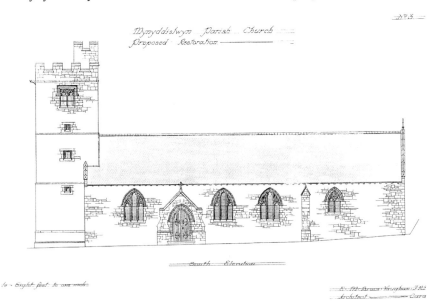

Mynyddislwyn Parish Church proposed restoration.

Abergelyswyn Church Proposed Restoration 1907

St. Tudor's Church as it would have looked if the proposed restoration work had been carried out in 1907. This was drawn by Michael Blackmore who made use of the original restoration plans.

In order to encourage the manufacture of woollen cloth the Statute of 18 Charles II c.4. was passed ordering burial in woollen; but not being sufficiently stringent it was repealed, and a second Statute, 30 Charles II c.3. was passed in 1679, which ordered that a fine of £5 should be imposed if an affidavit, duly signed and sealed, were not handed in within eighteen days of the interment. The Statute does not seem to have been enforced after 1696, and it was repealed in the reign of George III.

Certificate of Burial in Woollen 1696

'Wee Agnes Sawrey, widdow and Dorothy Tyson Spinster doe severally make oath yt ye Corps of Margaret Tyson of Gryzdale in the Parish aboves'd beeing Buryed the first of April 1696, was not put in wrapt wound up or Buryed in any shirt sheet shift or shroud made or mingled with Flax Hemp or any Coffin lined w'th Cloth or any materiall but what is made of sheep wooll only According to a late Act of Parliam't made for Burying in Woollen. In witness hereof wee the saide Agnes Sawrey and Dorothy Tyson have sett our Hands and Seals.

Capt: et jurat: primus dies (?)   *Agnes Sawrey*
Aprilis Ano Di 1696   *her mark X*
Coram me   *Dorothy Tyson*
    Myles Sandys   *her mark X'*

(This certificate is from Lancashire but was standard throughout England and Wales).

The Lych Gate at St. Tudor's, the roofed gateway to the churchyard, where in past times at a funeral, the coffin awaited the arrival of the clergyman. The coffin was then opened to check that the deceased was properly dressed in a woollen shroud.

Today only the top tier of the original three tier pulpit survives. The seats around the pulpit have also long gone, but were for the Churchwardens to sit in during a service. Each Churchwarden had a long wand, and if anyone was seen to be nodding off to sleep or to be misbehaving during a service, the wand was used as a gentle reminder that they had been noticed.

The Churchwardens' duties included reporting to the archdeacon concerning the state of the church fabric, the conduct of the parson, the attendance at church of the parishioners, their behaviour in and out of church, to keep order in church and in the graveyard during services, the conduct of alehouses and cases concerning sexual offences, defamation of character, brawling and disputed wills which were subject to trial in the archdeacon's court, sometimes referred to as the bawdy court.

The original three tier pulpit at St. Tudor's, in its original place in the middle of the south wall between the stained glass window and the clear glass window where the War Memorial plaque now hangs.

25

The interior of St. Tudor's showing the gas lighting, fuelled by bottled gas, which was installed in 1951.

In the summer of year 2000, following re-wiring, neat new powerful electric lights were fitted inside the church. This photograph was taken 28th September 2000 when the church was dressed for the Harvest Festival Service.

The last Bardic Chair won by Islwyn the poet at the 1877 Treherbert Eisteddfod, which has been at St. Tudor's for almost a hundred years. It was the property of Islwyn's last surviving niece Mrs Catherine Edmunds, of Pant Glas, who remarried to become Mrs. Lewis of Cwmcaesyngrug.

The event was recorded in the newspaper of the day. *'A solemn and inspiring service was held at the Parish Church of Mynyddislwyn on Sunday evening, when the Rev. E. J. Edmunds, vicar of St. Catherine's, Caerphilly, and grand nephew of Islwyn, dedicated the last bardic chair won by the celebrated Welsh poet, and which was bequeathed to the church by the late Mrs. Lewis, Cwmcaesyngrug, niece of Islwyn, and mother of the Rev. E.J. Edmunds.*

The chair was unveiled and formally presented to the vicar and churchwardens by Mr. T. Edmunds, Pennar, Mynyddislwyn, eldest son of Mrs. Lewis. Mr. T.C. Griffiths, senior churchwarden, formally accepted the gift on behalf of the church.

The service was conducted by Rev. B. Jones-Evans, vicar of Mynyddislwyn, and Rev. T. Williams, All Saints, Newport, read the lessons. An impressive address was given by Rev. E. J. Edmunds on the words "Blessed be the Lord God of our Fathers, who hath put such a thing as this in the heart, to beautify the house of the Lord". *Miss Doris Edmunds, granddaughter of Mrs. Lewis, played the organ.*

Other members of the family present were Mr. T. Lewis, Cwmcaesyngrug, Mrs. Stephens, Mrs. Thomas, Mrs. James, Mr. Morgan Edmunds, Mr. Islwyn Edmunds, and numerous grandchildren and other relatives'.

St. Tudor's choir in the early 1950s.
Back row - Holly Pritchard, Rita Morgan, Doreen Jones. Middle row - Cathleen
Symons, Ray Winnett, Christine Winnett, Danny Winnett, Rev. Fred Leslie Jones
(Vicar), Mr. Breeze (Lay Reader), Barbara Way, Mike Way. Kathie James (Organist),
Maldwyn Symons. Sitting - Glyn Symons, John Way.

The Rev. R.J. Summers
in his late teens as a
Church-Warden at
St. Tudor's, with the
Rev. J. McLaren Price,
Vicar of St. Tudor's,
The Bishop of
Monmouth, and
John Greedy,
Church-Warden.

The Bishop of Monmouth at St. Tudor's for a Confirmation Service in the 1950s.

Father Phillips receiving a thank-you gift from members of St. Tudor's after he had acted for nine months as Priest in Charge. The photograph was taken in the Church Inn in 1989.

Saturday 30th September 2000 saw a special Service at St. Tudor's to bless the new ring of bells. The Service was conducted in the presence of the Archbishop of Wales, the Most Reverend Rowan Williams. After the bells had been Dedicated, the bell ringers for the day stopped long enough for this photograph to be taken, with John James and Mrs. Rita Purnell (Church-wardens), Rowan, Archbishop of Wales, and the Rev. Ray Summers (Rector of St. Tudor's).

St. Tudor's Church before 1906, with two workmen on the roof over the Chancel. It shows the east wall rendered and partly white-washed.

Tithes

Tithes were payments made from early times for the support of the parish church and its clergy. Originally these payments were made in kind (crops, wool, young stock etc.) and usually represented a tenth part of the yearly production of cultivation and stock-rearing. Predial Tithes were the products of crop husbandry, such as grain, vegetables, woodland etc.

Tithes were divided into 'Great Tithes' and 'Small Tithes'. The great tithes were also called 'Rectorial Tithes' and were payable to the rector, and generally comprised corn, grain, hay and wood. The small tithes were also called 'Vicarial Tithes' and were payable to the vicar, and comprised all other produce.

Because the amount of crops, stock etc. collected annually in each district would have been large and bulky, Tithe Barns were built to store such Tithes. Also, because of its size, the parish of Mynyddislwyn was divided into three Hamlets, Penmaen, Mynyddmaen and Clawrplwyff, the latter covering the whole of the Mountain.

The ownership of Tithes within a parish could be bought and sold, which resulted in many of the Great or Rectorial Tithes passing into lay hands. They became the personal property of the new owner, or 'Lay Improprietor'. But the vicar usually continued to have the spiritual care of the parish and received the Vicarial or Small Tithes.

By the early 1800s there had been an increasing demand for the Commutation of Tithes, and in 1836 the Government got the Tithe Commutation Bill through Parliament. By that Act, a monetary value was worked out for the Tithe owned by each farm and piece of land in the country, and from that date money became a substitute for crops as a Tithe payment. Each land-user on Mynyddislwyn Mountain, and elsewhere in Wales and England, had to pay an annual Tithe Rent-Charge in lieu of payment in kind.

After the 1836 Act, the whole of the country was subjected to a Parish Tithe Survey, which provided an accurate measurement of the acreage of each parcel of land, each field, each home and garden, and recorded its state of cultivation. Such a record was an Apportionment, and in the parish of Mynyddislwyn, the Apportionment book was produced in 1839. (This has been much quoted in this book and is an accurate record of each landowner or tenant at that date, but only for that one year). In 1846 a Tithe Map was produced for this parish, with each field, building etc. accurately drawn on it.

The 1839 Tithe Apportionment Book gives us valuable information about life on the Mountain. All Titheable lands that had previously paid a Tithe on hay in kind, before the 1836 Act, now paid an annual sum of one penny from each and every farm instead.

As already mentioned, it was common practice for the Great Tithe to be sold to a Lay person. This happened in the parish of Mynyddislwyn, and the owner of the Tithe, the Lay Improprietor, was the Gore family for many years. The Apportionment Book tells us that the Great Tithes were payable to the Rev. Charles Gore and the Small Tithes were payable to the Lord Bishop of Llandaff, or his lessee. The fact that the owner of the Great Tithes was a Reverend gentleman was a pure coincidence. He had no connections with Mynyddislwyn Church.

The Bishop, or his Lessee, received £341 10s 10d by way of Rent-Charge. The Rev. Charles Gore received £240 14s 6d in lieu of corn, grain and hay as the lay owner of the Great Tithes. This gave a total of £582 5s 4d payable to the Tithe owners, annually.

The above named Rev. Charles Gore appears in the Land Tax Register for 1805, owning the following -

CARLLWYN TITHE FARM. Value £2 10s Land Tax 10 shillings
Landlord Charles Gore, Esquire. Occupier James Morris.

PENNER TITHE FARM. Value £4 10s Land Tax 18 shillings
Landlord Charles Gore, Esquire. Occupier James Morris.

The Land Tax was a non-secular tax imposed by the Government. Besides this tax, Tithes also had to be paid.

The County Record Office holds an account of *'Tithes collected from the Parish of Monythusloyne and Bedwellty for the Rev. Charles Gore for the Term of Ten Years ending Michelmas 1838'*.

		£	s	d	
1829	Mamhole Hamlet	66	8	6	
	Penmaine Hamlet	127	14	6	
	Clawrplwyve Hamlet	65	7	6	
	Monithmane Hamlet	64	19	6	total £324 10s 0d
1830	as above	65	3	0	
		110	3	6	
		70	3	0	
		60	2	6	total £305 12s 0d
1831	as above	71	1	6	
		82	7	6	
		55	13	0	
		55	6	0	total £262 8s 0d
1832	as above	71	2	0	
		82	9	0	
		73	9	0	
		57	0	0	total £284 0s 0d
1833	as above	71	2	0	
		84	9	0	
		73	19	0	
		57	0	0	total £286 10s 0d
1834	as above	70	5	6	
		85	1	6	
		59	6	6	
		54	15	0	total £269 8s 6d
1835	as above	67	7	0	
		91	8	0	

	£	s	d	
	50	3	0	
	53	12	0	total £262 10s 0d
1836 as above	56	18	6	
	92	4	0	
	53	2	0	
	51	7	0	total £253 11s 6d
1837 as above	53	8	6	
	133	1	6	
	65	0	0	
	58	10	0	total £310 0s 0d
1838 as above	61	10	6	
	132	17	0	
	57	15	0	
	65	14	6	total £317 17s 0d

On 30th March 1714 William Morgan of Penllwyn wrote to the Hon. William Gore, Esquire.

'Honored Sir,

Yours of the 27th instant I received and now return you thanks for your kind remembrances to your old servant in ordering Mr. William nothing better of wine to drink your health. Newporte fayre is upon the 6th of May next Sir that I conceive it best for Mr. Hipsly to come here the week following. Do desire to know punctually the day of his coming about a week before that I may give notice to all the tenants to come to him with their rents. As for tithe woods I conceive it a part of the Small Tithe and should belong to the minister of the parish, but Mr. Morgan of Penllwyn held the tithe clear and all the Small Tithe of the parish of Monythusloyne from the old Duchess of Beaufort and she from the Dean and Chapter of Llandaff for that all the Small Tithe of wood lambs and wool the minister and for it Mr. Morgan pays it him in money.

Long life and all prosperity. The constant prayers to the Great God of Heaven from him who is and desires to continue

Your most faithful servant
William Morgan

I have with thanks to God my health very well and my .... and have a good stomack to my meat.'

Another letter in the same bundle in the County Record Office reads -

'Endorsed

30th March 1717

The tithe of wood which Morgan of Penlloin claims. These for the Hon. William Gore, Esquire, at his lodgings in Charles Street, Covent Garden.'

- - - - - - - -

Another member of the Morgan family wrote from his home at Bedwellty Place (which became Plas Farm, and is now a public house in Blackwood) to Mr. Richard Eager of Post Office, Guildford, Surrey, on 25th July 1807.

'Sir,

After crossing the Passage (the Severn Estuary) I arrived home the same evening and the two following days spent in searching and inquiring into the particulars respecting the Tithes in the two following Parishes - Bedwelty hath three Hamlets, Ishlawcoed, Uwchlawcoed and Mamhole - and the Tithes divided as follows - Ishlawcoed and Uwchlawcoed all the Tithes Large and Small belong to the Bishop of Llandaff, and Mamhole the Large Tithes are the property of a Squire Gore and the Small the Bishop.

Monythusland hath three Hamlets, Mynyddmaen, Crospenmaen and Clawrplwyth, and the Tithes are divided as follows - all the Large Tithes in Mynyddmaen and Crospenmaen the property of Squire Gore and the Small Tithes are the Bishops, and Clawrplwyth, the Large Tithes are divided - the Customary or Copyhold (which are the greater part) the Large Tithes are the property of Squire Gore, and all Large Tithes on the Freeholds the property of the Bishop, and the Small Tithes in this Hamlet are the Bishops likewise - and hath being rented many years by Sir Charles Morgan of Tredegar - after inquierry I find there is a Modus given for hay, I think, two pence and no more to be paid let the quantity be great or small.

Sir, I think the above is corect as I have not spared pains or labour to gain every information as I promised you at the Passage House. Shall be obliged to you Sir for a line by return of post stating particulars. I will, if agreeable, Rent the Tithes or Colect them for you Sir - and have no doubt but can bring satisfactory Testimonials of my caracter etc from some of the Acting Magistrates in this neiberhood or from bonders of Bristol where I formerly dwelt.

Sir I remain your
Honourable Servant
John Morgan.

Sir as I understood you acted in behalf of Dr. Watson, Bishop of Llandaff, I have made all the inquiry I could respecting Machon, am informed it is a gift of Sir Charles Morgan and the Bishop have only the four following Parishes - Bedwelty, Monythusland, Coedkernue and St. Brides Wentlog - but (I think) Bedworst is the property of Dr. Watson.

Yours in haste
John Morgan'

The Primary Visitation of Bishop Ewer

In 1763 Dr. John Ewer, Bishop of Llandaff, made his primary visitation of his diocese, and in order to obtain a detailed knowledge of the state of each parish, he issued a questionnaire to be completed and returned by the clergy.

This questionnaire arrived at 'Mynithusloyne' just before the onset of the Industrial Revolution. The Bishop was interested in discovering what he could about his clergy and the ways in which they discharged their spiritual and pastoral duties, but he also inquired into charities, schools and almshouses.

In Ewer's time Llandaff diocese included almost the whole of Monmouthshire and Glamorgan, and it was largely unchanged from that of the first Norman Bishop, Ewer, at the beginning of the twelfth century.

The Bishop's letter -

Good Brother,
In order to obtain a proper Knowledge of the present State of my Diocese, I have sent you the following Queries, with vacant Spaces left for you to insert your Answers thereto. You will oblige me in sending as full and particular Answers as you can. I desire that this Paper, with the Answers inserted, may be return'd, sign'd by yourself, at my approaching Primary Visitation, and may be delivered either to the Register, or to my Secretary.

I heartily recommend both Yourself, and your Labours in the Church of GOD, to the Divine Favour and Blessing, and am,

Reverend Sir

Your very Affectionate Brother,

JOHN LLANDAFF

The return for 'Mynithusloyne' was signed *'Edward Hyett, Curate of Monuthisloyne'*, who at the same time was the Curate of Bedwellty. He was a graduate of Jesus College, Oxford, was ordained in 1740, and in 1741 was assistant to his father and namesake, who was Curate at Bedwas. He was also Rector at Wolvesnewton 1749-1771 and Curate at Kilgwrrwg 1756-1771.

The queries of Bishop Ewer and the answers of Edward Hyett are given below:

1. What number of families have you in your parish? Of these, how many are dissenters? And of what sort of denomination are they? Is there any licensed or other Meeting House of dissenters in your parish? Who teaches in such Meeting House?

Answer - We have about two hundred families in our parish, near one half of them dissenters, viz: Anabaptists have no meeting house in the parish, Presbyterians have a licensed meeting house, Philip David, Teacher, Independents have a meeting house. I do not know if it is licensed or no. William Edward, Teacher.

(The inhabitants would have attended either the Independent meeting house of Penmaen, erected 1694, or the Baptist meetings at Hengoed or Blaenau Gwent. The New Bethel brethren still met at a dwelling house).

2. Is there any Publick or Charity School, endowed or otherwise maintain'd, in your parish? What number of children are taught in it? And what care is taken to instruct them in the principles of the Christian religion, according to the doctrine of the Church of England, and to bring them duly to church, as the Canon requires?
Answer - We have no public or charity school in our parish.

3. Is there in your parish any Alms-house, Hospital, or other Charitable Endowment? Have any lands or tenements been left for the repair of your church, or other pious use? Who has the direction of such benefactions? Do you know, or have you heard of any abuses or frauds committed in the management of them?
Answer - We have no almshouse or hospital in our parish. We have lands valued at £1-10s. a year to the use of six poor widows. The curate and principal inhabitants have the direction of the benefaction. There are no abuses committed in the management of them.

4. Do you reside personally upon your Cure, and in your Parsonage or Vicarage-House? If not, where do you reside? And what is the reason of your non-residence?
Answer - I do reside upon my cure.

5. Have you a residing curate? What is his name? Does he live in your Parsonage or Vicarage-House? What allowance do you make him?
Answer - (No answer returned).

6. Do you perform Divine Service at any church besides your own?
Answer - I do not.

7. How often, and on what days is Divine Service perform'd in your church? If not twice every Lord's Day, with a sermon in the morning, for what reason?
Answer - Every Sunday and sometimes upon weekdays and holidays.

8. How often in the year is the Holy Sacrament of the Lord's Supper administered in your church?
Answer - Every month.

9. How many communicants are there in your parish? How many of them usually receive?
Answer - We have about forty that usually receive.

10. At what particular times, and how often, are the children catechiz'd in your church? Do your parishioners send their children and servants who have not learn'd their catechism to be instructed by you?
Answer - When the Welch Charity School was there once a fortnight.

(The Circulating Schools had been held in several parts of Mynyddislwyn parish. Hyett may have been referring specifically to that held in 1759-60, when thirty four children were taught).

11. Have you any chapels within your parish? What are the names of them, how far are they distant from the parish church, and by whom are they serv'd? Have you any chapels in ruin?
Answer - We have no chapels in our parish.
(The question referred to 'Chapels of Ease' erected in parts of a parish some distance from the 'other' church to enable the parishioners in those districts to attend worship with greater 'ease' than they could otherwise have done).

The Lewis Charity

The Van in Caerphilly was formerly the seat of one of the most important families in Wales. That family, Lewis of the Van, claimed descent from the ancient kings of Gwent and ruled as Lords in east Glamorgan. In the early 17th Century the Lewises acquired St. Fagan's Castle, along with many Manors and much land in South Wales. They were a very rich family.

A branch of the family became the Ap Richard, or Prichard, of Llancaiach, while another branch became the Lewises of Gilfach Fargoed Fawr (Bargoed).

In 1715 Gilfach Fargoed Fawr and its lands passed to Edward Lewis, and shortly afterwards he made his Will. That was a period in which considerable attention was being paid to the education of some of the poorer children in many districts. By 1720 there were schools in eighty-six parishes in Wales, and it is possible that Edward Lewis was aware of the good will being done in the district, for he left the bulk of his property for charitable works, including a school for the poor boys in his own parish (Gelligaer). This was eventually to become Lewis School Pengam.

Edward Lewis's Will appointed seven Trustees for certain property to be used to erect a school and pay a schoolmaster and to clothe and apprentice fifteen poor boys of the parish of Gelligaer; and to pay a 'Lecturer' to give sermons at 'Pedwelltee' (Bedwellty) and 'Monethuslin' (Mynyddislwyn) every three weeks.

The Trustees were to Elect one good learned and Orthodox Divine of the Church of England to preach two sermons on Sunday at the end of every three weeks, the one in the morning at the parish Church of 'Pedwelltee' and the other in the afternoon at the parish Church of 'Monethuslin'.

The Lectureship was restricted to the two parishes named above, and the school to the parish of Gelligaer. Why? A cousin of Edward Lewis was Gregory Perrott, Curate of the parishes of 'Bedwelte' and 'Munithuslan' so Lewis was probably aware of the spiritual needs of such a large area, served with difficulty by a single Curate. Perhaps that is why Edward Lewis was determined to assist his relative by a Lecturer to take part duly. The two parishes do not appear to have been in need of a teacher, for on 25th July 1704 Daniel Philip was licensed as 'Schoolmaster at Munith Istloyne' and on 30th November 1704 Henry Harris was also licensed to the same parish. So it seems that the two parishes had spiritual rather than educational needs.

In 1848 the Trustees of Edward Lewis's Will decided to rebuild the little school at Gelligaer as a much larger school at Pengam. The Trustees also agreed to apply to the Lord Bishop of Llandaff (Bishop of the Diocese) for a licence to authorise Divine Worship to be solemnised every Sunday, and on other days by the Church enjoined to be kept holy, not only in the adjacent portion of the parish of Gelligaer, but also to the inhabitants of the several crowded populous parts of the two adjoining parishes of Bedwellty and 'Monithislwyn', and which religious instruction would be additional to that furnished at the respective parish Churches at the two last mentioned parishes; and that in order to provide for the performance of Divine Worship the Trustees should be authorised to procure a good, learned and orthodox Divine of the Church of England to read prayers and preach a sermon. The Divine would be called a Lecturer, who would be paid from the Trust Fund of the Will, an annual salary of £150. In order to prevent any loss to the present Incumbents at Bedwellty and 'Monithislwyn' there should be paid to the present Incumbents the annual sum of £25 each.

The Lecturer should preach two sermons on Sunday at the end of every three weeks, the one in the morning at the parish Church of Bedwellty and the other in the afternoon at the parish Church of Monithislwyn, and should preach at the same Churches accordingly if allowed or permitted so to do by the present or future Incumbents of the parishes.

Over the years the Marriage Licence has altered. Below is a Licence of 1813 when the Bishop of Llandaff gave his permission for a wedding to take place at St. Tudor's, Mynyddislwyn. In fact, permission was granted by Benjamin Hall, Chancellor of the Diocese, the Bishop's legal adviser. This same Benjamin Hall was the father and grandfather of two other Benjamin Halls, both of whom were to became Lord of the Manor of Abercarne, and major landowners on Mynyddislwyn Mountain.

'Benjamin Hall D.D. Vicar General and Official Principal of the Right Reverend Father in God Richard, by divine permission Lord Bishop of Landaff lawfully constituted.

To our Beloved in Christ, *William George, Bachelor, and Ann Williams, Spinster, both of the parish of Mynyddyislwyn in the County of Monmouth and Diocese of Landaff, Health. Whereas it is alledged that ye have resolved to proceed to the Solemnization of true and lawful Matrimony, and that you greatly desire to cause and obtain that the same may be Solemnized in the Face of the Church,* ***We,*** *being willing that these your desires may the more speedily obtain a due Effect and to the End thereof That this Marriage may be Publicly and lawfully Solemnized in the Parish Church of Mynyddyislwyn by the Rector, Vicar or Curate thereof without the Publication or Proclamation of the Banns of Matrimony and at any time in the year,* ***provided*** *there shall appear no lawful Impediment in this Case by reason of any Pre Contract entered into before the twenty fifth day of March, One Thousand Seven Hundred and fifty four, Consanguinity, Iffinity, or any other Cause whatsoever, nor any Suit, Controversy, or Complaint be moved or now depending before any Judge, Ecclesiastical, or Civil, for or by reason thereof. And likewise that the Celebration of this Marriage be had and done Publicly in the aforesaid Parish Church between the hours of Eight and Twelve in the forenoon* ***We*** *for lawful causes graciously grant this our Licence and Faculty as well to You the Parties contracting as to the Rector, Vicar, or Curate of the aforesaid Church who is designed to Solemnize the Marriage between you in the Manner and Form above Specified according to the Rites of the Book of Common Prayer set forth for that Purpose by the Authority of Parliament.* ***Provided always*** *that if in this Case there shall hereafter appear any Fraud Suggested to us, or Truth suppressed at the time of obtaining this Licence, then the Licence to be void and of no Effect in Law as if the same had never been granted. And in that Case* ***We*** *inhibit all Ministers, if any thing of the Premises shall come to their Knowledge that they do not proceed to the Celebration of the said Marriage without consulting us or our Surrogate.* ***Given*** *under the Seal which we use in this behalf, this twenty seventh Day of March in the Year of our Lord, One Thousand Eight Hundred and Thirteen.*

E. Pearson
Registrar'

Benjamin Hall D.D. Vicar General & Official Principal of the Right Reverend Father in God Richard by divine permission Lord Bishop of Landaff lawfully constituted ———

To our Beloved in Christ William George Bachelor & Ann Williams Spinster both of the Parish of Trysyddyscwyn in the County of Monmouth & Diocese of Landaff Health Whereas it is alledged that ye have resolved to proceed to the Solemnization of true and lawful Matrimony

and that you greatly desire to come and obtain that the same may be solemnized in the Face of the Church We being willing that their wholesome desire may the more speedily obtain a due effect and to the End my Will that their Marriage may be Publicly and Lawfully solemnized in the Parish Church of Trysyddyscwyn

by the Rector Vicar or Curate thereof without the Publication or Proclamation of the Banns of Matrimony and at any time or the Year provided there shall appear no lawful Impediment on this Part by reason of any Pre Contract entered into before the Twenty fifth day of March One thousand seven Hundred and fifty four Consanguinity Affinity or any other lawful Cause whatsoever & nor any Suit Contrary to the Tenor of the Statute from henceforth before any Judge Ecclesiastical or Civil for or by reason thereof and likewise the Celebration of this Marriage to that End done & taking on the aforesaid Parish Church between the Hours of Eight and Twelve in the forenoon We for lawful Causes graciously grant this our Licence and Faculty as well the Rector contracting as the Minister who in or about the celebration of the ground Marriage between you on the Manner and Form above specified according to the Rites of the Book of Common Prayer set forth for that Purpose by the Authority of Parliament Provided always that in this Our Licence shall hereafter appear any Fraud suggested or any Truth suppressed at the time of obtaining this Licence then the same to be void and of no Effect as Law as if the same had never been granted And in that Case We inhibit all Ministers of any thing of the Premises shall come to their Knowledge that they do not proceed to the Celebration of the said Marriage without consulting us our Vicar General or Official Principal aforesaid Given this day of in the Year of our Lord One Thousand Eight Hundred and

Incumbents of Mynyddislwyn

Before 1744 the curates of Bassaleg and Llanhilleth held services at St. Tudor's

1744 - 1771	-	Edward Hyett (one bell hung in 1752)
1771 - 1815	-	John Rowlands
1815 - 1818	-	Thomas Thomas
1818 - 1840	-	Thomas Jones (Church restored)
1840 - 1843	-	John Evans
1843 - 1860	-	Isaac Hughes (two bells hung 1844)
1860 - 1899	-	John Griffiths - first Vicar of St. Augustine's
1899 - 1904	-	W.R. Compton Davies
1904 - 1907	-	J. Jones Lewis (Restoration work carried out)
1907 - 1915	-	H.P. James
1915 - 1951	-	B. Jones Evans
1951 - 1967	-	F. Leslie Jones
1967 - 1981	-	John McLaren Price
1981 - 1991	-	A. Brian Waters
1991 -	-	Raymond J. Summers

Monumental Inscriptions Inside St. Tudor's Church

At the side of the Altar

*The
remains of Edmund son of John Edmunds
were interr'd underne...
Jan the 2nd 1786 Aged
9 months 1...*

- - - - - - - -

On the east wall

*Sacred
to the memory of
William Edmunds
of Ty Gwyn in this parish,
(Yeoman),
who died April 16th 1850
aged 73 years.
Also Sarah
wife of the above
William Edmunds
who died October 29th 1857
aged 69 years*

- - - - - - - -

On the south wall

*To the Glory of God
and
in loving memory of
Rev. John Grifiths J.P.
for 39 years Vicar of this Parish
1860 - 1899
Born Aug 18th 1827
Died Mar 18th 1899
A faithful Minister and fellow
servant in the Lord.*

- - - - - - - -

*To the Glory of God
And in proud and Glorious Memory
Of those from this parish
Who sacrificed their lives by sea, land and air
During the World Wars 1914-1918 and 1939-1945
At the going down of the sun and in the morning
We will remember them.
Erected by subscriptions from the Mynyddislwyn Sheep dog
Trial Society and parishioners.*

Here lieth the body of Evan
Evans of Russiog in the
Parish, deceased February the
26 1749, aged 37 years
Here also lie Ye bodies of Anne,
Rachel and Thomas, son and
daughters of the aforesaid
Evan Evans by Sarah his wife.
Anne died June 29th 1744 aged 3 years,
Rachel died June 11th 1749
Aged 6 years,
Thomas died June 29th 1749 aged 2 years
- - - - - - - -
Sacred
to the memory of
Margaret, wife
of William George
of Abercarne who
departed this life
Nov 3rd 1795 aged
44 years
- - - - - - - -

Vestry Wall

.....
the a .....
trump ..... shall ....
blow and soul ... rd
bodys join ... millions
shall wish their lives
below had ... sh'd
as thine.

In Memory of John
Son of John Williams
of this parish who died
Jan 5 17783 aged ... years
- - - - - - - -
Sacred
to the Memory of
Henry Grant Hall,
third son of the late Benjamin Hall, Esquire, M.P.
of Hensol Castle in the county of Glamorgan
who after a long and painful illness
departed this life at Abercarne the 14th day of July 1822
in the 13th year of his age
the amiable qualities that he possessed
endeared him to all around him

43

continued   *And as a small testimony of love and respect*
                      for his memory
              this tablet was erected by his eldest brother
                      Benjamin Hall.
                      - - - - - - - -

On the north wall
                         Sacred
                    to the memory of
             John Jones of Abercarne in this parish
          who departed this life 23rd December 1865
                      aged 74 years.
                    Also in memory of
             Hannah Louise, daughter of the above,
      wife of Thomas Morgan Phillips of Llanhilleth House
             who died the 17th of December 1855
               and was interred at Glandwr
                        Also of
               Mary Jones, daughter of the above
                who died 6th December 1884.
            Also of Anne, daughter of the above,
             wife of Lodowick William Rees
                who died 17th October 1885.
            Also of Louisa, wife of the above
             John Jones who died June 21st, 1887
                      aged 84 years.
           Also of Sarah, daughter of the above
                who died Feb 12th 1927
                      aged 91 years.
                      - - - - - - - -

                    To perpetuate the
                   memory of Mr. Joseph
                    Phillips of Chapel in
                   this parish who departed
                    this life 27th of Dec
                   1804 aged 69 years.
            A faithful friend and husband dear
               a loveing father lyeth here
              the loss is great that we sustain
            but Christ has made our loss his gain.
             Also here lies the remains of Mrs.
             Margaret Phillips, wife of the said
             Mr. Joseph Phillips, who died Feb 9th
                   1806 aged 71 years.
              Mr. Daniel Phillips of Chapel di'd
                Nov 2nd 1820 aged 60 years.
          Also William, son of Mr. Daniel Phillips who

44

continued *died Oct 3rd 1821 aged 17 years.*
David son of Mr. Daniel Phillips died M'ch 11th.
1828, aged 43 years.
Mary wife of Edmund Llewelyn the youngest
daughter of Mr. Daniel Phillips di'd April 14th
1843 aged 36 years.
Also
of Mrs. Mary Phillips of
Chapel Farm
who died August 12th
1855 aged 82 years.
- - - - - - - -

In Memory of Mr. John Phillips
of this parish who died August 26
1832 aged 59 years.
Dywedwch mae da fydd I'r cyfiawn
Canys ffrwyth eu gweithredoedd
a fwynhant.
Also Mrs. Mary Phillips
of Troed rhiw Penner in
this parish who died February 1st
1850 aged 84 years.
- - - - - - - -

Sacred
to the memory of
Margaret Phillips
of Penher House in this parish
died May 31st 1837
aged 19 years.
Also
Daniel Phillips
died January 22 1842
aged 27 years.
Also
William Phillips
died November 3rd 1842
aged 65 years.
Also
Rachel Phillips
died July 7th 1843
aged 18 years.
Also
of Ann, wife of the above named
William Phillips
Died June 23rd 1847, aged 65 years.

Sacred
to the memory of
Margaret
wife of John Watters of Pantglase in this parish
who died Nov 6th 1774 aged 49 years.
Also the above John Watters
who died Dec 27th 1790 aged 69 years.
Also Elizabeth, wife of Thomas Edmunds
of the above named place and youngest daughter of the
above John Watters, who died November 28th 1806, aged 50 years.
Also the above Thomas Edmunds who
died November 14th 1808 aged 44 years.
Also to the memory of Margaret wife of John Edmunds of
the above named place and eldest daughter of
Mr. Daniel Phillips of Chapel Farm in this parish who died
July 6th 1826 aged 24 years.
Also
of the above John Edmunds who died
May the 27th 1866 aged 77
Years.
- - - - - - - -

FLAT STONES
Within the communion rails.

... Edmund Morgan
... departed this life the
... Anno Domini 1708
aged 51 years
... lieth the body of
... of the above Edmund
Morgan of Penllwyn Sarph, Esquire
who departed this life the twenty eighth
day of April in the year of our Lord
1757, aged 70 years.
- - - - - - - -

In the north aisle

Here lieth ye body of William
son of Joseph Phillips
died December 4th 1776
aged 9 months.
Here lieth the body of William
son of Daniel Phillips
who died the 27th of April 17..
aged 7 months.
- - - - - - - -

Here lieth the body of William
Ye son of Joseph Phillips of this parish
who died December 31st 1768
aged one year and 6 months.

46

In memory of Mr. William Phillips
of Penner in this parish
who died Nov 3rd 1842
aged 65 years.
Also Rachel, daughter of the said
Mr. William Phillips
who died July 7th 1843
aged 18 years.
Also of Anne,
wife of the above named Mr. William Phillips
died June 23rd 1847
aged 65 years.
- - - - - - - -

Here lies the body of John Phillips of this parish
who died August 26th 1832
aged 59 years.
Also Mary Phillips of Troed-rhiw-penner in this parish
who died February 1st 1850
aged 84 years.
- - - - - - - -

Here lies the body of Rachel
daughter of William Phillips of Penner in this parish
died March 23 1824
aged 11 months.
Also Margaret, daughter of the said William Phillips,
died May 31 1837
aged 19 years.
Also the body of Daniel Phillips
son of the above named William Phillips
died Jan 22nd 1842
aged 27 years.
- - - - - - - -

In memory of Lewis Thomas
of Abercame in this parish
who died Dec 29th 1762
aged 59 years.
Also the body of Thomas George of Abercarne
who died April 16th 1812
aged 59 years.
Also of Mary
wife of the said Thomas George
who died July 2nd 1833
aged 91 years.

A day trip from St. Tudor's to Barry Island in 1930.

A St. Tudor's Church outing in 1935.

Under a churchyard yew tree, to the south of the church, in 1924 were Mrs. E.M Thorne, Mrs. Peggy Morgan, Vera Suter and Emily Hughes.

Mrs. Rita Purnell, Churchwarden, explains the 'Gambler's Stone' to two pupils of a class group from Pentwynmawr Junior School, who were at St. Tudor's Church during an educational visit.

Why do Yew Trees grow in Churchyards?

There has been much speculation over an answer to this question, but there can be no proof after such a long time span, because the connection between yew trees and churchyards can be traced back to pre-Christian times.

The yew tree would have played an important role in many early cultures. During the Bronze Age it is known that yews were often planted at burial sites, but it is not known why. One suggestion is that early burial sites were located near an underground spring, or supply of water. Yews would have been planted to mark this area, often in the shape of a circle, a symbol thought to possess magical properties. It is possible that the yews, the circle and the burial site combined, could have cultivated a strong sense of place and shelter, which in time could have grown into the idea of protection from danger, or evil spirits. It has been speculated that the Celts viewed yew trees as symbols of immortality and continuity because of their longevity and evergreen appearance.

These pagan symbols remained, even after Christianity began to take root. Early Christians continued to use the same burial sites as their ancestors, thus continuing the association between burial and yew tree. Such yews became useful meeting places providing shelter for the early Christians. In time, churches were built to provide that shelter, with the yews remaining.

Yew trees kept their significant presence in churchyards into Medieval times and beyond. They were incorporated into many Christian ceremonies. Yew branches were placed in graves at funerals. On Palm Sunday yew branches were used as substitutes for palms. The Medieval name for Palm Sunday was in fact Yew Sunday. On Ash Wednesday, in some parts of Wales and England, the foreheads of the congregation were smeared with yew ash.

Yew trees also served practical uses. In 1307 Edward I ordered that yew trees should be planted as shelters from high winds near church doors. Churchyard yews could also be used to provide makeshift weapons in times of emergency. Yews were also used to keep grazing cattle off consecrated ground as its leaves and berries were poisonous to them. This would also serve to remind farmers of their obligation to keep boundary walls well maintained.

By Medieval times the relationship between churchyard and yew tree had been firmly established. From pagan mysticism to a popular Christian symbol of resurrection, the yew continues as a potent symbol of death and resurrection today.

Mynyddislwyn Church
by John Rowe

Sacred it stands serene and old,
That grey old church built long ago.
Thy tower still pointeth to the sky,
And links the earth to Heaven on high.

Within thy walls sweet peace was found,
To many who sleepeth under yonder mounds.
They served their church and did their best,
Their souls are numbered with the blest.

Oh monuments of stone you tell a tale,
Of friends I knew within those graves.
I read their names and breathe a sigh,
And wipe the teardrops from mine eye.

As daylight fades I look again,
At yonder church farewell to say.
Ring out thy bell in call to prayer,
Inside thy walls find solace there.

Those mystic yew trees seem to say,
We'll mark a spot for thee some day.
Thy days are numbered like us all,
To thee some day will come the call.

So down the rough old mountain road,
I wend my way towards my home.
Good-bye old church and if I'm spared,
I will come again thy joys to share.

Like the flowers that grow in yonder glen,
We too will fade we know not when.
The tolling bell in yonder tower,
Will indicate that solemn hour.

In thy churchyard let me lie,
Near the tower that points to the sky.
And there to sleep in sweet repose,
And lay my head beneath a rose.

Thoughts While Tramping the Hilltops of Gwent

by Roy Saunders

(Taken from a newspaper article of January 1939)

A cold wind and a flurry of sleet occasionally swept over my road between Newport and Risca, but inside the car it was warm and comfortable. I contemplated tramping over Mynydd Islwyn, but with every mile of the Sirhowy Valley I was losing my enthusiasm.

At the foot of a steep hill near Cwm-felin Fach I stopped to consider the prospects. Things looked pretty grim. After donning heavy shoes and mackintosh I felt more ready, though there was still the hiss of rain on the waterlogged road and the roar of the wind in the trees. But over it all came my sheep-dog's eager whine, a siren call of the hills. A waft of moorland scent came down, and the long, lonely mountain road claimed me.

A mile brought me within sight of the hilltop church of Mynydd Islwyn, surrounded by its great yews and the strange earth mound, Twyn Tudur, outside the churchyard. From that distance it stood out a lone, grey silhouette against the rainy sky at 1,100 feet up.

Cairn of Celtic Saint. It made me think of a lighthouse on a high rock above the ebb and flow of life in the valleys below. It has been a worshipping place for 1,500 years, so near and yet so far removed from the industrialism that surrounds it - a Soar-y-Mynydd of Gwent.

Many strange tales are told of this ancient mountain. A tradition exists that St. Paul preached here when he went on a pilgrimage to the Isles of the West, and that Caractacus here introduced Christianity to Monmouthshire on his return from Rome.

In the sixth century Iddon, son of the King of Gwent, by way of thanksgiving for a successful battle, turned hermit and lived on Mynydd Islwyn. Ton Iddon, a local farmhouse, still retains his name.

The huge burial mound, Twyn Tudur, adjoining the Churchyard, is traditionally believed to be his burial place. It is interesting to think of this early Celtic saint lying under his vast cairn beside the church he is supposed to have founded.

The present church was rebuilt in 1820 on the site of one erected probably in late Norman times, which might have been built on the site of Tudur's original sixth century chapel of wattles and clay.

Church Twice Collapsed. There is an old belief that the first church was built near the scene of pagan druid rites. On two occasions the finished church collapsed during the night. Eventually the builders heard a celestial voice bidding them 'Myned is y llwyn', so the hallowed grove was abandoned and the church built farther away, hence the name Myned is y llwyn - Mynydd Islwyn.

A thirteenth century document describes the place as Menet Eslin. In Pope Nicholas's taxation of 1291 it appears as Menedusteley. The living was then worth £4 a year.

Leland, writing in 1533, described the region as *'plentiful of woode as it were a forest ground myngelid with feldes but having little corn'*.

How different Leland would find the appearance of the Western Valleys today. In old writings such as his we get glimpses of the paradise that South Wales must have been.

This was the district that gave us William Thomas, the Welsh poet Islwyn, a famous and popular preacher. It was as a poet of wild nature that Islwyn rose to his greatest achievements. He was born at Ynysddu at the foot of Mynydd Islwyn and died in 1879.

Buried Treasure. When I reached the hilltop the elements seemed to be venting their rage on my lonely, mudsplashed figure. The grey bluff of a church resembled some old ship reaching out on the crest of some gigantic wave, taking the blast of the storm that poured up from the Sirhowy Valley. Even the sturdy yews had been forced back by the prevailing winds and seemed like waves along the ship's side.

I went inside to shelter from the storm, and in a corner behind a boarded partition a Sunday School was being held.

During a lull in the rain I walked through the graveyard and over the fields that sloped up to the church, the venue of one of Monmouthshire's sheep-dog trials. I climbed the 20 ft mound, Twyn Tudur, which legend says is the burial-place of an army of Roman soldiers. Another belief is that it contains treasure. One mercenary son of Gwent started digging for it, but a thunderstorm arose as he fled in a panic. The digging was never continued.

As I stood on the ancient tump the sound of thunder was rumbling in the distance again, far away among the Western Valleys now drenched under a pall of rain and gloom, and like the treasure seeker of old I thought that Mynydd Islwyn and I had better say farewell.

Ancient Gwent
A Peep at Pre-Reformation Times

by Mr. T.H. Phillips

(Taken from a newspaper article of November 1927)

To understand Mynyddislwyn Parish we must review its position in relation to the rest of the county of Monmouthshire. It forms an important part of the Princedom or Lordship of Gwent, which later comprised the hilly district enclosed between the rivers Usk on the east, and the River Rhymney on the west, extending from the Severn on the south, far up the hills of Breconshire on the north. The name Gwent means 'Smiling Land'.

Part of Gwent was designated Wentlooge, a corruption of Waun Llwch; Waun - a plain or meadow, Llwch - a lake. For the sake of Government, a family of ten or twelve was called a 'tithing'. In 1295 Wentlooge was called a county, which sent a jury of six free men and six burgesses to the Council of Newport, which dealt with the matters relating to Newport and Manor of Wentlooge. Mynyddislwyn, Abercarne, Penllyn, Bedwellty etc. were parts of Wentlooge. According to records, the population of the area in 1801 was 8,764, consisting of 4,261 males and 4,503 females, who inhabited 1,764 houses. Of the male population 2,136 were engaged in agriculture, and 1,025 in trades, manufactures and handicrafts.

Gwent was sometimes named 'Glywysg' after its first king, Glywys, son of Tegid, and its seat of government was Caerleon. Glywys flourished in the fifth century and was the founder of Machen Church. It was even said to contain mineral wealth.

Origin of Mynyddislwyn. Mynyddislwyn was one of the most ancient parishes in the district and was, prior to the introduction of Christianity into this country, without doubt a Druidical place of worship. The Patron Saint of Mynyddislwyn Church is Saint Tudor, one time spelt Tewdwr, who lived in the sixth century, and the mound near the church, Twyn Tudur, in all probability was built over the grave in which his remains were buried. In all likelihood he was an Archdruid. His residence is supposed to have been in an old building near the present church, which is called Hafod Tudur. Close by are several farms, respectively named Caerllwyn Mawr, Caerllwyn Ganol, Caerllwyn Isaf and Caerllwyn Bach, Caerllwyn meaning 'the field of the tree', which 'tree' had great prominence in Druidical worship. We can now conclude that Mynyddislwyn means 'The mountain of the grove'.

Served by Monks. According to the Bishop of Monmouth's speech at Abercarn in September 1924, there are records of 1102 which say that a great landowner in the area, Robert de la Hay, made a gift to the Abbot of Glastonbury of the old central parish church of Bassaleg, with its dependant chapels of Bedwas, Machen, Mynyddislwyn, Manmoel, and other little chapels such as Chapel Farm, Abercarn, scattered about the district. His son-in-law Roger de

Berkerolle (who had married Robert's daughter and had built a castle at Rogerstone) ratified his father-in-law's gift, and for a considerable time the chapels were served by the monks sent across the Severn by the Abbot of Glastonbury, or by monks who lived at Bassaleg. But in 1254 they had surrendered their property and the cure of the churches to the Bishop of Llandaff, on a perpetual lease, because they found it difficult to work the district from across the Severn. Right up to the Reformation, and even up to the date of the Disestablishment, the Bishop of Llandaff paid to the monks, and after their day to the Crown, the rent with respect to the Bassaleg Church and the dependant chapels. The Bishop of Llandaff appointed the Vicar of Bassaleg and Rectors of Bedwas and Machen, but for a long period Mynyddislwyn remained a dependant chapel of Bassaleg, served by a Chaplain, and the people came from Bedwellty to worship at Mynyddislwyn. But in 1441 the people of Bedwellty petitioned the Bishop for a chaplain, which was granted them, and later those chaplains became vicars.

Mynyddislwyn Parish, in my recollection, was much more extensive than it is now, for it reached from the Carne Brook in Pontywaun to near Llanhilleth in the Ebbw Valley, and from North Risca (Newtown) to Cwm Corrwg (Argoed), but now it is divided into Penmaen, Aberbeeg, Newbridge and Ynysddu Parishes, each with its respective vicar.

Along The Ridge

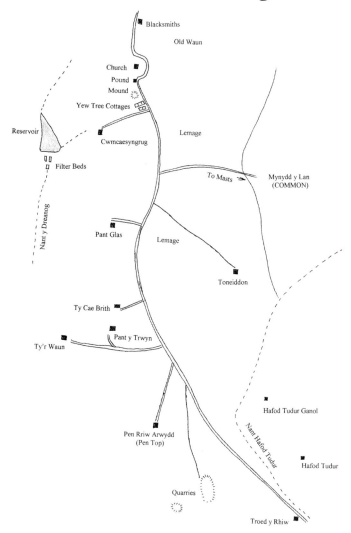

Blacksmiths

Old Waun

Church
Pound
Mound
Yew Tree Cottages

Reservoir

Lemage

Cwmcaesyngrug

Filter Beds

To Masts

Mynydd y Lan
(COMMON)

Nant y Dreanog

Pant Glas

Lemage

Toneiddon

Ty Cae Brith

Pant y Trwyn

Ty'r Waun

Hafod Tudur Ganol

Pen Rriw Arwydd
(Pen Top)

Nant Hafod Tudur

Hafod Tudur

Quarries

Troed y Rhiw

Leaving St. Tudor's Church behind, the road running south along the ridge is an ancient way. In fact, it does not run actually along the spine of Mynydd y Lan, but is lower down the slope in a slightly more sheltered position. The fact that the church and the mound of Twyn Tudor have been here for a very long time is an indication of the age of the road.

Immediately outside the graveyard gate is the position of the Parish Pound. Nothing remains of it now, but it was still in use into the 1940s. It was about the size of a house, with its four walls unroofed. The walls were high enough to stop anyone looking over into the enclosure and possibly retrieve their animals, high enough to have a door and not a gate, so that impounded animals were hidden from view. Animals that strayed, particularly into the graveyard, were put into the Pound and their owners had to pay to redeem them.

Tom Lewis with children John and Rachel, walking towards the Pound in 1930.

Almost a stone's throw from the Pound was Twyn Tudor, the great earth mound, or Twmp. Mention has been made of it in the previous chapter. Some say it is the last resting place of Saint Tudur, and maybe he was buried there, but under a much smaller mound, or cairn. That older mound could have been greatly enlarged, because as we see it today, Twyn Tudor was undoubtedly a Motte from the Norman invasion of our area in the early twelfth century. When Robert de la Hay arrived to plunder, he needed a secure base, and probably built the mound and erected a wooden stockade on top of it. All evidence of that stockade has now gone after eight hundred years. From the safety of his little 'castle' his soldiers could have controlled movement of the natives along the ridgeway.

The road forms the boundary of an area of land called The Lemage, which is opposite Twyn Tudor and stretches to left and right. The name has puzzled people, and there has been no satisfactory explanation. This author believes that the name could go back to the time that Twyn Tudor was a castle tump in the days of the Normans. They came from France, and Lemage could be the French words 'Le Mage' the margin, border or boundary. The edge or margin of a no-go zone for the native Welsh?

Whatever its meaning, today the Lemage is divided between two farms, Cwmcaesyngrug Lemage at 83 acres and Toneiddon Lemage (or Cae Rosser) at 54 acres, giving a total of 137 acres. The Lemage goes up-hill to the boundary wall of the Common, or Mynydd y Lan. For almost a hundred years the Lemage, and adjoining Old Waun, has been the home of the annual sheep dog trials on the Mountain. That topic is covered in the next chapter of this book.

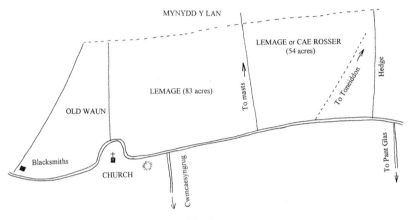

The Lemage.

The Common is a remnant from medieval times. It was traditionally the less productive part of a Manor that was used for the grazing of cattle and sheep. Local farmers with the right to 'Pasture' still graze on the common. These farmers, or Commoners, used to have the right of Estovers, to cut wood and bracken for fuel and bedding, and of Pannage, which allowed pigs to eat fallen acorns and beechnuts. But contrary to popular belief, it is not common to you and me, the public.

On the common can be seen ditches and banks that divide up the land. After countless years of nature taking its toll, the banks are now much lower than they used to be and the ditches have been silted up, but they can still be traced. Alongside the banks and ditches there are still some of the boundary stones, probably making it very clear whose land was whose. In the past, the ditches marked each farm's grazing rights, and the animals would have been accompanied by a shepherd whose job was to keep his master's animals on his own land. Today, a number of stones can be seen with initials carved on them - MWM, H, B. Legend tells us that it is here that Oliver Cromwell's troops lost some cannonballs as they passed this way. They may be found one day!

Just along the road was the site of Yew Tree Cottages. There were five cottages, three facing northwards towards Twyn Tudor, and two facing south, with gardens separating the two blocks. They were also known as Jacob's Cottages. In 1839 they covered an area of 23 perches, and were owned by Rev. William Lewis. The land that was to become gardens was in 1839 listed as pasture, with its tithe rated at two pence a year.

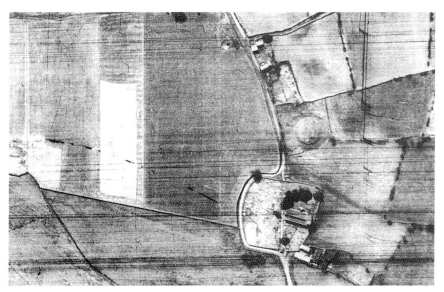

An aerial photograph taken in 1947. Showing the five Yew Tree Cottages a short distance from St. Tudor's Church. It also shows how farming has changed in the last half century. Almost filling half the photo is the Nineteen Acre Field, with crop marks. Today that field is used only for sheep grazing, and is the venue of the annual Sheep-Dog Trials.

The author's two dogs guard this boundary stone on the open common. Two of these stones survive, but old O.S. maps show that there were originally many more. The 'H' could be Hanbury of Pontypool Estate which still owns Toneiddon Farm near to the stones. The date of 1789 could be the date when Hanbury exchanged lands with Abercarne Estate, giving him a small foothold on Mynyddislwyn Mountain.

Quite a number of boundary stones survive on the common with the letters M.W.M probably meaning Mathew Weston Moggridge descendant of John Hodder Moggridge who started the Moggridge Estate in 1804.

This aerial photograph centres on St. Tudor's Church. Above it can be seen Twyn Tudor, and above that again are the five Yew Tree Cottages. Nearest to the Church were three cottages, and fronting on to the lane leading down to Cwmcaesyngrug Farm were two cottages. At the bottom of the photograph, in the fork in the road, is Coedyridder Cottage.

Looking towards St. Tudor's Church, with the motte of Twyn Tudor to the left of the photograph. In the immediate left foreground were the five Yew Tree Cottages, also known as Jacob's Cottages.

At the end of the 1947 winter, a group sit on a snowdrift outside Yew Tree Cottages. The snow has gone from the roofs of the cottages.

Christine Winnett and Olwen Waters outside Yew Tree Cottages. Behind the railings can be seen the road that runs from St. Tudor's Church towards Rhiw Hill.

Gary and Graham Waters with Zena Suter outside Yew Tree Cottages.

Two of the forenamed cottages fronted on to the lane leading down to Cwmcaesyngrug Farm. Mrs. Meyrick's little booklet* says *'once the home of the vicars of Mynyddislwyn, before the beautiful Vicarage, which is now called Glebe Farmstead or Homestead, was built'.* The 1839 Tithe Apportionment Book tells us that Cwmcaesyngrug was owned and occupied by Rev. John Davies. At that time it covered an area of 30 acres, 2 roods and 31 perches, and its annual tithe was rated at £1 15s 1d.

The little booklet of the childhood memories of Mrs. Ann Meyrick, of the Parish of Mynyddislwyn, about the years 1880-90.

In 1904 the widow Mrs. Catherine Edmunds, married Mr. Thomas Lewis. The couple are photographed outside their home at Cwmcaesyngrug Farm sometime after that date. Mrs. Lewis (above) died in 1924. Her obituary in the newspaper read - *'Amid tokens of respect the funeral of the late Mrs. Catherine Lewis, Cwmcaesyngrug, took place at Mynyddislwyn Churchyard on Thursday. Mrs. Lewis was the youngest daughter of the late Daniel and Elizabeth Howells, of Greenmeadow, and the last surviving niece of the bard Islwyn, to whose memory she had always been devoted. In the year 1879 she married Thomas, the only surviving son of Edmund and Elizabeth Edmunds, of Pant Glas, and in the year 1895 she was left a widow with nine children, eight of whom survive her. She married Mr. Thomas Lewis, The Caerllwyn, Mynyddislwyn, and the Electricity Department, the Town Hall, Newport, in 1904. Mrs. Lewis had many interests, but the work of the Church was nearest her heart always. She enjoyed the distinction of having been for several years Vicar's Warden of the undivided parish of Mynyddislwyn, and for about 20 years until her last illness she was Sunday School superintendent at the Parish Church. The funeral service was conducted by the Rev. B. Jones-Evans, vicar and rural dean. At the church Islwyn's famous hymn 'Gwel uwchlaw Cymylau Amser' and 'Lead, Kindly Light' were sung. Mrs. Jones-Evans presided at the organ. There were numerous floral tributes including a wreath from the Sunday School, and the children of the Sunday School threw bunches of lilies into the vault after the committal'.*

Down hill from Cwmcaesyngrug is still to be seen the site of Nant y Draenog Reservoir, in a little valley largely hidden from view.

The dam wall of Nant y Draenog Reservoir, with Cwmcaesyngrug Farm uphill.

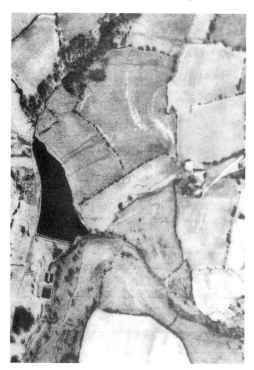

A view facing north, showing Nant y Draenog Reservoir and Filter Beds, photographed in 1947. To the right, or east, is Cwmcaesyngrug Farm.

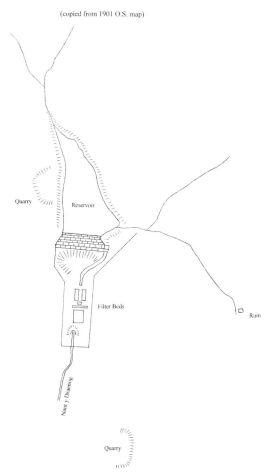

NANT Y DRAENOG RESERVOIR

(copied from 1901 O.S. map)

Quarry

Reservoir

Filter Beds

Ruin

Nant y Draenog

Quarry

Towards the end of the 19th century, the drainage and water supply for our area was in the hands of the Western Valley Gas and Water Company. By 1894 they had set in place their network of water supplies, which included Draenog Reservoir. The local need for a water supply was acute and was met by a local agreement. Draenog Reservoir was built without Act of Parliament or official authority, so officially it did not exist. The above date is borne out by the fact that that no reservoir, of any size, is shown on the 1880 Ordnance Survey map, but a completed reservoir is shown on the 1900 O.S. map which was surveyed in 1899. That map shows a reservoir with filter beds. This tells us that from the outset it was built for domestic drinking water. But why?

It has been assumed that it was built for Cwmfelinfach, but at the dates above, Cwmfelinfach did not exist, (other than a few scattered houses and farms), nor the Nine Mile Point Colliery. A clue *could* lie in Wattsville, where an old black

65

water pipe runs down the valley, parallel with the road, and crosses over Nant Hafod Tudor Brook. Water from Draenog Reservoir was piped down the Draenog valley and was turned away southwards across the breast of the hill, with the pipe sunk below ground level, to carry drinking water to Wattsville and Newtown (North Risca), two communities that had existed before 1894, having been built for the workmen at Risca Colliery.

Almost ten years after the building of the reservoir, Nine Mile Point Colliery was sunk and Cwmfelinfach came into existence. There can be no doubt that Draenog Reservoir then served the coal mining village of Cwmfelinfach.

It is possible that there was a natural hollow in the ground near the head of the Draenog Valley. If so, it would have been excavated much bigger and deeper, and the earth so removed was used in the dam wall, and held in place behind a stone facing. That stone probably came from the quarry below Pant Glas, while there is a small quarry beside the reservoir on its western side. That same quarry below Pant Glas would have given the stone for the buildings over the filter beds. During building work eight horses were used, three being stabled nightly in the yard at Caerllwyn Isha, while five were stabled in a barn in a field a little further north.

In 1909 the Urban District Councils of Abertillery, Abercarn, Risca and Mynyddislwyn sought Parliamentary powers to set up the Abertillery and District Water Board to meet the urgent water needs of the area, caused by the huge increase in people coming in to the new collieries. The Act received Royal Assent in August 1910. It was an *'Act to constitute and incorporate a Water Board consisting of the Councils of the Urban Districts of Abertillery, Abercarn, Risca and Mynyddislwyn in the County of Monmouth, and to authorise the Board to construct waterworks to vest in the Board the waterworks undertakings of the said Councils, and for other purposes'.*

The new Board took over from the Western Valleys Gas and Water Company. To get sufficient water to our area, the new Board set about building the Grwyne Fawr Reservoir in the Black Mountains, far to the north of Abergavenny. The new reservoir was at 1800 feet above sea level, so high in fact that water would flow by gravity to the service reservoirs in the mining valleys, and have no need to be pumped.

A small temporary reservoir was built at Grwyne Fawr in 1915 while the main reservoir and dam wall were being built, a job not completed until 1928. From 1915 Grwyne Fawr water flowed through a 16 inch mains pipe below ground to Cwmtillery Service Reservoir at 1330 feet above sea level. From there it flowed twelve miles in a 12 inch mains pipe to Nant y Draenog Reservoir, at 750 feet above sea level.

Abertillery and District Water Board ceased to exist in 1970. In 1974 the newly formed Welsh National Water Development Authority came into being, which closed Nant y Draenog Reservoir in 1979, when there was sufficient water from Llandegfedd Reservoir to make our little reservoir surplus to requirements.

The first reservoir caretaker was Daniel Jones of Caerllwyn Isha, who died in 1921, to be followed in that job by his son William until 1940. The next caretaker was John Waters, and then Alf Brazington, the last keeper.

In the last years of its existence the reservoir was used by a local angling club, but unfortunately the reservoir suffered at the hands of mindless vandals, and the club was forced to leave.

Today, the buildings over the former filter beds stand as roofless skeletons and the reservoir itself is dry, except for a short time after heavy rain.

The author was told that occasionally the reservoir would dry up and be unable to supply enough water for the locality in the early twentieth century. In the communities that depended upon the reservoir's water, springs would have to be used, where water ran pure out of the hillside, to be carried home in a variety of convenient vessels.

Running into the reservoir from the eastern bank are two small streams, both now dry except after heavy rain. The one running down from Cwmcaesyngrug has a broken grave headstone lying long discarded. Was it made in the nearby quarry below Pant Glas and was in the course of being taken to a graveyard when it broke? The other small stream, from Pant Glas, has a stone built ruin alongside. Two of the older generation of local farmers have said that this was once a Woollen or Flannel Mill. Both streams would have been running with water in the past, but with so much coal mining under the Mountain, the water table has been seriously affected, and when steady rain water falls, it now soaks down through the fractured strata of the Pennant Sandstone into the great voids below.

A broken, unfinished headstone which lies long forgotten near the Reservoir.

Leaving the reservoir behind, we will return to the road along the ridge. A little further on is the track up to Toneiddon Farm, the Layland of Gorse. It is supposedly the oldest farm building remaining on the Mountain, and is certainly the most remote. It was here that Tudur settled as a hermit when he came to the area, according to local legend.

This is the only farm on the Mountain which is part of Hanbury's Pontypool Park Estate, or is known to have been. In 1839 it was listed as 121 acres and 19 perches, with its annual tithe rated at £3 7s 2d. It was here that Oliver Cromwell spent a night during a Civil War campaign in South Wales.

Mrs. Meyrick's little booklet tells us *'At Toneiddon we find the home of the Williams', a very genteel family. The mother was left a widow when the children were rather young. She re-married, changing her name to Nicholas. Toneiddon was a very good Mountainous farm. They kept a large number of sheep, together with cattle and other animals. When their children grew up, married, and left them, they saw no point in living at Toneiddon, so they moved to lower pastures, taking over Caerllwyn Bach. Toneiddon was then taken over by the Thorne family. They soon adapted themselves to their new surroundings and became a strong link in the chain of friendship that bound the people of Mynyddislwyn together'.*

Mrs. Rita Purnell has delved into her family history to provide the following information on the farm. *'John Thorne, my great grandfather, moved into Toneiddon about 1897 with his wife Margaret and six children, John, my grandfather, Tom and Billy, and Susana, Rachel and Gwenny.*

My great grandfather was a carpenter, but had other skills. He farmed, owned a quarry just below Pen Top, built houses in Wattsville, and provided some of the stone for Wattsville School and the school at Ynysddu. He moved out of Toneiddon after his wife died and went to Wattsville to live, leaving the farm to John and Billy. Tom had married and moved out.

Susana married a Mr. Jones and went to live in Duffryn Farm, Wattsville, and later to Nine Mile Point Road. Rachel married a Mr. Stone and lived in Waunfawr Road, Crosskeys. Billy never married. He lived at Toneiddon most of his life but went to live with his sisters from time to time.

John married Ethel Thomas when he was 35 years old and she was 17. They had three children, Peggy, Mervyn and Vena. Grandfather John had rented land at Little Mill (Pontypool) and walked his sheep there. He would stay overnight and walk home again the next day. He also walked cattle to the moor at Goldcliffe (Newport) for the winter months. He would buy sheep at Brecon market and convey them home on the Brecon and Merthyr Railway to Maesycwmmer, then walk them up the Mountain. John died in 1950 at the age of 70. Mervyn Thorne then ran the farm with his mother (my grandmother) until she retired in 1960. She kept herself very busy, being involved with the church, was on hand to help if anyone was ill or having a baby, being actively involved with the Sheep Dog Trials, where she was the only woman on the committee for a number of years. She was involved with cooking the refreshments for the day of the Trials. She could also work in the fields with the men.

When my mother was a child my grandmother would buy a sack of flour, 28 lbs. of sugar, and most other food products in large quantities. She would butcher a pig and take the chitlings to a stream on the Lemage to wash them before cooking them, because there was no running water at the farm. She made black pudding and faggots and rendered the fat down into lard for cooking. She would then take the meat to Wattsville to sell it to her customers. The farm also had a milk round in Wattsville. The milk was taken down on horseback in side-churns.'

*Peggy and Ethel Thorne, mother and daughter, leaving Toneiddon Farm at the start of
their daily milk round, with the milk carried either side of the horse in a pair of saddle
churns, which were halfround, with a flat side against the horse's body. They walked the
horse daily down the Rhiw to Wattsville to deliver the milk to the doorsteps, into the
customers' own jugs, in the days before milk bottles. The round came to an end when
The Ministry stated that all milk had to be pasteurised.*
(The author apologises for the quality of this particular photograph due to the original camerawork).

*Mr. and Mrs. J. Thorne
of Toneiddon Farm, on
a day trip to Barry
Island in 1930.*

A little further along the road a track on the right leads down to Pant Glas. Although it is an old Long-House, as it stands today the farmhouse doesn't look that old, and certainly has no long-house look about it, with the beast house gone, and alterations to the outside of the farmhouse. The 1839 Tithe Apportionment Book tells us that it was owned and occupied by John Edmunds, and that it covered 100 acres, 2 roods and 23 perches, with its annual Tithe rated at £4 1s 8d. The Edmunds family lived here for a long time. Mrs. Meyrick's little booklet tells us *'Pant Glas Farm, where Mr. Edmund Edmunds and his family once lived as owner occupiers. Quite an aristocratic family, an air of superiority could be noticed on entering the farmyard. Dairy utensils gleaming on the wall in readiness for use. The lady of the house, a very dignified person, was always ready to extend a welcome to anyone who happened to call upon her. The old oak and mahogany furniture were a shining example of good order. An old oak dresser covered with pewter ware and other things that were used to adorn the old farmhouses of distinction'.*

Mrs. Catherine Edmunds outside Pant Glas in 1904. She had been widowed and in that year married Thomas Lewis. She sold Pant Glas and the contents of the house, which was the custom of the day, and moved with Mr. Lewis into Cwmcaesyngrug Farm. She is photographed with the last Bardic Chair to be won by her uncle, Islwyn, won at the 1877 Treherbert Eisteddfod, which was later presented to St. Tudor's Church.

70

Catherine Edmunds
photographed in 1880, a year
after her marriage to
Thomas Edmunds.

Below: The family of Catherine
and Thomas Edmunds outside
their home, Pant Glas, about 1883.
The little girl to the right of the
photograph was three-year-old
Elizabeth Edmunds, born 9th June
1880. Today the farmhouse is
unrecognisable from this photograph,
with the attached beast-house
and front wall long gone.
The house walls have been
raised and the roof angle
altered. Local artist Illtyd David
told the story of how the beast-house
was the venue for boxing bouts
between himself and Trevor and
Edmund Edmunds in their youth,
although their different sizes made
such bouts something of
a miss-match.

The Rev. Edmund John Edmunds and his sister Mrs. Elizabeth Stephens, photographed outside St. Tudor's about 1960. They were born at Pant Glas, two of the children of Catherine and Thomas Edmunds. His church was St. Catherine's, Caerphilly.

A newspaper article from November 1859 says *'Mr. Thomas of Pennar Colliery, lessee of a coal level at Pantglas, south of the church, has won a seam of coal three feet thick. An incline is to be constructed to take it down to the Llanarth Railway'.* If built, that tramroad incline could only have gone down into the Draenog Valley to Cwmfelinfach, where it would have joined John Jones's Tramroad near the later Nine Mile Point Colliery.

The farm has another link with coal, because in the 1880s Mr. W.E. Beddoe, who owned Black Diamond Colliery, near Gilwern House, sold that colliery and moved to Pant Glas Farm. Was he involved with coal mining there at that time?

Continuing along the old ridge road, lanes lead down to three farms, Ty Cae Brith, Pant y Trwyn and Ty'r Waun.

Ty Cae Brith is an old Welsh Longhouse built end-on into the hillside. It has a later extension giving it today an 'L' shape. Above the porch that covered the through passage from front to back, is a date stone with 'RP 1738'. In fact, this porch is probably a later addition to the original longhouse, so goodness knows when it was originally built.

In the early part of the twentieth century it was the home of the Morris family, who had eighteen children. Mr. Morris was from a family of twenty-one children, having been brought up at Pen Chwarra on the next hillside over. Mrs Morris was formerly Jenkins, and was also one of twenty-one children, having been brought up at Ty Llwyd Farm.

In 1839 the farm was owned by Colbrith Derby and covered 19 acres 1 rood and 26 perches, with an annual Tithe rated at £1 0s 5d.

In the field immediately below the farmhouse was a coal level. As there is little evidence of waste tips nearby, it is to be assumed that it was not a very profitable venture.

The date stone above Ty Cae Brith porch.

Close enough to be almost within talking distance of Ty Cae Brith was Pant y Trwyn, another old longhouse built end-on into the hillside. In 1839 it was owned by William Jones of St. Mellons and occupied by William Williams. It annual Tithe was rated at £1 9s 6d. The last occupant was Hubert Morgan. In the early 1990s the farm was in a very bad state of repair and was pulled down to be replaced by a new house (photographed over page).

Below the farmhouse were a number of coal levels and waste tips, suggesting that coal was actually worked from here, but it was probably of an inferior quality.

Pant y Trwyn Farmhouse, an old Ty Hir or Welsh Longhouse, with living accommodation, and the attached barn downhill from the house.

Pant y Trwyn was the home of Mr. John Lewis. He has written of his upbringing on The Mountain, which I now include.

'I, John Lewis, was born in 1926, the eldest child of Thomas and Doris Lewis, living then I believe at Birch Cottage, opposite Cae'rllwyn Bach. I had two sisters, Rachel born 1929 and Dorothy born 1931.

My father Tom Lewis was born 21st December 1868. His family, I believe, farmed at Pentre Farm. He had one brother George and a sister who married John Morgan, a blacksmith at Gelligroes.

Panty Trwyn, the modern house that replaced the old farmhouse in the 1990s.

My father had a previous marriage to Catherine Edmunds, whom he married in 1904, and they lived at Cwmcaesyngrug Farm. She was a widow with numerous children, namely John, Tom, Islwyn, Morgan, Rachel, Bessie, Louisa, these I can remember.

My mother was the eldest daughter of William and Rebekka Morgan, who at one time kept the Church Inn. They later moved to Pant y Trwyn Farm. We shared that farmhouse with my grandparents from about 1930 to 1934. We then moved to Yew Tree Cottages, which was close to the church. Pant y Trwyn had been the home of my great-grandparents John and Leah Jones in the late 19th century. John was killed in an accident in 1880, aged 32. I remember one Sunday afternoon being taken on a picnic to Ty Pwcca on the Machen Mountain, walking all the way there and back to Yew Tree Cottages.

My father walked from Mynyddislwyn to Newport to work in the General Strike. He then worked for Newport Corporation as clerk in the Electricity and Tramway Department and retired at 65 in December 1933. Father also helped out on the farm at Pant y Trwyn until we moved to Yew Tree Cottage. He then walked every day to Pennar Farm for 5 a.m. milking, for which he was paid two shillings per day. Father's stepson Tom Edmunds owned Pennar Farm.

This photograph, taken in 1930, shows the infant John Lewis with his parents and sister Rachel.

John Lewis feeding the pigs at Panty Trwyn in the early 1930s.

One item of interest is that my father was born in 1868 and my grandfather on mother's side was born in 1874, so he was older than his father-in-law. Both attended New Bethel School and talked to me about paying two pence per week for their education.

I attended Cwmfelinfach Council School from 1931-34, with sister Rachel starting two years later. We walked every day from Pant y Trwyn, and also from Yew Tree Cottages. We attended at Pentwynmawr for a couple of weeks. We went to school at the same time as Colwyn, Frank and Lavinia Cook, Trevor and Margaret Jones, and Katy James, to mention just a few. Other children that we played with were Arthur Arnold, Arthur Benham, John and Jean Cobley, and Doug Jones from the Church Inn.

Mother had sisters Nancy, Leah, Mary, Peggy and Dinah. Peggy died early in life, about 1922, whilst my grandparents kept the Church Inn.

Leah Jones, my great-grandmother, was a close friend of Islwyn the poet. She was renowned for being a good horse woman with an aptitude for riding side saddle. Her mare was called Doll.

My mother related to me her life in the early 1920s, before she was married, having to walk a cow from Pant y Trwyn to Newport Market. Gran Morgan would put a reserve price on the cow and if it failed to make the price, mother had to walk it back home. She then had to walk that cow to the next market, at Nelson.

Mother had great-grandparents Jones and Evans, one family came from Duffryn Farm (Wattsville) and the other from Glan yr Afon (across the river from Babell Chapel). Mother's great grandfather Jones drove teams of horses on the tramroad to Newport.

We moved from Mynyddislwyn in early 1936 to the village of Llangwm, but I returned to this area in the early years of the War and attended Pontllanfraith Technical School.

I stayed during the week with my grandmother at Gelligroes, going home at weekends. Sometimes I cycled to Llangwm on a Friday evening, and back again on Sunday'.

John Lewis's family at Panty Trwyn in the 1930s.

76

Tom Lewis with sister-in-law Leah Morgan sitting on the machine, making hay at Panty Trwyn in 1934.

Back up to the road, and the journey soon takes us to the top of The Rhiw, a steep hill leading down into Wattsville. The road is on the side of the Hafod Tudor Valley, with the stream way below. At the top of the hill is Pen Rhiw Arwydd, or Pen Top. The name translates as Head or Top of the Signal Hill. Is this name remembering the activities of the Norman soldiers nine hundred years ago when they occupied their Motte of Twyn Tudur?

Pen Rhiw Arwydd or Pen Top. Working the sheep ready for winter are Hubert Morgan (with his back to the camera), Morgan Cook and son Stuart.

77

However, the 1839 Tithe Apportionment Book called it Penrhyw Argoed. Probably the English speaking scribe had difficulty with the Welsh language. It was listed then as being part of the Llanarth Estate and tenanted by Henry Morgan. It covered 79 acres, 1 rood and 30 perches, with its annual Tithe rated at £3 13s 6d.

Mrs. Meyrick's little booklet tells us *'At Pen Top two spinster ladies lived, having come from Brecon about eighty to ninety years ago (about 1800). They knew their work and farmed the place well with the help of a local man, who entered their service as a boy and grew with them into fine manhood. The elder sister looked after the home and the farmstead, while Elizabeth (the younger) did the shopping. She rode her pony as Pen Top was very outlandish. She collected all the money that was due to them, did the marketing, the dealing and buying and selling. It would take a very smart farmer to outwit Lizzie Pentop'.* At the beginning of the 20th century it was the home of the Edmunds family. Mr. Edmunds married twice and from his first marriage he had Harold and Jinny, and from his second marriage he had Annie and Ivor. When Mr. Edmunds died his second wife moved to Abergavenny, leaving Harold as the farmer. He was known to all as 'Harold Pen Top'. He married Queenie, who at one time lived at Three Cocks Cottage, but they had no children.

A farm worker called Ginger Amblin from Wattsville worked at Toneiddon for five years, then went to Pen Top for the rest of his working life. Ginger was known for his mild swearing, everyone was called a 'Budder'.

Harold Pen Top had a milk round in Wattsville and Cwmfelinfach. The milk was taken down Rhiw Hill by horse and cart. During the War the Ministry zoned the selling of milk. In Wattsville there were a number of milk men - Jack Thorne, Toneiddon; Harold Pen Top; C.W.S; Mr. Lewis (Skimmer Lewis) from Crosskeys.

Harold farmed Pen Top until he died.

The barn is part of the original Pen Rhiw Arwydd Farm. The left end of the barn shows a crease or roof line where the original farm house was attached, making it a Longhouse.

*Rita and Verlie Morgan
in 1947 at Ben's Gate
on Rhiw Hill.*

Towards the bottom of The Rhiw is the aptly named Troed y Rhiw Farm, the Foot of the Hill. It was part of Tredegar Estate, which owned a small amount of land on the Mountain. The 1839 Tithe Apportionment Book tells us that its boundary was the Nant Hafod Tudor stream, and that its land stretched steeply up the north side of the stream until it reached Pen Top land. It is listed as having been 82 acres, 3 roods and two perches with its annual Tithe rated at £1 1s 10d.

From the front, the Cottage Farmhouse has the two gables which are typical of Tredegar Estate houses. It was probably built in the mid 1700s. Inside is the usual Inglenook fireplace and bread oven, but no spiral stone stairs. Instead the house had a straight flight of wooden stairs, unusual in an old house on the Mountain.

Outside, a Victorian extension which shows on an old photograph (now sadly lost), on the up-hill side of the house, was built on an older structure, as foundations show. That extension has now been replaced by a larger structure which has the appearance of being original, but it isn't.

The present owner, Tony Edwards, has come home. His great-grandparents had lived here. Today it is a Carehome for special needs people, and has been since 1990. The owner has bought land across the Nant Hafod Tudor stream, which was once Moggridge Estate, where a purpose-built Carehome called Ty Hafod Tudor is part of the complex.

Troed y Rhiw Farm as it was in the early 20th century. This brass etching was taken from an old photograph which has since been lost in a house fire. The original photograph did not show the girl in the upstairs window, but the person who did this etching saw her, and included her. Was there some supernatural force here?

Troed y Rhiw Farm as it is today. The original little extension shown in the previous photograph was removed and a much larger one was built in its place in the 20th century.

As already mentioned, across the stream, and stretching up to the top of Mynydd y Lan, was originally part of the Moggridge Estate. This little Empire was started when John Hodder Moggridge arrived in the Blackwood area in 1804. He was succeeded by sons John and Mathew, and they bought land in the Sirhowy Valley stretching up the side of Mynyddislwyn Mountain. In the latter part of the nineteenth century Mathew Weston Moggridge was the head of the Estate.

In the Nant Hafod Tudor valley, much of the old Moggridge Estate is now owned by the Forestry Commission, and covered by their dreadful conifers. In amongst those trees it is possible to find, with difficulty, the remains of an old farm called Hafod Tudur, or was it three farms? One part was listed as Ruin on the 1846 Tithe Map, probably a barn. The 1839 Tithe Apportionment Book called another part Hafodtowdwr, measuring 39 acres and 21 perches, with its annual Tithe rated at 13s 5d.

All that now remains of Hafod Tudor Ganol

In amongst the forest it is also possible to find Charcoal Platforms. These were small areas of land levelled out of the sloping hillside, where charcoal was made. Charcoal was used in the manufacture of iron until Abraham Darby came up with coke smelting in the mid 1700s. It was also used for re-heating iron for it to be shaped in a forge. There were no known iron manufactories in this part of the Sirhowy Valley, so where did the charcoal go? Close by, in the Ebbw Valley, was Abercarne Ironworks, with its Rolling Mill, Forge, Osmond Forge etc. which dated from 1750, and it would have needed all the charcoal that it could get. Another outlet for that charcoal could have been near Bassaleg, where the

Tredegar Forge was established on Tredegar Estate land by John Mayberry in 1764. That place has given its name to Forge Lane between Bassaleg and the M4 motorway.

The valley of Nant Hafod Tudor with Troed y Rhiw Farm to the bottom left, and the newly built Ty Hafod Tudor across the stream. The dense conifer forest hides the old Hafod Tudor Farm.

The old track along the ridge has come to an end down in the Sirhowy Valley. Earlier in this chapter, mention was made of The Lemage and its links with the annual Sheep Dog Trials. That topic is covered in the next chapter.

Mynyddislwyn Sheep Dog Trials Society

The Society was formed in 1904, a date that comes from a newspaper report of the 1938 Annual Dinner when the Chairman, Mr. T. Edmunds, said that the Society was formed 34 years ago and that he was one of the two founder members still alive.

The idea of a local competition between sheep dogs and their handlers came about when two men had a discussion in the Blacksmith's Arms as to who had the best dog. They were John Thorne (known as Jack) of Toneiddon and Bob Phillips. Soon afterwards a committee was formed which led to the formation of the Society.

Certainly up until the Second World War the Society had no permanent base from which to hold its regular Committee Meetings. It would appear that every public house in the area had its turn to play host to the committee - Nailer's Arms, White Hart, Greyhound Hotel, Red Lion (Newbridge), Carpenter's Arms (Blackwood), Pant yr Esk Inn, Llanarth Club, Blacksmith's Arms, Ivor Arms, Church Inn, Beaufort Arms (Newbridge), Pioneer Hotel (Cwmfelinfach), Three Horseshoes (Pentwynmawr).

The sheep dog Trials became so successful that in 1928 the Society formed an Agricultural Show to connect with it. The agricultural industry was one of the most essential for the life of the country and the Mynyddislwyn Society did all in its power to promote the welfare of that industry. For many years the President of the Society was Lord Tredegar.

Before the Second World War the Society was called The Mynyddislwyn Sheep Dog Trials and Agricultural Show. Its aim was to promote sheep dog trials and exhibitions of live stock, agricultural produce and horticulture. It was to become a very big event in the local calendar, as the 1938 programme shows, with classes as follows.

Sheep Dogs -   Open
Novice
Local novice

Horses -   Best mare and gelding suitable for underground work but which has not been underground.
Best mare and foal suitable for underground purposes.
Best cart foal.
Best yearling cart foal or filly.
Best two-year-old cart, gelding or filly suitable for agricultural purposes.
Best mare or gelding which has been working underground.
Best mountain pony.
Best pony to be ridden by a boy or girl under fifteen years of age.

	Best jumper to be ridden by a boy or girl under sixteen years of age.
Cattle -	Best dairy cow in full profit.
	Best pair of heifers most suitable for dual purpose.
	Best heifer.
	Best heifer calf.
Goats -	Best female goat in milk.
	Best female goat that has not borne a kid.
Sheep -	Best pen of three Welsh Mountain ewes.
	Best pen of three Welsh Mountain Ewe lambs.
	Best Welsh Mountain yearling ram.
	Best collection - ram, ewe and lamb.
	Open best Welsh Mountain ram lamb.

There was also a horticulture section. Best 1lb of butter.
Best home made fruit cake.
Best dressed foul.
Best pot plant.
Best four vases of summer annuals, four distinct varieties.

There was also space for stalls, and a booth for the supply of wines, spirits, beers, minerals and tobacco. Was this the reason for the presence of at least one police officer at the show each year?

An indication of the popularity of the show was that two car parks were provided for visitors, outside car park at one shilling parking fee and inside showground at two shillings. In 1938 the R.A.C. and the A.A. were invited to supervise the car parks but both declined because the event clashed with the National Eisteddfod in Cardiff and no staff would be available. But not all spectators had a car, and for those people a regular bus service was run by Gibbs buses, and later by Howells and Withers Bus Co. Today, entry into the Lemage field is through a wide pair of double gates. These were put up by Tom Cook to provide a wide enough opening for the buses to enter and turn.

Gate receipts and car park charges added up to respectable funds in the bank and for many years the Society gave generous financial support to the Royal Gwent Hospital and local Nursing Associations. Such donations had begun in 1913.

The Society's trials have always been held near the top of the Mountain, at the Old Waun on land jointly owned by the Blacksmith's Arms and Mr. Cook of Pant Glas, then at Toneiddon Lemage, and then at the Lemage opposite St. Tudor's Church (where it is now held), but at times it reverted back to one of the previous sites. Until recently, the Trials were always held on August Tuesday, at the beginning of August. The Society has always had an all-male committee, with the exception of a short period when two ladies served on that committee. They were Mrs. James, a schoolteacher from Ochr Wyth, and Mrs. Ethel Thorne of Toneiddon.

When World War Two came the Trials were suspended. In 1943 the Committee agreed to hold a Trial for the benefit of the Red Cross agricultural funds, which was held on the Old Waun site. In anticipation, two thousand entry tickets were printed at the admission price of one shilling, and a record crowd did attend. At the event, besides the sheep dog trials themselves, there was a demonstration by the War Agriculture Committee, which included hill grazing, potato diseases, utilisation of straw, diseases of dairy cows, fertiliser rationing, liming, and the care and use of machinery.

Following the very successful 1943 event, the committee agreed to hold another Trial in August 1944. In addition to the sheep dog trials there was musical chairs, children's horse jumping, and a local Galloway Race of one mile for horses not exceeding 14.2 hands. The newspaper report of the event stated that more than five thousand miners, on holiday with their families, and hundreds of evacuees in the district attended, making it the most successful Trial ever at Mynyddislwyn. Mrs. Thorne of Toneiddon Farm donated a basket of eggs to be raffled. The prize was won by her granddaughter Miss Rita Morgan, who gave them back, and they were sold to the highest bidder. Again, financial support was given to the Red Cross Agriculture Fund, handed over at the Annual Dinner.

In 1945 it was felt that the Society's title, Mynyddislwyn Sheep Dog Trials and Agriculture Show was misleading the public into thinking that an agriculture show was being run each year, and that the name should be changed to Mynyddislwyn Sheep Dog Trials Society. Galloway racing was done away with in 1946 and gradually over the years the annual event has become a sheep dog trials only.

Originally the Mynyddislwyn Trials were South Wales style only, but in the 1950s the National Style was introduced, so that for nearly half a century both classes have been run by the Society.

The Society has produced many celebrated trialists, and the Mynyddislwyn Trials has attracted the highest quality of competitor from far and wide to compete on the Lemage. The mid 1950s saw Harry Greenslade and dogs in his best winning form.

Another regular competitor was Herbert Worthington. His parents started married life at Penyrheol Caerllwyn (Three Cocks) but moved to the northern edge of the parish of Mynyddislwyn before Herbert was born. (He was a cousin of the author's mother). In 1963 he won The Supreme Championship of Great Britain at York with Juno. In the same year he was Welsh Aggregate Champion and International Aggregate Champion. In 1964 and 1965 he was Welsh Driving Champion, while in 1967 he was Welsh National Champion and Welsh Farmers' Champion. Besides Juno his other winning dogs were Hemp and Fly.

Mr. Les Suter was born in the shadow of the Mountain and was a member of the Society. His best year was 1964 when he won the Welsh Aggregate Championship and the Captain Whittaker Outwork Cup, and went on to become Supreme Champion of Great Britain at Drymen with his dog Craig.

Harry Greenslade, mentioned above, was a product of the coal mining valleys which produced men who worked their 'shift' in such unpleasant conditions that they sought relaxation in a variety of ways. Some kept pigeons, some took

Mr. Les Suter with Craig,
the Supreme Champion of
Great Britain in 1964.

up boxing, rugby, sung in choirs, or some, like Harry, worked dogs. He practised his art in an era when the 'hobby trialist' (as opposed to the farmer or hired shepherd) was a rare sight.

He was born in 1913 and was a collier. A serious accident underground in 1948 left him with two broken legs He was forced to take a less arduous job underground. As he recovered he built up his strength walking the hills with a dog at his side, and he turned to his favourite pastime, sheepdog trialing. He had no sheep of his own and owned no land on which to practise so he borrowed sheep from farmer friends who let him use their land.

In 1955 running at his first Welsh National, he became Welsh Singles Champion at Beaumaris, with Glen. He became Captain of the Welsh Team at the Edinburgh International. In 1956 at Haverfordwest, he was Welsh Champion again, with Glen. He also won the Driving Championship at the same event. In September he won the International Farmers Championship at Llandudno.

In May 1956 there was an invitation sheep dog trials at Hyde Park in London. On Saturday 19th May he was second with Glen, then on Monday 21st he was first with Gary. On that Bank Holiday Monday the newspapers reported a crowd in excess of 200,000 spectators standing ten deep around the mile long perimeter of the field. After his success at Hyde Park he was invited onto the popular radio programme 'In Town Tonight' sharing top billing with film stars Debbie Reynolds and Eddie Fisher. The following year there was another Hyde Park Trials and the Daily Express newspaper did Harry the honour of publishing a Gren cartoon.

SEE YOU IN HYDE PARK TODAY . . . . by GILES

'Certainly they're mine. Finest team of Welsh sheep dogs that ever came to London, mam.'

Sheep Dog trials in Hyde Park, London, on Whit Monday 1956. The crowd, estimated at 200,000 around the mile long perimeter of the field, saw Harry Greenslade take first prize.

The Society split into two groups in 1988 so that today there are two separate Societies on the Mountain each holding its own sheep dog trials. The new society is the Islwyn Sheep Dog Society which was formed in 1989 and held its first trials in that year.

87

Presentation of prizes at the end of the Daily Express invitation Sheep Dog Trials at Hyde Park, London, Whitsun 1956. Harry Greenslade is to the left of the photograph. On the Saturday he was second with Glen, and then on the Monday he was first with Gary.

THE BRITISH BROADCASTING CORPORATION

Head Office : Broadcasting House, London, W.1

Broadcasting House, 38-40 Park Place, Cardiff

TELEPHONE AND TELEGRAMS CARDIFF xxxx 72291.

Reference: 03/STS.   7th September, 1959.

Dear Mr. Greenslade,

    On Saturday, 1st October, we are organising a television programme from near Cardiff in which we hope to feature Sheep Dog Trials. We are taking the Captain of the English International team to come down and to bring with him a member of his team and we are extending the same invitation to yourself and another member of the Welsh team (to be decided later).

    I have spoken to Mr. Roy Saunders about this matter and he has proved most helpful. I gather that you and he will be seeing each other on Saturday and he will be able to give you most of the details. However, I would be most grateful if you could ring me at the above number as soon as you can before then. Please reverse the charge.

    Yours sincerely,

    (Selwyn Roderick)
    Television Producer, Wales.

Harry Greenslade, Esq.,
Jamesville,
Cwmcarn,
Mon.

SWR.

THE BRITISH BROADCASTING CORPORATION

HEAD OFFICE : BROADCASTING HOUSE, LONDON, W.1

AEOLIAN HALL, NEW BOND STREET, LONDON, W.1

TELEGRAMS AND CABLES BROADCASTS, LONDON, TELEX • INTERNATIONAL TELEX: 2-2182
TELEPHONE MAYFAIR 8411

Reference: 03/V/PD

    7th June, 1957

Dear Mr. Greenslade,

    This is to confirm that you are taking part in this week's "In Town Tonight", Saturday, 8th June 1957. The rehearsal is 5.30 p.m. in Studio 8, Broadcasting House, London, W.1., and the transmission is 7.30-8.00 p.m. in the Home Service of the BBC.

    We shall be pleased to offer you an expense fee of £5.5s.0d.

    Yours sincerely,

    (Peter Duncan)

H. Greenslade, Esq.,

The committee of the Sheep Dog Trials Society in the 1930s. On the left of the photograph is the tarpaulin cover for the secretary.

At the Mynyddislwyn Sheep Dog Trials in 1947.

At the Mynyddislwyn Sheep Dog Trials in 1951.

At the Mynyddislwyn Sheep Dog Trials in the 1950s.

In recognition of his captaining the Welsh team at the International Sheep Dog Trials, Harry Greenslade was presented with a shepherd's crook by Mr. Col Cook at the annual dinner of the Mynyddislwyn Sheepdog Society.
The photograph shows Mr. Morton, Trevor Griffiths (President), Harry Greenslade, Major Powell (Secretary), Col. Cook, Tom Butler, Tom Jones (Treasurer).

Trials of Tomorrow?

by Harry Greenslade

Winter is a time for thinking. For sheepdog men it's a time to remember the past season's trials, the days when hill men gather, when old friends meet, when you couldn't go wrong, when nothing went right. It's a time to assimilate the things learned from mistakes made and the advice given. It's a time of preparing and remembering.

Walking the hills on a bleak day - with a hard wind and a white sky breaking through sooty clouds; with a good dog scouring the fields and never tiring; with the knowledge, deep in your marrow, of generations of men and dogs having done the same tough task before you; with the sense of the task well done - is what sheepdog work is about. It's a natural skill, a craft married to the land, to a particular landscape. We all have our own, but for me it's the landscape of my native valley, and the mountain, Mynyddislwyn, which towers above it. A patchwork of small hill farms and forestry plantations, Mynyddislwyn is where I learned about dogs. Since I first climbed its slopes, farms have changed hands, and the valley, with its new road, shows a different face to the men looking down from the mountainside.

It's a mountain with a long history of sheepdog trials. The Mynyddislwyn Sheepdog Society, one of the oldest in Wales, and now running towards its 68th Year, first held its annual trial where it is still held, on Toneiddon Farm, Mynyddislwyn.

Founder members of the society are still well remembered. One of the founders, a young exponent of the South Wales style, was Mr. Robert Phillips. A winner of many prizes on Mynyddislwyn, Mr. Phillips' home was Ty Gwyn farm, on the Pennargraig side of Mynyddislwyn. For many years he shepherded Cilfynydd, but when he retired Mr. Phillips moved away to Pandy. Although separated by 20 miles from the mountain he loved, Mr. Phillips' long association with the Mynyddislwyn Sheepdog Society didn't end here, but in a way that, perhaps, can't be explained by coincidence.

Another founder, and treasurer for many years, was Mr. Thomas Jones, who lived at Pennar Farm, near New Bethel Chapel. Death unites us all, but perhaps not as closely as these two friends. Although separated, after Mr. Phillips' retirement, for 30 years, both men eventually died, and were buried on the same day at Beulah Chapel, Newbridge.

Since its foundation, when the first trial entry fee was a princely half-a-crown, the Mynyddislwyn Sheepdog Society's annual trial, which suffered only slight interruptions during two World Wars, has been a stronghold of the South Wales style. The National style was only introduced in the early 1950s.

Many famous sheepdog men have come to Mynyddislwyn to compete on Toneiddon Farm's long, testing and very natural course. Mr. J.M. Wilson, a legend among sheepdog men, and nine times Supreme Championship winner, came to Mynyddislwyn in 1949, and although unfamiliar with the

South Wales style, swept the board by taking 1st, 2nd, and 3rd places in the Open South Wales class. On that memorable day he ran the famous Glen, Mirk and another Glen.

Mr. W.J. Evans, Supreme Championship winner with Roy in 1953, and with Tweed in 1958, was another regular runner.

Names, familiar on trial fields and almost too many to mention, come to mind. From the many more that deserve mention, other fine handlers who have run dogs on Mynyddislwyn are Mr. H.J. Worthington, Supreme Championship winner with Juno in 1963; Mr. D.W. Daniels from Ystradgynlais, Supreme Championship winner with Chip in 1949; and Mr. E.L. Daniels, Supreme Championship winner in 1960.

The mountain has also bred local men who have reached the top in the trial game. Mr. L.R. Suter, who left the foot of Mynyddislwyn in 1963 for his present home at Gellifiniog Farm, Crosskeys, won the 1964 Supreme Championship with Craig, and the 1969 Welsh National with Sally.

At the risk of sounding immodest, I include myself and two great dogs here. It was with Glen that I won the Welsh National in 1955 and 1956, and the International Farmer's Championship in 1956, and with Gary that I won the 1956 Hyde Park International.

Winter's a time for remembering; and perhaps I've done enough for one evening. But remembering and preparation go together. I'm not simply remembering old friends. I think there is something about Mynyddislwyn's Toneiddon course and the quality of the good dog handlers I've remembered which go together. They are linked by a quality which, I'm sorry to say, the trials of today are losing.

Such statements are never entirely true and need some explaining. The successes of the men I've mentioned need no comment; rather, let me describe Mynyddislwyn's trial course. Set on the mountain's top, where winds carry across what weather comes, it is a long course. With an outrun of a good 700 yards, and a width of 350 yards, it's an open and natural course giving a good dog plenty of room to do a good outrun. This kind of terrain is surely the essence of sheepdog trials. Farmers want dogs to do the running for them, to be handled far out and not to have the dogs racing sheep and breaking their necks.

In trials today, too many dogs - even at the highest level - are lacking in a good outrun. In the 1971 International at Trelai Park, Cardiff, on the final day, where 12 of the finest dogs in the country were running, I didn't expect (and I know I wasn't alone in this) to see dogs coming in early on their outrun, some before they had gone 200 yards. It wasn't only the outrun; at Trelai Park the shedding on the final was almost non-existent; the thrills and rules of shedding were almost non-existent.

This failing off in standards comes from the increase in what I like to call 'football pitch' trials. Too many trial fields today are too short and don't test the dog's outrun at all. Many dogs, largely as a result of these trials, are being bred too soft. I wonder how many of such dogs could stand up to a day's work on a mountain. Sheepdogs are working dogs and a dog who's blowing after ten minutes work would be of little use.

Too many handlers are going to trial courses unprepared, without having done their homework. Standards of handling are falling, with the resulting over-commanding of dogs, especially on the outrun.

The International Sheepdog Society is trying to maintain standards but what can be done when dogs are coming to the Supreme Championship unprepared for the big task. It's not just in the Supreme Championship; standards are being watered down in too many trials today. But they are not being watered down at Mynyddislwyn and a few other courses. These tougher courses, to my mind the essence of sheepdog trials, are unfortunately being neglected by handlers who expect to reach, and are working for, the top; and as a result, dogs and handlers are found wanting in the Supreme Championship.

The neglect is lowering trial standards, standards which ideally test a working dog and man doing a tough and skilful job. I'm accusing no one, and I'm sure most sheepdog men, with a knowledge and sense of what a good working trial should be, will agree with what I'm saying. Let's be honest about the situation, and now, looking forward to a new season, think seriously about what can be done to maintain trial standards.

Mynyddislwyn's Toneiddon Farm course will be offered to the International Sheepdog Society as a possible venue for the Welsh National. I believe it is a trial field that will fit their needs better than most others.

Winter's a time for preparation. The Mynyddislwyn Sheepdog Society has been preparing its course to maintain the rigorous standards of open mountain work. It is a course which shouldn't be neglected; it is an example which should be followed.

Mynyddislwyn's annual sheep auction has now become firmly established in local farmer's diaries. It is held each year on the first Monday in September.

The sheep auction.

Ebbw Valley

The eastern slopes of Mynyddislwyn Mountain drop down steeply to the Ebbw Valley. In its bottom is the Ebbw River, which forms the eastern limit of this book. In 1799 Archdeacon Coxe toured in Monmouthshire collecting information for his book, and while walking southwards down the towpath of the canal, he described his journey thus - *'Below the Ebwy... here pent up in a narrow gulf, there spreading its devastations in a wider channel. The contrast between the tranquil waters of the canal, and the rapid eddies of the torrent, bursting through groves of alder and foaming over fragments of rock, is particularly striking.*

Between Newbridge and Risca, numerous houses, mills, forges and hamlets are scattered on the side of the canal, and on the banks of the Ebwy, and the whole valley became a scene of bustle and activity.

I passed on the left not less than four of those wooded glens which are frequent in these parts; they are called cwms by the natives. On the right (Mynyddislwyn Mountainside) the mountains are less broken with dingles; their lower parts are covered with underwood, and their heathy tops overhang and darken the torrent.

Below Abercarne I entered the stony road leading through the vale, which here expands to the breadth of half a mile, and is rich in wood, pasture and corn'.

In September 1750 an agreement was entered into to build a blast furnace for the smelting of local iron ore. Immediately afterwards the area had an Osmond Forge, Wiremill, Foundry, Tilting and Turning Mill, Great Forge, Rolling Mill and various Premises and Residences. Abercarne Iron Works had begun. Unfortunately, all of the above, and the later Abercarne Tinplate Works, were on the east side of the Ebbw River, and just outside the area covered by this book. But the eastern slopes of Mynyddislwyn Mountain had their part to play in the running of the works. When built in 1750, the Furnace was charcoal fired, as was the Osmond Forge where iron of the highest quality was drawn out to make wire, mainly for the woollen industry (carding machines etc.) Charcoal was made locally by heating wood in earth covered clumps, on small platforms cut into the hillside, and many remnants of those charcoal platforms can still be found today on Mynyddislwyn Mountain. The charcoal burners were a breed of men who moved along the hillside cutting down trees sixteen years old, so they weren't very big trees and didn't need much splitting. After cutting down just above ground level, the trees grew again, with many stems, and the charcoal burners would return to the same trees sixteen years later to repeat the process. The trees were cut again, and re-sprouted, in a process called coppicing. Again, evidence of these multi-stemmed trees can be found on the steep slopes of the Mountain. In those days only the native broad leaved hardwood trees grew here. The conifers that cover so much of that part of the Mountain today are of twentieth century origin.

One part of Abercarne Works was to the west of the river, Pennar Foundry, which is today covered by a children's playing field at West End, Abercarn. The date when it was built is unknown, but it was undoubtedly later than the preceeding parts of the Works. The earliest proven date is to be found in the Minute Books of the Monmouthshire Canal Company for February and April

1832, when there is an agreement with John Llewellin (agent to Benjamin Hall, Lord of the Manor of Abercarne) to form a junction from the 'Foundry Branch' from Hall's Tramroad, with the Canal Company's own tramroad, and on into Abercarne Works.

Part of West End, Abercarn, in the eastern shadow of Mynyddislwyn Mountain. To the right of the photograph was Cwm Pennar Foundry. The River Ebbw, in foreground, is the eastern boundary of this book.

A record of the accounts of Hall's Tramroad for the 1840s reveal that the Foundry was an integral part of the tramroad. Its prime function at that date was the manufacture of tramplates (an early form of rail) for Hall's Road, while the records show that tramplates were also made for the Monmouthshire Canal Company and various Colliery owners on Hall's Estate. One unusual order was for cast iron pillars for the house of Sir Peckham Micklethwaite in London, the iron for which was brought in from Blaina Ironworks.

In July 1844 Hall's Road Account Book tells us that a pond was excavated in a field on Church Farm, to impound water to drive machinery in the Foundry. The Account reads *'Paid expenses of excavating and completing a Pond in the Church Farm, for supplying Cwm Penner Foundry with Water. Cost £77 11s 2d'*. (That pond still exists behind Church Farm, but is today a small nature reserve with nest boxes for water birds).

In July 1853 Hall's Road and the Foundry were leased to the Ebbw Vale Company for twenty-one years. Included in the Agreement was a Schedule which included the buildings and equipment therein - *'A Foundry at Cwm Pennar with a yard, pond water course, wheel pit, culverts, and other erections attached thereto. Also the machinery belonging to same, consisting of water wheel fourteen feet in diameter, a driving wheel four feet two inches in diameter, sundry other wheels and sheaves, driving bands, and a fan Blast machine, diameter of fan four feet, and eighteen inches wide. One tram house near the Foundry'.*

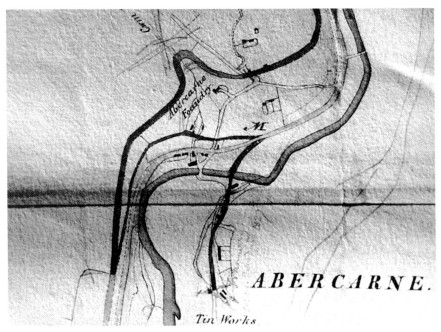

Part of a map showing the Abercarne or Cwm Pennar Foundry, being fed by water from the Cwm Pennar stream. At the head of that valley was a pond, dug in 1844, to top-up the stream in dry weather. On the map the dark lines are Benjamin Hall's Tramroad. Also shown is the road over the River Ebbw which becomes a winding track going up steeply to Pen Graig Pennar, and beyond.

An entry for 13th July 1844 mentions the cutting of the Pond at the head of Cwm Pennar, at the cost of £77 11s 2d.

For reasons unknown the Ebbw Vale Company appear to have given up the lease of the Foundry before the expiry date of 1874. In March 1872 a lease of the Foundry was entered into between Benjamin Hall's widow, Lady Llanover, and William James and James Davies, for a term of 99 years. Two years later another lease for 99 years was entered into when Jesse Bailey bought his way into the Company. Between 1890 and 1896 the Company entered into contracts with

> W. Simmons, Gloucester
> Vallotta & Girvone, Genoa
> Drysdale & Co. Glasgow
> E.C. Laybourne, Seattle
> Capt. Cremonini, Genoa
> Calo Girvone, Genoa
> John Birch & Co. London
> E. Dates & Co. Liverpool

The above mentioned contracts were mainly in connection with floating pontoons for lifting sea going vessels. (It seems hard to imagine such a thing happening in the shadow of the Mountain).

The Foundry ceased to operate in the early twentieth century.

Hall's Tramroad, mentioned above, was the tramroad built by Benjamin Hall. He had become Lord of the Manor of Abercarne, and owner of Abercarne Estate (two separate items) in 1808. The Manor was rich in coal, as the Mynyddislwyn Seam covered much of it. Hall was not a colliery owner, but was keen to lease land to anyone who wanted to open a coal level, for which Hall would receive a royalty for every ton of coal, or quarry stone, removed from the ground. He knew that any prospective colliery owner would need to get coal to market (which in those days meant the riverside quays in Newport), so Hall set about building a tramroad as the only means that those colliery owners had of getting to Newport.

In 1809 he had started building his tramroad from Abercarne, north-west towards the present Oakdale. The end of his tramroad was to be the Monmouthshire Canal at Abercarne. From there it crossed the River Ebbw at West End, Abercarn, and climbed gently through Tilla Cox (or Cock's) Wood, through the grounds of the present Trecelyn House, and skirted around the northern boundary set for this book to Pentwynmawr, and onward. Some years later his son, also Benjamin Hall, extended his father's tramroad when it by-passed Abercarne and ran along the lower slopes of Mynyddislwyn Mountain before crossing the Ebbw Valley by a seven-arched bridge to Pontywaun. That tramroad eventually became a railway line carrying millions of tons of coal from Oakdale, Markham and Llanover Collieries, as well as countless smaller collieries and levels.

The lower slopes of our Mountain were to be despoiled by another tramroad, running parallel with Hall's Road, and just below it. That was the tramroad built by the Monmouthshire Canal Company.

When the canal was opened in the late 1790s, it ended at Crumlin. Tramroads ran through the Ebbw Valleys carrying iron and coal to the canal, from where it was shipped to the riverside quays at Newport. By an agreement of 31st December 1827 between the Canal Company and Benjamin Hall, the Canal Company would build a tramroad from Crumlin, along the lower slopes of Mynyddislwyn Mountain, on Hall's Estate, and Hall would build his own tramroad (mentioned above) to by-pass Abercarne, both joining together at Risca, before heading down to Newport. That tramroad of the Canal Company forms the line of the railway to Ebbw Vale, which is still running at the time of writing this book.

Before Benjamin Hall became Lord of the Manor of Abercarne in 1808, the title was held by Samuel Glover. He had financial difficulties and sold off parts of his Estates. In 1804 he had sold the Bedwellty Estate to Sir Henry Protheroe, a large area of coal rich land stretching between the Sirhowy and Ebbw Rivers, very roughly from Penyfan Pond northwards to a line drawn from the bottom end of Tredegar to the bottom end of Ebbw Vale. Protheroe intended opening a coal level into the hillside opposite Argoed, along with Penyfan Colliery overlooking Aberbeeg, both on his new Estate.

The market for that coal was the riverside at Newport, and to get there he had to travel over the Abercarne Estate. If he had started his colliery immediately he would probably have reached an agreement with Samuel Glover, but his long delay meant that Benjamin Hall was the new Lord of the Manor, a man who adopted a much more business-like manner to the running of his Estate than Glover had done.

In 1809 Protheroe got permission from the Canal Company to build a tramroad from his intended collieries to join the canal at Pontywaun, a tramroad that would have to run very largely over Hall's new Estates. Protheroe did not ask permission of Hall, but went about building his tramroad as an act of trespass. In part, Protheroe's tramroad would run alongside the tramroad that Hall was building himself The last miles of Protheroe's intended tramroad would be along the lower slopes of Mynyddislwyn Mountain, before crossing the Ebbw Valley by a bridge to join the canal at Pontywaun. Such a route passed through fields belonging to Chapel Farm (across the river), owned by Daniel Phillips.

By late 1809 Protheroe was on those Chapel Farm fields, surveying his route and cutting down trees, but without Daniel Phillips' permission. At the same time another gang of Protheroe's workmen was trespassing on Hall's land, surveying and cutting down trees in Tilla Cox Wood, opposite and in view of Hall's house (Abercarne House). The damage of digging was *'upwards of 100 yards in length and 5 yards in breadth'* and trees were cut down over a length of 500 yards. Hall had to stop him, and went to Court of Chancery for an injunction against Protheroe. It led to the court case that Hall won.

In the meantime, on 1st January 1810 Hall bought a small parcel of Chapel Farm land off Daniel Phillips and on the very same day he directed his agent, John Llewellin, to start work on building six houses for his (Hall's) Estate workers. The six houses were a terrace up the steep hillside to obstruct the line that Protheroe had marked out for his tramroad. They were built to stop Protheroe.

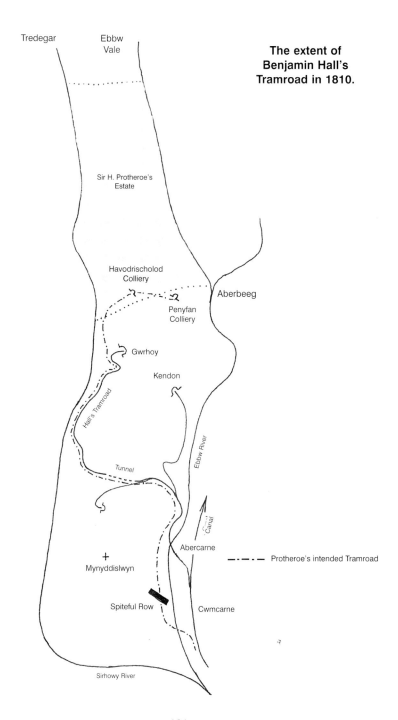

Tredegar

Ebbw
Vale

**The extent of
Benjamin Hall's
Tramroad in 1810.**

Sir H. Protheroe's
Estate

Havodrischolod
Colliery

Aberbeeg

Penyfan
Colliery

Gwrhoy

Kendon

Hall's Tramroad

Ebbw River

Tunnel

Canal

Mynyddislwyn

Abercarne

Protheroe's intended Tramroad

Spiteful Row

Cwmcarne

Sirhowy River

101

On 7th February Protheroe employed workmen to tear down the hedges on both sides of Hall's piece of land, and to throw the earth into the interiors of the houses that Hall was having built, and to tear down the door and window frames. That action continued for several days afterwards.

Those six houses on the lower slopes of Mynyddislwyn Mountain have become known as 'The Spiteful'. But whose action was spiteful to whom?

The Court of Chancery stopped Protheroe's actions. However, twenty years later, Hall's son, also Benjamin Hall, decided that Hall's Road would by-pass Abercarne and carry on along the lower slopes of Mynyddislwyn Mountain. It is interesting to note that Hall's by-pass ran on the route surveyed by Protheroe, and crossed the Ebbw Valley by a bridge where Protheroe intended crossing the valley. At The Spiteful, Hall's Road ran through the terrace of houses, possibly through the gap left by Protheroe's vandalism, so that until recently there were four houses above the line and two below it.

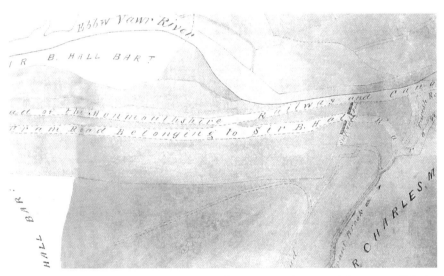

The papers for the law suit brought by Hall against Protheroe, and the sworn affidavits that follow, are in the Court of Chancery Archives in London.

Affidavit of Edward Rowland Farmer. Sworn at Cardiff 22nd February, 1810.

'Saith that he is informed and believes that said Defendant Sir Henry Protheroe is now forming a tramroad from a certain field in the parish of Risca in the county of Monmouth, called Carne Field, to a certain colliery in the parish of Monythusloin called Penyfan Colliery. And that the said tramroad is intended to run parallel with a tramroad of the Plaintiff's (Benjamin Hall) in the same parish, now nearly completed. And that about 10 o'clock in the morning of the 7th day of February instant, he, Defendant, together with John Morris and Edward George, both of the same parish of Monythusloin, yoemen, went to a certain piece of land situate in the said parish of Monythusloin, the property of the Plaintiff and upon which said piece of land the Plaintiff was then erecting several dwelling houses, and saw there the Defendant, Roger Hopkins, John Thomas, Watkin Jones,

Thomas Morris and William Thomas Edmund, and that immediately after he went there, he observed the said William Thomas Edmund, Thomas Morris and Watkin Jones tearing down the hedges which divided the said piece of land from the adjoining lands, and after that they dug up a large portion of the said piece of land and threw the earth which was so dug up into the interior of one of the said dwelling houses (which was then in an

The end house of Spiteful Row, showing how close it was to Hall's Road.

unfinished state) for the purpose of forming the said tramroad of him, the said Defendant Sir Henry Protheroe. And further saith that about 11 of the clock in the morning of the 6th of February instant, he went to Tilla Cox Wood in the said parish of Monythusloin, and which is the property of the said Plaintiff, and there saw the Defendant, Roger Hopkins, David Jones, John Thomas (labourer) and two other persons, the said Roger Hopkins a-levelling and the said David Jones and John Thomas cutting down the wood, and the said other two persons digging up the ground for the purpose of forming the said tramroad of the said Defendant Sir Henry Protheroe, and that he, Defendant, immediately after he came up to them, the said Roger Hopkins, David Jones, John Thomas and the said other two persons, he desired them to desist from working and quit the premises, but to such desire they paid no attention and continued working on, and Roger Hopkins told Defendant that he had a better right in the said wood than he had, and that they (meaning the said Roger Hopkins and the other workmen) intended pulling down the said houses on the following morning. And further saith that when he went to the said Roger Hopkins and the said David Jones and John Thomas and the said two other persons, as aforesaid, they had cut through the soil of said wood about eight yards in length and *about four yards in breadth, and that they had cut down about 100 yards in length and five yards in breadth of said coppice wood. Saith that they continued working in said wood for several days afterwards and that a great number of other persons afterwards joined them and continued working there, and that several persons are now daily digging up the ground in the said wood, and cutting down the coppice and other wood'.*

A memorial on the wall of St. Tudor's Church to the Phillips family of Chapel. The Chapel in question was Chapel Farm. Daniel Phillips sold the land on which Hall built Spiteful Row. Chapel Farm is also mentioned towards the end of this book in connection with the letter from Australia. In that letter the names of Mary and Edmund Llewelyn (at the bottom of the memorial) are mentioned.

Affidavit of John Hopkins Master Mason. Sworn at Cardiff 22nd February 1810.
'*Saith that the Defendant Sir Henry Protheroe came to him about 12 of the clock at noon on the 5th of February instant, when building some dwelling houses for the Plaintiff (Benjamin Hall) upon a piece of land in the Chapel Wood in said parish of Monythusloin, the property of Plaintiff Benjamin Hall, and asked him whether the said Plaintiff had directed him to build across his tramroad, upon which Defendant Sir Henry Protheroe said "I will have it all down tomorrow"'*
   Saith that between the hours of 9 and 10 of the clock in the morning of the 7th of February instant, when he was at work upon said dwelling houses, Roger Hopkins, John Thomas, Watkin Jones, Thomas Morris and William Thomas Edmund came there and the said Roger Hopkins measured the length, height and breadth of part of two of the said dwelling houses which were then built up nearly to the square, and then the said Watkin

Jones, Thomas Morris and William Thomas Edmund tore the hedges on each side of the said piece of land and then proceeded to dig up the same thereof on each side of the said houses and to throw the earth so dug up into the interior of one of the said houses. Saith that in about half an hour afterwards, and in consequence of the said proceedings, he, together with four of his workmen were obliged to quit their work and went home. And that he, between 7 and 8 of the clock the following morning went to the said dwelling houses again in order to observe what had been done, when he saw the same persons working there as before, and that they had knocked down the walls and gone completely through one of the said houses so built, as aforesaid, and had formed part of the said Defendant Sir Henry Protheroe's said road over the same'.

Affidavit of Morgan Thomas Yeoman. Sworn at Cardiff 22nd February 1810.

'Saith that about 10 of the clock in the morning of the 7th February instant, he was working in a quarry then opened in a piece of land situate in the Chapel Wood in the said parish of Monythusloin, the property of the Plaintiff (Benjamin Hall) and upon which the Plaintiff was then erecting dwelling houses. Saith that about 11 of the clock in the morning of the 7th of February instant, he saw the said Watkin Jones go into one of the said houses and take the wooden frames of two inside and one outside door and the wooden frame of one of the windows, and carried them away. And that in about half an hour after this the said Watkin Jones took a pick axe and pulled down the side wall of one of the said houses and then threw the stones thereof, with a quantity of earth, into one of the other houses over which part of the said Defendant Sir Henry Protheroe's road was formed'.

Tyr Shams yr Ellwr, a farm besides Hall's Road.

The steeply sloping eastern side of Mynyddislwyn Mountain contains far fewer farms than the western slopes that drop down to the Sirhowy Valley. One of those farms is Tyr Shams yr Ellwr, which could possibly have monastic origins. The Old Book of Llandaff dates from the twelfth century and gives an early history of this part of the Ebbw Valley. It takes us back to the time of Gulfrid, the 27th Bishop of Llandaff, who succeeded to his position in 929. In the time of Bishop Gulfrid a Gwent chieftain named Llywarch ab Cadwgan went on a plundering expedition, during which he burned some Church property. The powerful Bishop soon brought him to book, and Llywarch humbly sought pardon. He made peace with the Church and presented to the Bishop of Llandaff for ever 'the village of Trefcarn y Bont, and 27 acres'. Trefcarn y Bont became known as Chapel Farm just across the river and outside the area of study of this book. However, as we have already seen at The Spiteful, Chapel Farm had land across the river at the foot of Mynyddislwyn Mountain.

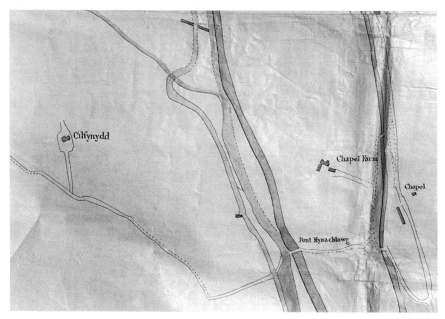

A map of 1847 showing the two tramroads already mentioned. Alongside Hall's Road is Spiteful and Tyr Shams yr Ellwr. Pont Mynachlog crossed the Ebbw River and led to the track up the steep hillside, past Cilfynydd Farm, and on to St. Tudor's Church.

That track was the boundary of a land sale mentioned in March 1790, when Samuel Glover, then Lord of the Manor of Abercarne, sold land to Thomas Jefferys.

'*The said Samuel Glover did grant, bargain, sell, alien, release and confirm unto the said Thomas Jefferys all that piece or parcel of wood and rough ground, with the woods, trees and underwoods thereon, commonly called or known by the name of Caeyenny, Pont Cae, Yr Pania, Cady Coalhouse, Caeti Clover, and Carri Ffain, and containing by estimation 10 acres, be the same more or less, theretofore in the possession of Charles Vann, Esquire, situate lying and being in the Hamlet of Clawrplwyth, within the parish of Monyddysloyne or Monnydisloyne, otherwise Mon y Dasloyne, in the said county of Monmouth, between the lane leading from Pont Monathlog towards Monyddysloyne Church on the north to the lands of the Hon. William Morgan of Tredegar, Esquire on the west and south, and to the River Ebow or Eboth on the east'.*

Tyr Shams yr Ellwr has been linked to Chapel Farm. Between the two is a bridge over the Ebbw River known as Pont Mynachlog (the Monk's Bridge). Alongside Tyr Shams is an old track, possibly a Parish Road, leading up to Mynyddislwyn Church. In its early days St. Tudor's Church would have been served by monks, so does that track link the Church to a monastic establishment in the valley bottom? Was Tyr Shams a Grange where food was grown by the monks for their own use?

In the Tithe Apportionment Book of 1839 Tyr Shams is listed as belonging to Tredegar Estate, its 14 acres and 35 perches leased to Leah Edmunds. Its annual tithe was rated at £1 9s 2d.

When Benjamin Hall built his tramroad in 1828 to by-pass Abercarne that tramroad passed within touching distance of Tyr Shams. That would have placed the farm in an ideal position to be used by the tramroad company for the horses on the tramroad.

The name Tyr Shams yr Ellwr means James the nailer's land, suggesting that at one time it was owned by a James who could have worked in a nail-making

The lower slopes of the steep eastern side of Mynyddislwyn Mountain. Top centre is Cilfynydd Farm. To the extreme left is Tyr Shams yr Ellwr, besides Hall's Road, while to the extreme right is Spiteful Row. In the foreground is Chapel Farm, pulled down to make way for Cwmcarn Comprehensive School.

107

Mrs. Rees standing at the corner of Cilfynydd Farm, before she moved out in the mid 1980s

business associated with Abercarne Ironworks, or he could even have bought iron there and ran a nail-making business on the farm. But we will probably never know.

Another old farm on that steep hillside is Cilfynydd, now owned by Mr. and Mrs. Col Cook, who succeeded Mrs. Rees. Until the mid 1980s it was a very small farmhouse set into the hillside. The walls were four feet thick. The down-slope end wall still has the big Inglenook fireplace with its bread oven with an unusual stone door, and the stone spiral stairs. The original oak beams survive. In the mid 1980s there was no mains water, no electricity and no telephone. Today, the original house survives as the lounge of a greatly enlarged house. It now has electricity and its own water supply. Water from a spring down the hill is pumped up to a settling tank above the farm, from where it feeds the house by gravity.

Previous owners Mr. and Mrs. Rees had their own way of collecting water. They used the same spring down the hill and carried it up to the house using a donkey with panniers strapped to its sides. Monday was Mrs. Rees' washing day and extra water was needed. Mrs. Rees remembers that the donkey could never be found on a Monday morning. She had to search for it in the woods above the farm. The donkey knew his days of the week.

Two legends are associated with Cilfynydd. One is that Oliver Cromwell and his troops passed by, on their way down from Toniddon Farm. Another is that it had links with the monks of Chapel Farm.

The 1839 Tithe Apportionment Book tells us that the 148 acres of Cilfynydd was owned by Rev. William Price Lewis and Henry Lewis, but occupied by Daniel Williams. Its annual tithe payment was rated at £2 0s 2d.

Another view of Cilfynydd Farmhouse, this time a painting, showing how it looked at the time Mr. and Mrs. Col Cook bought it in 1985.

A little to the north of Cilfynydd Farm is the steep little valley of Nant y Crochan. Northwards of that the wooded hillside of Mynyddislwyn Mountain is called Craig y Darren, until we reach another steep little valley, Nant Pennar, (which has already been mentioned as starting from the pond on Church Farm). Close to this little valley was an old farmhouse, last occupied by Mrs. Keeble. Unfortunately, in the 1930s, the farmhouse burnt down and Mrs Keeble died in that fire. Immediately above the farmhouse was West End Board School, built in 1876 at the cost of £3,220, and enlarged in 1883 at a further cost of £1,500. It was designed for 626 children. In its early days Mr. James Hughes was the Master. Northwards again the hillside is called Tyla Coch (or Cox) Wood, which was the scene of Sir Henry Protheroe's illegal actions in 1810. A possible explanation for its name is that it abounds in native beech trees which are a glorious golden red colour (Coch) when the leaves turn in the autumn.

Opposite Tyla Coch Wood was South Celynen Colliery. It deserves a mention because it was to the west of the River Ebbw, so within this book's area of study.

It was sunk in 1873 by the Newport Abercarn Black Vein Steam Coal Company. When sunk, it was known only as Celynen Colliery, but when another colliery was sunk a little further north at the start of the First World War, this one was called South and the new Celynen was called North. By the beginning of the twentieth century a massive bank of coke ovens had been built to the south of the colliery. The colliery produced steam, house, manufacturing and coking coals, and the sole agent for the coals was Beynon & Co. Ltd. There were three shafts eventually, two for winding the coal and one for ventilation.

Mrs. Keeble outside her little cottage close to Pant yr Esk Crossing. She died when the cottage was burnt down in the 1930s.

No.1 shaft was sunk in 1873, with Nos.2 and 3 being sunk in 1880. The winding engine for No.1 shaft was a Robey steam engine, and operated for almost 100 years until electric winding was introduced in 1970.

In the mid 1930s the Newport Abercarn Black Vein Co. was taken over by Partridge, Jones, and John Paton. The colliery was one of the locality's largest employers with two thousand men in the colliery and coke ovens at its peak. That resulted in the demand for houses for the colliers, and much of Newbridge was built. Some of those houses can be seen on the next page surrounding Blaenblodau Farm.

South Celynen Colliery closed in September 1985.

The above mentioned Blaenblodau Farm has long disappeared, along with the nearby Newbridge Mill. Blaenblodau Farm is mentioned in the 1839 Tithe Apportionment Book as being part of Benjamin Hall's Abercarne Estate, being 31 acres, 1 rood and 12 perch, with its annual tithe rated at £2 12s 5d. Newbridge Mill was also part of Hall's Abercarne Estate. It was a corn mill with six fields, covering 5 acres 1 rood and 39 perch, being rated in 1839 at 6s 10d. It was at Newbridge Mill that the Steward of the Manor of Abercarne held his Court Leat. When a farmer died, to be succeeded by his son and heir, or if a completely new family took over, the new farmer had to appear before the representative of the Lord of the Manor where he 'Prayed to be admitted a Tenant of the Manor' for which he had to pay an annual rent. (See the chapter on Cwmbrynar Farm).

South Celynen Colliery 1873-1985.

The north-east corner of Mynyddislwyn Mountain sloping down towards Newbridge. On the skyline, in the centre, can be seen Pennar Fach Farm, today a ruin. Lower down the photograph and running across it from right to left is Hall's railway line, and beside it is Ivy Cottage, Penrhiwbica. Below that, at the extreme left of the photograph is Ty Celyn. The houses in the centre of the photograph form Blaenblodau and Beynon Streets, built to house the colliers of South Celynen Colliery. In front of those houses can be seen Blaenblodau Farm, which no longer exists. In the shadows to the left of the photograph stood Newbridge Mill.

111

Ivy Cottage, Penrhiwbica, built so close to Hall's Road.

Newbridge Mill, and just above it the Monmouthshire Company's railway line from Ebbw Vale to Newport. The mill's waterwheel can be seen at the left (west) end of the building.

Lower Sirhowy Valley

When Archdeacon Coxe toured the area in 1799 he journeyed down the Ebbw Valley, stayed at Risca, and then travelled up through the Sirhowy Valley to Penllwyn House. On entering the valley above Risca he wrote '*Soon afterwards we ascended the side of the hill (Mynyddislwyn Mountain), which bounds the vale, and continued along an elevated ridge, through thickets, corn fields and meadows, sprinkled with hamlets, watered by numerous torrents, and overlooking the Sorwy (River Sirhowy). The features of this vale are more wild and romantic than those of the Ebwy (Ebbw). It is narrower and deeper, and the shelving declivities, laid out in meadows, stretch to the edge of the torrent, which roars in a profound abyss, obscured by overhanging trees*'

Travelling northward from Newport, on reaching Risca the imposing land mass of Mynyddislwyn Mountain is in front of you, and the huge man-made feature that cannot be missed is Cox's Quarry. Nearby is the confluence of the Sirhowy and Ebbw Rivers. On entering the Sirhowy Valley the first settlement is Newtown, then, Wattsville, Brynawel and Morrisville, Cwmfelinfach, and Ynysddu, all in the shadow of the Mountain, and all owing their existence to coal. Each was a coal mining community.

In this lower part of the Sirhowy Valley the 1846 Tithe Map shows a sparsely populated area. The steep hillside leading onto the Mountain was called Coed Prince, and near the valley bottom were Troed y Rhiw and Duffryn Farms. There was a rough road leading up the valley with a road branching off it near Troad y Rhiw Farm leading up the steep Rhiw to the Parish Church and beyond, while near Cwmfelinfach Mill another road branched off up Twyn Gwyn Hill.

The third quarter of the Nineteenth Century saw the sinking of North Risca Pit which led for the demand for colliers houses. Two settlements were built, Newtown, with Tredegar and Llanover Streets, and Wattsville.

WATTSVILLE - Named after Edmund Hannay Watts, Chairman of Watts Ward and Co. who sunk North Risca Colliery, and also owned nearby Old Blackvein Colliery and later bought Abercarn Colliery. Watts Ward and Company eventually merged in the London And South Wales Coal Company. E.H. Watts was also involved in the coal industry of the Rhondda Valley and gave his name to Wattstown. As North Risca Colliery was opened in 1875 we have a date from when houses were needed. The 1901 O.S. map shows thirty-six houses built on the south side of the road, and also a reservoir built across the Nant Hafod Tudur. As the Reservoir did not have filter beds it would not have been built for domestic water, but for the boilers and coolers of the colliery. About 1920 another reservoir was built a little higher up the dingle joining the tail of the first reservoir. By the time of the 1920 O.S. map Wattsville had been completed, with the main road through the village called Islwyn Street. The village then had a school, a Baptist Chapel at the end of Duffryn Terrace, and Zion Congregational Chapel at Hafod Tudur Terrace. Earlier in the twentieth century the local policeman lived in a house near the Co-operative Stores in Islwyn Street. On a lane at the rear of these houses Mr. B. Hoskins had his blacksmith's shop on the corner of a row of buildings consisting of stores and horses' stables.

Wattsville, in the bottom of the Sirhowy Valley. Above the conifers is the barren hillside of Mynydd y Lan. To the extreme left of the photograph is the valley of Hafod Tudor.

At the top end of Wattsville is the Hafod Tudor valley. On the left of the photograph lies Troed y Rhiw Farm. On the horizon to the left is Pen Top Farm, while to the right is Toneiddon Farm.

BRYNAWEL - Leaving Wattsville behind, the road goes up the hill to Duffryn Road. This community was made up of twenty-three houses on the north side of the road and Mrs. John's shop on the south side, built in the first decade of the twentieth century.

Behind Duffryn Road are the twenty-seven houses of Llanarth Terrace. Brynawel was built for the colliers and officials of Nine Mile Point Colliery. Falcon Terrace was for the Officials. At the end of Llanarth Terrace was the colliery Manager's house, Craig y Trw'n. Behind this was Craig y Trwyn (or Adams) Quarry, now filled in as a landfill site. The quarry and others higher up the hillside provided the hard Pennant Sandstone for the building of these villages, also for the colliery buildings and the shaft lining.

Brynawel Village on the lower slopes of The Mountain, just north of Wattsville.
On the skyline can be seen the masts on Mynydd y Lan.

In common with other valley communities, and the scattered homes on the Mountain, in the early years of their existence the only means to light the houses were with candles or oil lamps, with cooking done on an open range around the coal fire.

It seems strange that while Brynawel was built for the workers at Nine Mile Point Colliery, their children did not attend Cwmfelinfach School, but went to Wattsville School in a village built for Risca Colliery.

Adjacent to Brynawel was Morrisville which was built 1925-26.

One of the early residents of Brynawel was Mr. C. Fish who was born there in 1911. His memoirs make interesting reading of life there during his childhood about 1920. *'The Wattsville School was set up below the Prince's Street rough roadway. The infants section and playgrounds were about thirty feet below the boys playground. These looked over the houses of Islwyn Road.*

At 8.50 a.m. the school bell that hung under the barge boards at the apex of the building would start ringing until 8.55. When it stopped all the children would line up in their classes in the playgrounds, with no talking, then walk into assemblies. The infants had theirs in their small hall while the seniors had their assembly in a large hall area on the first floor. The usual hymn was "New every morning" *or a special hymn for such an occasion as storms or disasters, followed by The Lord's Prayer, then a passage of scripture was read, another hymn, then any details for the day were given out.*

Anyone who had not been in lines was held in the foyers until after assembly, when the girls had their names entered into a late book while the boys got the cane once, twice if they had been late before. Girls were never caned. They were spoken to by the headmaster which always ended with the girls in tears.

There was complete silence at all times inside school. A ten-minute playtime was granted during the mornings and afternoons. At 4 p.m. the headmaster would ring a large bell which was the signal for each class to walk to the cloakroom. It was only then that talking was permitted. Running was never allowed.

Lessons were so arranged that singing and games came in the last part of the day. Arithmetic and English came at the start of the day, interspersed with History and Geography. Nature Study was always brought into the week's work, with English and Poems. The first of March was kept in mind at every opportunity - Saint David's Day. For that morning each class had been preparing its own show to put on in front of the whole school and parents. The afternoon we had off.

In 1914 the Great War commenced. School life passed by each day with a pleasant happy feeling. It was only when we saw men coming into the area in khaki coloured clothes, and no lights were allowed at night, that there was a war on. Search lights would light up the night sky at times. Mr. Lawrence, the headmaster, got the senior boys to clear about three acres of hillside of bracken and made a garden for vegetables, surrounded by a fence to keep out the sheep. Parties of senior children picked blackberries, the juice of which made a blue dye. Food rationing had been introduced; sugar (1lb Per person per month), cheese ($^1/4$ lb Per person per week), bacon, all fats and jams were restricted. Mother would send my brother George and I down to a butcher friend in Cross Keys who did his own killing in his slaughterhouse. We would get half a bullocks head from which mother made many savoury dishes and stews. Father would help or advise local farmers concerning their horses and cattle. In payment we would get a sack of potatoes or swedes dropped on the door step. During the war we would always come home past the shops to see if any of them had notices stating that there was an item off rationing. If it was jam or treacle, mother would give us the money and we would take empty jam jars down in a frail to make it safer for us to carry home.

Each day the papers would give news of what was happening on the war front. Our first knowledge of the peace declarations came by the railway signal box messages, our usual news spreaders. Mr. Phillips and Mr. Burford, the Station Master and Signalman, were waving the green flags of the railway to let all who could see them that there was a peace conference being held to end the war. That night all lights were put on, candles were put in jam jars, lit, and put on window sills, and any pieces of rags or dusters were strung out to celebrate. Gradually life became less tense and food rationing eased, but the home grown produce from the allotments was still needed. A few hens had helped with eggs, and small potatoes given to neighbours who kept pigs also helped. A cut of pork would be given back at times. Other items of exchange were bottles of herb beer and bee wine.

116

Any accident in the mine, large or small, was the concern of everyone. Hot water was always kept on the fireplace at all times, usually for the colliers to have their bath in front of the fire, but also in case of an accident, so that the doctor had plenty of hot water to deal with the case.

The usual village activities flowed along; Sunday School, Band of Hope, Young Men and Young Women's groups in the chapels and churches, football and cricket games, the Sunday School Anniversaries, a day out to Barry Island by train, a trip to Saint Bride's Lighthouse by a two horse brake or waggonette. Contributions to pay for these outings came from funds raised in chapel, church, or sales of home made items.

At one time each chapel or church had its own anniversary and tea party, on a different day to another group, but this caused problems with school attendances. Mr. Lawrence (Headmaster) was able to get the officers running these activities together and arranged to have all the various tea parties held on the one day. Some children felt that they had been deprived of an extra tea party because they often attended one chapel or church for the morning and evening service but a different one for afternoon Sunday School.

We rarely saw a car pass through the village. Horses and carts or traps were the only traffic. A few French cars were brought by military officers on leave, and these were used to carry walking wounded soldiers, in their blue uniforms and red ties, to concerts put on for them at tea parties arranged by chapels or churches. Our Dr. Smith had a Model T Ford. He would stand it outside his surgery on Islwyn Hill. To get it started up the hill he would wait for a group of boys to give him a push. We never got a ride.

In 1922 a firm called Howells commenced to run a local bus service from the top of Stow Hill in Newport through Risca and Cross Keys up to Cwmfelinfach, where it stopped and turned round at the Pioneer Hotel. The road beyond was too rough, just an old cart track. The service started with a charabanc with solid rubber tyres and a folding canvas cover for the inclement weather. Lewis and Jones took over the service and experimented with a wireless on board. An aerial was secured to the roof of the coach and passengers could use headphones, but this did not last very long as there was too much interference.

Warm woollen clothes were usually worn with Welsh flannel vests. Most boys had woollen jerseys and shorts with a long top coat. The girls wore long white pinafores with dainty lace collars, woollen stockings and laced up shoes, while the boys had hob nailed boots with steel toe and heel protectors.'

How many readers have similar memories of those by-gone days?

DUFFRYN ISAF FARM. Situated between the village of Wattsville and the Sirhowy River. The 1871 census tells us the following about the farm's occupants -

John Evans	age 56	Widower	born Mynyddislwyn
Ann Evans	27		"
John Evans	19		"
Leah Evans	20		"
Ben Evans	14		"
Sarah Powell	26		"
Edward Powell	8 months		"
John Pugh	62	General Labourer	born Brecon

Duffryn Isaf Farm was taken over by Risca North Colliery in 1890 and its fields were used for the building of much of Wattsville. The farmhouse stayed as a residence until it was condemned about 1980. The above named residents of the farm have their own little history.

John Evans. Widower. His wife Jane had died in 1870. As a young man he had hidden in a barn when the Chartists marched on Newport in 1839. He wanted to be buried with his wife near the entrance door to St. Mary's Church, Risca, but as the grave was not brick lined his request was refused. He was one of the first to be buried by the main gate of the Old Cemetery in Risca.

Ann Evans. She stayed at home as the housekeeper.

John Evans. No information.

Leah Evans. She married a Mr. Jones of Glanyrafon Farm, across the river from Cwmfelinfach. Her husband was killed in Risca Colliery. The 1881 census lists her as a widow with two small children, at Pant y Trwyn Farm. The 1891 census has her living at Caerllwyn with her son William, aged 13. He was killed in the 1920s when he was crushed between a gambo and a fence post.

Ben Evans. Ben took over the farm when his father died. He was re-housed at Penllwyn Farm between Machen and Trethomas.

Sarah Powell (nee Evans). She married a sea captain on the Spanish iron ore run to South Wales. She moved to Newport where her son, Edward, became an accountant before emigrating to Kansas, U.S.A. in 1913.

John Pugh. The labourer was housed and fed for one year and received a horse as his payment. A man and horse could get good wages working on the nearby canal in the 1870s.

The Infants Department of Wattsville Council School in 1922-23.

Outside Oxford House (Wattsville Social Service Centre) in 1950.
Billy Payne, Jeffrey Evans, Jim Regan, Rita Morgan, Marie Williams.

Risca Colliery

The first pit in Risca was sunk in 1841 and with it started the series of Risca explosions. In 1842 Risca Collieries got a contract to supply the Royal West India Mail Steam Packet Company with 72,000 tons of coal for their West Indian Station, and to meet this demand the Old Black Vein Colliery was opened in 1845 (outside the area covered by this book). By 1849 the East India Company included only Welsh Coal (Risca Black Vein) in its list of acceptable coals.

There was an explosion at Old Black Vein Colliery on the 1st December 1860 killing 145 men and boys. The local coroner complained of the extra work that the disaster entailed. The dead were buried on the hillside across the valley, above the canal, with a plantation of pines marking the spot. (The cemetery was tidied up and rebuilt in the spring of 1993).

The 1873 Coal Mines Regulation Act laid down that in any mine where gas had been found there was to be an inspection for gas between each shift. Both Old Black Vein Colliery and New Risca Colliery (built on the lower slopes of Mynyddislwyn Mountain) were very gassy. The New Risca Colliery was opened in 1875, having been sunk by Watts, Ward, and Company. Two eight-hour shifts were being worked at Risca by 1880 (although the Eight Hour Act was not passed until 1908). An account of the new pit in The Hereford Times of July 1880 says *'about 800 men are employed in the colliery and they work in two shifts - 400 or thereabouts going to work at 6 o'clock and remaining until two, and another shift of repairers, about 119 men, then went down to remove falls and to prop'.*

Soon after sinking, 1,050 men and boys were employed, with 102 horses. The colliery was 840 feet deep, not as deep as the later collieries in the mid Sirhowy Valley, because Risca was closer to the southern rim of the coalfield, where the seams of coal were closer to the surface.

A Western Mail article of 21st September 1892 said *'Risca Collieries are amongst the largest in South Wales. They were the first in the South Wales Coalfield to be illuminated by electric light. An installation not only provides the light at the surface but also at the bottom. The underground traction is dealt with by a very complete system of compressed air haulage'.*

When Risca Colliery was sunk, the shaft was aimed to connect with the bottom of a slope from the Old Black Vein Colliery, which it did exactly. Then there was an upcast and a downcast shaft and a return airway to take the foul air over the fresh.

Risca Colliery was the first pit in the valleys to use fans and its layout was thought to be the most modern, but it contained features that would not have been allowed years later. One road ran as a line for 1,000 yards from the bottom of the shaft. Better ventilation INCREASED the risk of gas exploding - there was always a lot of dust blowing about. No one believed in those days that coal dust could explode, and Risca was one of the last pits in the valley to adopt dust control.

The Risca Colliery explosion happened about midnight on the 14th July 1880 when the night shift was down. Some masons were strengthening the arches at the bottom of the shaft and were using naked flame lights, naptha flares. They were supposed to be safe at that spot with so much fresh air coming down the shaft, and normally they probably would have been, but a 900 feet long drift came down to the bottom of the shaft from the Old Black Vein Colliery workings, with the new shaft being sunk deliberately to meet that incline. A great deal of gas had accumulated in the old workings which should have gone up, not down. But there was enough draught to draw it down the incline to the naked lights, which exploded it. The explosion killed everyone in Risca Colliery that night. No one came out alive. The straight road where you could have seen a safety lamp 1,000 yards away was blown in, all blocked tight. The cage and winding gear were gone. One hundred and twenty men and boys, and every horse, were killed.

The top of the fan had been blown off. Men worked like mad to get it back so that they could get the fan working again to get the foul air drawn off.

The best that could be done was done for the bereaved. The Company allowed widows to go on living in Company houses and gave them their coal free. There was a public appeal. They were months getting the bodies out. The rescuers wore camphor bags around the neck as a sort of precaution against infection from the dead bodies - bodies of horses as well as men. Most of the dead could only be identified from their lamp check numbers.

The disaster was reported at length in the newspapers of the day. One report read *'At half past ten Allsop, the night foreman, came up and reported all safe. At twenty past one this morning (Thursday) a loud report of an explosion was heard in the village, and from the volume of smoke which emanated from the pit, it was seen that the gas had exploded. When the smoke had cleared away, Evan Evans, Underground Manager, and John Bond, a pumpman, and several others, volunteered to descend, but the force of the explosion had blown part of the engine house into the air and the fan was damaged'.*

According to the Hereford Times, Mr. Watts (Chairman of the Company) telegraphed, hoping fears of the safety of the men were unfounded. Then *'Mr. Watts and Mr. Thomas Williams, Secretary, arrived at the colliery about 6 p.m. The former gave an immediate order for coffins to be provided and the expense of the interments to be borne by the Company'.*

The Mayor of Newport issued an appeal for £20,000 to provide for 302 dependants. There was a public meeting at Newport on 20th July at which it was moved that subscriptions should be collected by the banks.

The Risca fund ran out before the need was fully met, but the deficiency was made good out of the Abercarn Colliery Disaster Fund (1878). A report of Abercarn Trustees' annual meeting says *'The Trustees again voted £500 from their anticipated surplus to the recipients from the Risca explosion of 1880, the funds in this case having been for some time entirely exhausted, there being still dependent 27 widows, 19 orphans, and 8 relatives. The total amount now granted from the Abercarn Fund to help Risca fund is £1,600'.*

It was reported that *'the bodies of 45 horses have now been got out - a necessary thing as the stench arising from them was most intolerable'*. There were 70 horses altogether in the pit at the time of the explosion. *'The place of working is so warm that the men have to be changed every few minutes'*. *'The pit is in a terribly shattered condition and any further serious disturbances would practically mean the closing of the pit altogether'*.

The manager at the time of the explosion was Mr. Llewellyn Llewellyn. Mr. Kelly is mentioned in newspapers as 'late manager', and was among the many colliery managers and mining engineers who came to give advice. Mr. Wilkinson, Mr. Christopher Pond, and Mr. J.T. Green were present.

Risca colliery closed in August 1967.

Risca Colliery 1875-1967 with Mynyddislwyn Mountain behind.

The Risca Colliery Explosion of 15th July 1880.
The widow from the 1860 explosion comforts the widow from the 1880 explosion.
(Illustrated London News).

Risca Colliery, 1875-1967.

Cwmfelinfach and Ynysddu

These two villages have similarities in their origins. Up to one hundred years ago both were a loose collection of farms and workers houses built alongside the road down the valley that had crossed the Sirhowy River at Gelligroes Mill and ran along the lower slopes of Mynyddislwyn Mountain (not the present A4048), or the Penllwyn Tramroad, which had been built in 1824 by John Jones of Llanarth Court.

Both became villages as a result of the sinking of Nine Mile Point Colliery, which event began in 1902. Both villages were built soon after that date to house the families of the workers at the colliery. Of the two villages, Ynysddu seems to have been the most important in the early years. When Nine Mile Point Colliery was being sunk, its address was *'Ynysddu'*. Also, when the Pioneer Hotel in Cwmfelinfach was planned in 1903, its address was *'Ynysddu'*.

Cwmfelinfach

This village was nearer to the Nine Mile Point Colliery than Ynysddu so the colliery workers had less distance to walk to work. Before the village was formed there were many scattered farms and houses, mostly built alongside the Penllwyn Tramroad or the old road down the valley that was to become Commercial Road. What was to become Stanley Street had been the Parish Road to Machen, linking up with the Parish Road to Mynyddislwyn. The name Cwmfelinfach comes from the little flannel mill that was situated close to the river, but was powered by water from the Nant Draenog than ran down off Mynyddislwyn Mountain.

The rows of houses and shops that were to form the new village were started to be built soon after the Nine Mile Point Colliery began sinking in 1902. In 1903 the Pioneer Hotel was planned, and it was built in 1906. This area was known to be very rich in coal reserves which would be mined for countless years to follow. Any commercial venture here would have been believed to be a solid investment, and when the Pioneer Hotel was sold at an auction at the Westgate Hotel, Newport, in October 1909, it fetched £26,000. To put that into perspective, at the same auction, the Viaduct Hotel in Crumlin sold for under £300.

In 1907 the colliers at the newly opened Nine Mile Point Colliery had two pence a week stopped out of their wages to go towards a planned institute, which opened in 1913. It went on to have a library, reading room, cinema, swimming pool, billiards room and dance hall. It was to close in 1986, but re-opened as a snooker hall, bar and leisure centre, but was not the success that was hoped for. On Saturday 21st October 1995 it mysteriously burned down and has now been completely demolished.

In 1913 also, a new bridge was built over the Nant Draenog, just to the south of the Pioneer Hotel, and a new road was built through the village, a more direct route than the original road from Ynysddu which ran past what was to become

St. Theodore's Church and along Commercial Road, before dropping down to the Pioneer Hotel.

The first school for the children of the emerging village of Cwmfelinfach was on Twyn Gwyn Hill. A temporary corrugated building had been put up by the Church in 1905, called the Mission Church. That doubled up as a school in 1907. Its one room was the school for 141 Cwmfelinfach children. In March 1909 the children moved out of Twyn Gwyn into a temporary school at the end of Maindee Road, much nearer to the heart of the village. That temporary building had previously served as a temporary school in Machen, while the permanent school there was being built. Because of lack of space up at the Mission Church, some of the older Cwmfelinfach children had attended the old Ynysddu School, which they would have walked to each day. These entries from the School Log mention the move from Twyn Gwyn to the temporary building.

> March 29th Recommenced school again after having been closed for a fortnight. We reopened in the new temporary building which has been erected at the end of Maindee Road, having now sufficient accommodation the children from Stds V. VI & VII who had hitherto gone to Ynysddu school were transferred to this school.
>
> 6th May
>
> 1909.
> "Mixed, and infants":-
> The temporary premises occupied at present are of a much more suitable character and the class discipline now is generally satisfactory. The spring rush of babies has caused a serious overcrowding of the babies' room which however has been somewhat relieved today by drafting some of them to the higher class of Infants.

125

As at Ynysddu School, it would be expected that with so many children attending school from Welsh-speaking homes, then Welsh lessons would have been taught.

> Welsh is making fair progress; the instruction in this subject is well given but care will be needed to see that the English speaking children take an intelligent interest in the lessons & their fair share in the work.

The temporary school at the end of Maindee Road served the village from March 1909, at which date a new permanent school was in the process of being built. Part of that new school was opened in 1910.

> — 1910 —
> The Cwmfelinfach Infants' Council School commenced as a separate Department on January 10th. ~~1909~~ 1910.

In September 1910 another three classrooms were put into use.

> Sep. 20th Started at the premises of the new school – using three classrooms – School Unfinished

126

The official opening of the new school was in January 1911. That school-building still serves the village.

> 1911.
>
> Jan 9th Reopened school after the holidays in the new permanent buildings, there being present in the morning for registration 240. In the afternoon the formal opening took place.
>
> Jan 13th In the afternoon there was no school but instead the children to the number of 425 assembled and tea was provided them in order to celebrate the opening of the new school.

When sinking began at Nine Mile Point Colliery in 1902, the London and North Western Railway (who ran the railway from Tredegar to Newport, across the river) agreed to re-lay part of the old Penllwyn Tramroad to link the new colliery to the main line. A new railway bridge was built over the Sirhowy River, and all was completed by March 1908. Small goods depots were built at Wattsville (1913) Cwmfelinfach (1911) and Ynysddu (1911). Wattsville goods depot closed in August 1929.

Ynysddu depot was the largest of the three depots, with goods sheds, offices, stables and crane. The depots were the lifeline to the outside world for the new villages, providing them with building materials, furniture, food, clothing etc. Ynysddu depot closed in December 1937.

Babell Chapel was opened in 1827, and into the twentieth century the worship was conducted in Welsh. For the sake of the English speakers in the new community a small church was started above a shop in Stanley Street which in 1911 moved into a bigger building, that had been a dance hall and billiards room. It was re-named Bethany.

Nine Mile Point Colliery

Of all the Collieries in the South Wales coalfield Nine Mile Point was certainly one of the most famous, or infamous, depending on which side of the fence you belong. Most of the troubles were not the usual wrangle between owners and workmen, but a political battle between rival unions.

The colliery got its name from its proximity to The Nine Mile Point, about a mile away across the river on the Sirhowy Railway Line. As a result of the 1802 Act of Parliament, the Sirhowy Tramroad Company could not build their tramroad all the way from Sirhowy (Tredegar) to Newport. Working from the other direction northwards from Newport, the Monmouthshire Canal Company agreed to build a tramroad eight miles long, running up to the Sirhowy Valley. However, it had to go through Sir Charles Morgan's Tredegar Park, and being an influential man, he insisted on building any tramroad that ran on his land, himself. This was built in a sweeping curve and was exactly one mile long. Either side of Morgan's tramroad was the Mon. Canal Company's line. Their eight miles and Morgan's one mile added up to Nine Miles, hence the name of its terminal, where it was joined end-on by the Sirhowy Company's line.

The colliery was sunk by the Cardiff company of Burnyeat Brown, and sinking began in 1902. It was at that time called Coronation Colliery after the coronation of that year. During sinking, seven men died in a shaft accident in August 1904. Coal production started in 1905.

At sinking, the owners anticipated eight seams of workable thickness coal, totalling thirty five feet. Assuming 45,000 tons of coal to the acre, and an unworked area between Risca Colliery and Pontllanfraith of 5,000 acres of untouched coal, there would be about 225 million tons of coal to be produced in the lower Sirhowy Valley.

There were three shafts at the Nine Mile Point Colliery - East Pit, West Pit and Rock Vein Pit. By 1922 it had changed ownership to United National Collieries Co. (who owned Risca Colliery). Rumours were rife over the possible closure of N.M.P. Colliery. The manager was assaulted and almost thrown into the feeder pond. Sixteen men were charged with the offence and some were gaoled.

March 1923 saw more troubles at N.M.P. when the South Wales Miners Federation (The Fed.) tried to make all collieries belong to their union. Again, N.M.P. colliers landed in court, with some gaoled.

In October 1923 the owners announced the closure of the colliery at the end of the month, due to prohibitive working costs, but the threat was withdrawn. Ownership of the colliery again changed hands, to The Ocean Coal Company.

1928 saw further troubles at N.M.P. over wages, resulting in an 'all-out strike' by The Fed. It carried over into 1929. There were nineteen men from a rival union at The Point who were prepared to work, making feelings run very high. In February 1929 six non-Fed. men were offered greatly increased pay, plus police protection, to go down The Point. Extra police were called in. Four men agreed to work, and they were escorted to work by police. Running home they were met by a crowd of about seven hundred men, women and children. That evening their homes were attacked. Next day only two worked, and returning home they

128

were again attacked. The Riot Act was read by the police and batons were drawn. Some of the rioters were gaoled. Work slowly and reluctantly restarted at The Point after a four month stoppage.

Nine Mile Point Colliery.
The waste tip to the left of the photograph almost engulfed Babell Chapel.

September 1935 saw another strike caused by the political battle of rival unions. Again The Fed. wanted a closed shop at The Point. All Fed. men reported for work but only two hundred of them were taken on, plus eighty-eight non-Fed. colliers. In October 1935 non-Fed. men were again being escorted to work by the police. The Fed. tried to stop them with such tactics as nail studded boards across the road at Ynysddu to stop buses, and by pushing coping stones off a bridge onto the Sirhowy railway line to stop trains. But on the afternoon of Saturday 12th October, the non-Fed. men were already on pit top ready to descend to work. Some Fed. Men were underground finishing their shift when they agreed that if they stayed down the pit the non-Feds. would not be able to go down. Word spread underground and seventy-eight Fed. colliers stayed down the pit that Saturday afternoon. On Sunday three of them came up. On Monday Fed. men were allowed down the pit to work as normal and tried to persuade the strikers to come up. This was a mistake because there were now two hundred strikers below. Boys were sent up to the surface.

Non-Fed. men did get down the pit to work, but by Wednesday morning there were none of them at The Point. The Fed. men refused to return to the surface until there was a written guarantee that no further non-Fed. men would be employed at N.M.P. An agreement was reached, and on Saturday afternoon, a week after the 'Stay Down' started, the men came to the surface. A hundred and eighty four men had been underground, some for 177 hours.

129

In 1916 there were 2,440 men employed on three shifts at N.M.P. Colliery. When it closed in July 1964 there were 699 men employed.

Nine Mile point Colliery 1905-1964, with Mynyddislwyn Mountain looming over it. The coal wagons show 'BB' which was Burnyeat Brown, the Company that sunk the colliery, and 'Ocean', the Company into which Burnyeat Brown was amalgamated.

Nant y Draenog, running down from the reservoir on Mynyddislwyn Mountain, flowed through the arches and under the main road to Newport, in Cwmfelinfach. Today, the Park is to the right of the photograph, while the houses in the background are on Twyn Gwyn Hill.

The same view as in the last photograph, but the cameraman has moved round a little. This photograph must have been taken on a Monday, the traditional day for having a line full of washing.

Nant y Draenog, running down off The Mountain, was used for Baptisms, as seen here in April 1909.

Cwmfelinfach and District Juvenile Choir in 'Queen Lily' in May 1922. Photograph taken at the back of the Institute. Just off the photograph to the left was a First World War Field Gun (known locally as The Canon) which was well anchored to the ground. It remained in place until the Second World War when it went for scrap.

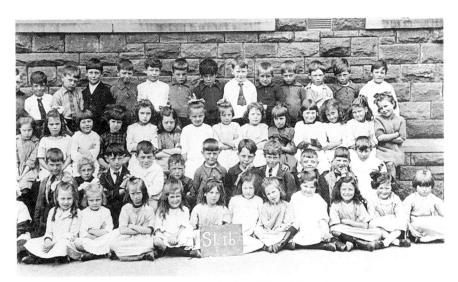

Standard 1b outside Cwmfelinfach School.

A wartime photograph taken in Cwmfelinfach quarry, opposite the Pioneer Hotel. On the right at the back, standing on the running board of the lorry, was Eddy Rees, who owned the lorry, and worked it at Mynyddislwyn Quarry.

A 1906 photograph of Cwmfelinfach. The boy with the sack truck was Arthur Wilkes, standing outside the London and Provincial Bank.

Harvest Festival at Cwmfelinfach in the early years of the village. 'The Harvest is great but Labours are few'.

Dr. Bob.
Dr. Robert Ellis Roberts was born in Caernarfonshire, North Wales, and arrived in South Wales to practise medicine. He became doctor to the Nine Mile Point Colliery. The villages of Ynysddu and Cwmfelinfach, and the district of Mynyddislwyn, where he became Medical Officer of Health, were his world for twenty six years, when he would visit his patients on horseback. He married a local lady, Elvira Evans, in 1912. She had chosen a nursing career and they ran the practice together. Their house was called 'Castell', part of which was the surgery. The 6 feet 2 inch tall man was known to the people of Mynyddislwyn as 'Dr. Bob Bach'.

Opposite the Pioneer Hotel. Cwmfelinfach. The group were off on a trip to Newport Lighthouse.

Cwmfelinfach Flannel Mill by local artist Mr. Granville Davies. This sketch is believed to be an accurate representation. Plans have been scaled and the artist had first hand information about the building from his father and grandfather. The Fellmongers' wool store near the River Sirhowy was burnt down in the very early 1900s.

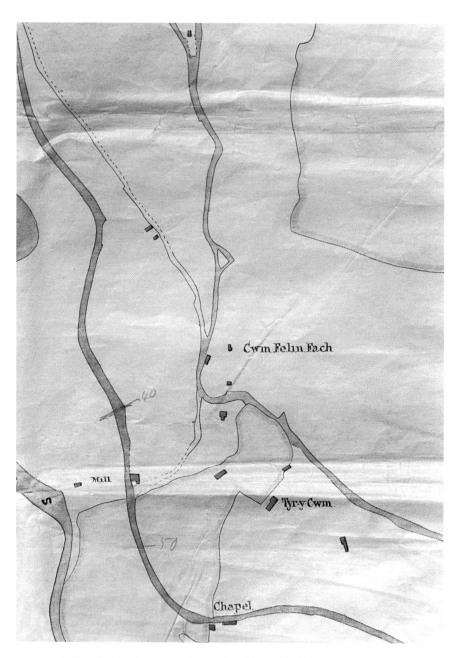

A map of 1847 showing how sparsely populated Cwmfelinfach was. To the extreme left is the Sirhowy River, and next to it, beside Babell Chapel and the Mill, was the Penllwyn (or Llanarth) Tramroad. Twyn Gwyn Hill runs up through the middle of the map.

Ynysddu

Soon after 1902, Ynysddu had about 280 houses in various length rows in the village, and in the outlying terraces of Pontgam, Caerllwyn, Glenview and Greenfield, which were built alongside the original road down the valley, which was to become Commercial Street and Glyn Terrace as it passed through the new village of Ynysddu.

Soon Ynysddu boasted a large Police Station (built in 1911) and Glyn Baptist Chapel, as well as the school that had been built earlier in 1877. In 1910 a temporary corrugated iron building was erected for the Infants Department because the old school was not big enough for the population explosion.

> Infants' Department,
> This department is still accommodated in a temporary corrugated iron building erected in 1910. There are five classrooms giving accommodation for 250. The number on books is 272. but, so far, owing to the low attendance there has been no overcrowding.

The present Ynysddu School was built in 1926, the same year that the Deeds were signed for the Welfare Ground.

> 8.9.26. A half holiday has been granted for this afternoon, for the official opening of the New Mixed School.

Taken from the Old School Log Book, 1924.

> The temperature of the classrooms on Wednesday and today has not risen above 36 degrees, and it has been impossible to keep the children warm

In those early years of the twentieth century, when holidays were unheard of the Sunday School Outings were the only chance to get away from the area, albeit only for a day. The first extract is from 1920, and the second is from 1928.

> July 15th: A holiday will be given on Monday July 19th. The Sunday Schools having united to take the children away for the day. by permission of the Director

> July 27th: A holiday will be given on Monday. The Sunday School children of Twyn Gwyn. The Church, Bethany & Pisgah are going for their annual outing to Barry.

In 1928 the old Penllwyn Tramroad between Ynysddu and Gelligroes (which had been unused for many years) was relaid as the modem A4048, and became the main road up the valley.

> June 25th: Work has commenced on the new road which runs by the School gates. The two gates opening on to the road has been closed for the present. and all the children enter by the gate leading, out to Alexandra Rd.

> October 3rd: A Part of the School wall, and the old Cloakroom adjoining the new road is being pulled down today. for the extension of the new Road.

The old school Log Book shows that the Welsh language was much used in the area in the early years of the twentieth century. The native population on Mynyddislwyn Mountain was probably Welsh speaking at that time, while some of the colliery workers would have come into the district from Welsh speaking areas, bringing with them their language and customs. Welsh was also the language of many of the local chapels at that time.

Welsh is intelligently taught under somewhat more favourable conditions than usual, as the teacher is Welsh speaking and a proportion of the children come from homes where Welsh is habitually spoken

Despatched 6th April 1911

Oct 5th   Miss Cecelia Jones of Rehymney joined the Staff of this school; she will for the present take the babies class, and take First Class in Welsh for one lesson each day, the Head mistress taking the babies class during the Welsh lesson.

Ynysddu was no different to other valley communities in the early twentieth century, when diseases were prevalent. The county Medical Officer would have had no alternative but to shut the schools for prolonged periods.

Dec 2 1910. (Week ending)
          Number on Books 171
          Average attendance 91.2
          Percentage   53.3 %.

Nov 30th 10. School closed until Dec 14th 1910, on account of an epidemic of measles and whooping cough. Notice of closing of school received from Dr. W. E. James, Glendwr. Newbridge. Mon.

Dec 11th Received notice from Dr. W. E. James
         Ty. Glany-Dwr. Newbridge. Mon that this
         school is to be closed until after Xmas
         on account of measles and whooping cough
1911
Jan 9th School re-opened after Xmas vacation
         The long holiday of 5½ weeks has
         retarded the progress of the children
         very much
              There are still many children absent
         who are suffering from whooping cough

March 28th This school will be closed mid day for the
           Easter vacation. and will reassemble on April the 8th
April 8th School opened today. Attendance very bad owing
           to epidemic of measles. Percentage for the day - 70%
April 12th Number on Books 286. Average Att. 197.8. Perc: 69.1%
April 18th This department closed today. until after the
           Whitsun Holidays owing to Epidemic of measles.

Nov 11th This school opened today after been closed
         since Oct 23rd for Influenza.

Jan: 5th 1920, School opened this morning. There are many
               scarlet fever cases.

27.4.23 This School will be closed until May 28th
         owing to epidemic of measles.

1918
Jan 16th Owing to the heavy fall of snow only six
         children attended School. Therefore the school
         was closed for the day.
17th   On Thursday not one child attended.

140

Life in the Depression 1920-30s

Life was no different here than anywhere else in the locality - the same hardships were felt. Application could be made to Mr. Jenkins the Relieving Officer for financial assistance. He would pay a visit to the home. If he saw anything of value, the applicant was expected to sell it. The 'lucky' people were awarded two shillings and six pence ($12\frac{1}{2}$p) or a food voucher. During that period the 'Blue Pilgrims', a well-to-do body from London, frequently visited. They hired an empty shop in Commercial Street and issued boots and clothing in an effort to alleviate the effects of the depression.

Evacuees

This community became the home of wartime evacuees during the Second World War. How many of those children from cities would have stood unbelieving at the wonderful countryside of Mynyddislwyn Mountain? How many of those children played in their spare time on the Mountain?

Sept 4th School closed until further notice because War has been declared on Germany.
Sept.18th School commenced this morning. Thirteen children under four years old were sent home. They did not have gas masks and I consider they were too young to attend under the present circumstances.
Twelve children has been admitted from various places. and will attend this school for the duration of the war.

> June 5th School was closed on Monday June 3rd. On Sunday June 2nd the boys and girls from Barton Rd Schools. Dover were evacuated to this district owing to war conditions, Dover being in a dangerous area.

The Bomb

During Saturday night the 1st November, 1941, a 1,000 lb bomb was dropped on Ynysddu and penetrated deep into the old ash tip between the river and Alexandra Road. Fortunately, it did not explode. Partial evacuation of the residents took place from the 17th to 23rd November for its removal to an open space on top of Machen Mountain (Mynydd y Grug) for its final disarming.

Tea Party

During the Second World War when rationing of foods was in force, a tea party for the children must have been a wonderful treat.

> Jan 10th a tea party was given to the children of the Mynyddislwyn Area, by the members of the M.U.D.C.

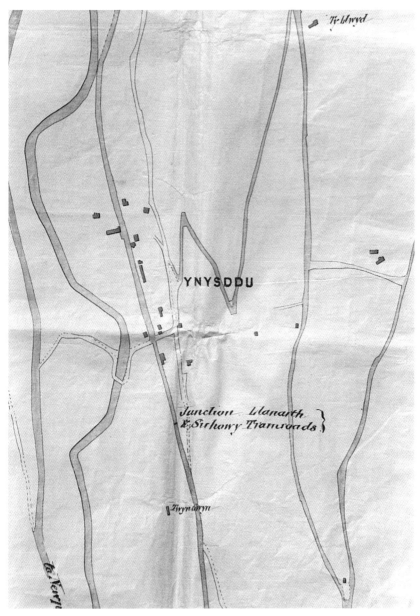

A map of 1847 showing that at that date Ynysddu had more houses and farms than Cwmfelinfach. Most of those houses were built alongside the tramroad, opened in 1824 by John Jones of Llanarth Court (near Raglan). The village got its name from Ynysddu Farm (shown between the river and tramroad), which was bought by John Hodder Moggridge in 1804, and became part of the Moggridge Estate.

143

Ynysddu before 1900. In the foreground can be seen Ynysddu Railway Station, which was on the line from Nantybwch to Newport. In the background, on Mynyddislwyn Mountain, can be seen Hen Ysgoldy (Old Schoolhouse), Ty Lloyd Farm, Pant y Ffynnon Farm, a barn (in centre), Twyn Gwyn Chapel and Tyla Du. The scattered buildings that were to become Ynysddu were built alongside the Penllwyn Tramroad, or the road down the valley that was to become Commercial Road. From the left can be seen Well House, Ynysddu Farm, Myrtle Cottage, the chimneys of Black Prince Inn can be seen over Ynysddu School, The Ranks, numbers 2 and 3 Garden Cottages, number 1 Garden Cottage, Duffryn House (the first Post Office in the village), a barn with outside steps (for Ynysddu Farm), numbers 1 and 2 Station View, Ty'r Agent, Forest House and Y Glyn.

144

Ynysddu before 1900. From the left can be seen Well House, Ynysddu Farm, Myrtle Cottage (became Green Cottage, then Green House, then Garden Club, then Garden Cottage, then Garden House), the chimneys of the Black Prince Inn can be seen over Ynysddu School, the Ranks (the northernmost of which was the school Headmaster's house.

The Ranks were built in the late 1820s by John Hodder Moggridge, who came to the area in 1804 from Gloucestershire, and settled in Blackwood. These were one of three small settlements built by him. The others were at Blackwood and Fleur de Lys.

The Ranks were founded as a social experiment after Moggridge became alarmed at the dreadful living conditions of the poor. He called them his 'Village System'.

He offered a small number of selected workers a lease of a small plot of land, on condition that a small rent would be paid to him, and that a substantial cottage be built, with a garden laid out in the form of an allotment.

Of course, if those workers could look after themselves and their families, they were unlikely to need Parish Relief which was a great burden to the ratepayers, such as Moggridge. Such workers were also more likely to be interested in maintaining law and order.

Ynysddu Ranks were built fronting on to John Jones's Penllwyn Tramroad, opened in 1824. Close by was the Black Prince Inn, also opening onto that tramroad.

Ynysddu before 1900. From the left can be seen Numbers 2 and 3 Garden Cottages, Number 1 Garden Cottage, Duffryn House, a barn for Ynysddu Farm, Numbers 1 and 2 Station View, Ty'r Agent, Forest House and Y Glyn. On the hillside of Mynyddislwyn Mountain can be seen Twyn Gwyn Chapel and Tyla Du.

In 1804 John Hodder Moggridge bought Ynysddu Farm with its 161 acres, and 40 acres of woods adjoining. On part of this land the village was to develop.

Ynysddu School

William Thomas, Islwyn the poet, was one who was responsible for, and supervised the building of the school, opposite the Black Prince Inn. He became Chairman of the Governors. The school was due for completion in 1876, but due to a dispute with the builders it was not opened until 30th April 1877. It cost £1,500 to build. On completion of his education at Bangor Normal College, Glynfab Williams took over the headship on the opening date, when sixty pupils were enrolled. It was later enlarged to accommodate 170 pupils. The opening of the school probably led to the decline and closure of Hen Ysgoldy (the old Schoolhouse, seen at the top left of the photograph on page 144) opposite Ty Llwyd farm on Mynyddislwyn Mountain. In July 1877 'Islwyn' approached Glynfab Williams and requested the school keys. Islwyn and the children locked themselves inside the school and demanded three months summer holiday. The outcome was the grant of three weeks holiday.

In 1926 a new school was built to the south end of the village, which survives today. Ysgol Islwyn School was commenced in 1914 but was abandoned because of World War I. It was finally completed and opened in 1926. One of the provisions in its design was for an open-air classroom to accommodate ex-T.B. suffering children, a disease that was widespread at that time. The original school then became a Junior School, and survived until it was pulled down in the early 1980s, to be replaced by Alexandra Court, a home for the elderly.

An Obediah Hodges painting of Ynysddu Farm, painted in 1916. The man, who lived at the farm, was Mr. George, known locally as 'Squire George'. One of his brothers kept the Black Prince Inn, while another was a blacksmith at Ynysddu. The farm house stood alone, with its barns and outbuildings a short distance away. This painting was anonymously donated to be auctioned, with the proceeds going to St. Tudor's Church tower restoration fund. At the time the building and man were unknown, and in March 1994 there was an appeal in a local newspaper for anyone with information to come forward to solve the mystery. The farm gave its name to the village that was built on its land, and passed from Abercarne Estate to Moggridge Estate in 1804.

The outbuildings to Ynysddu Farm, and behind, Well House.

148

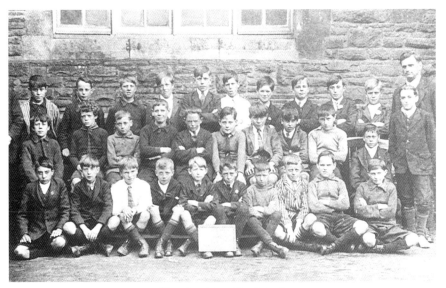

Class I at Ynysddu School.

Ynysddu Mission Church Sunday School treat in 1908.

St. Theodore's Church

At the start of the twentieth century Cwmfelinfach and Ynysddu were each a collection of farms, houses etc. Neither was a village. The sinking of Nine Mile Point Colliery changed that, with an influx of colliery workers causing a population explosion. This caused Ynysddu to become a Conventional District within the parish of Mynyddislwyn, with its own Priest. The congregation met at the Mission Church, a corrugated sheet structure half way up Twyn Gwyn Hill out of Cwmfelinfach, which was destroyed in a storm in 1916.

In 1920 the Church in Wales became Dis-Established and parish boundaries were re-aligned. The parish of Ynysddu came into being, covering the area from Gelligroes to Wattsville, and a parish Church needed to be built. The site chosen was half way between Ynysddu and Cwmfelinfach. The first church built was temporary, another corrugated building, next to the present St. Theodore's. The Priest-in Charge was elevated to a Vicar.

In 1925 the Foundation Stone was laid for the present stone-built St. Theodore's Church, and the Church was completed and consecrated in July 1927, with a seating capacity for about 300 in the congregation.

The Induction Service at St. Theodore's Church, Ynysddu, of the Rev. I.G.H. Bowen Harris, by the Ven. Archdeacon Griffiths, on 6th. May 1925.

Laying the Foundation Stone for St. Theodore's Church on 23rd September 1925.

Ivy Curtiss and Milly Long at the rear of King Street, Cwmfelinfach. The wooden fence was the boundary of the old Penllwyn Tramroad, which became a railway running as far north as Ynysddu. In the distance, to the ladies' left, can be seen Saint Theodore's Church.

Islwyn

(The Sweet Singer of Sirhowy)

William Thomas (Islwyn) was born in Ty'r Agent at Ynysddu on 3rd April 1832, the youngest of nine children of Morgan and Mary Thomas. His father was a native of Ystradgynlais and his mother was from Blaengwawrne Farm near Crumlin. After their marriage they moved to Ynysddu where Morgan took up his position as agent to John Jones of Llanarth, who had just completed the building of the Penllwyn (or Llanarth) Tramroad (which is today the main road down the valley between Gelligroes and Ynysddu). Ty'r Agent, their home, was alongside that tramroad.

William was born to middle aged parents and was not a strong child, suffering many chest ailments. When he grew up his father wanted William to become a surveyor, so he was given a good education in private schools in Newport, Tredegar, Cowbridge and Swansea.

A great influence on his life was his brother-in-law Daniel Jenkyns, Minister at Babell Chapel, Cwmfelinfach. Apart from his religious influence, Jenkyns also encouraged and sharpened William's use and understanding of the Welsh language. Another who influenced him greatly was Aneurin Jones (Aneurin Fardd) the miller at Gelligroes Mill, who wrote Welsh poetry and who competed at eisteddfodau.

William's youth coincided with the times of the annual eisteddfod at Abergavenny, one of the most important in Wales at that time, which was sponsored by such wealthy patrons as Sir Benjamin and Lady Hall (later Lord and Lady Llanover) and the Guests of Dowlais Ironworks. Under the watchful eye of his two local tutors William began writing poetry. Soon he was competing at various eisteddfodau, using many pseudonyms, but legend has it that after winning at Abergavenny one year he was encouraged by Lady Hall to compete under the name of Islwyn.

While completing his education at Swansea he met Anne Bowen and they became engaged to be married. But she died suddenly in 1853, aged 20. Her death was to have a devastating effect on the 21 year old William, which he described in this poem

> ...y... cartre'n barod -
> Ond yr angau'n mynd rhyngom,
> Y dodrefn wedi'u trefnu
> Hefyd, a'r gain fodrwy gu,
> Rhwymau ein bore amod,
> A'r ysblennydd ddydd ar ddod,
> Ond yr angau'n mynd rhyngom,
> A'm heinioes I mwy yn siom,
> Yn siom oll, fy enioes mwy
> Yn fedd I mi tra fyddwy.

....the home ready
But death went between us
The furniture arranged
Too, and the lovely ring,
The bonds of our early agreement
And the splendid day about to come,
But death went between us,
And my life is henceforth a disappointment,
All a disappointment, my life henceforth,
Will be a grave for me while I live.

Soon after Anne's death William entered the Ministry (in 1859) and followed his brother-in-law as a Minister of the Calvinistic Methodist Church of Wales. He was never to have charge of his own chapel, which was not unusual at that time. His weekends were spent away from home on preaching engagements.

Under the name of Islwyn, he concentrated more on his poetry. But of all his many works his fame rests mainly on his 'Storm' poem of 5,500 lines, and later another 'Storm' poem of the same length, which have become known as Storm 1 and Storm 2.

Throughout his life he continued to compete for the Chair at the National Eisteddfod, but he never won it. But he did win many minor prizes at the National, and was a regular adjudicator there, for which he received a payment to supplement his low Ministerial income. He did win Chairs at lesser, but important, eisteddfodau; at Rhyl 1870, Holyhead 1872, Caerphilly 1874 and Treherbert 1877 (the last named Chair is in St. Tudor's Church).

Elizabeth Thomas,
sister of Islwyn.
She married Daniel
Howells, and was the
mother of Catherine
(see photograph
on Pant Glas).

He returned to Swansea in 1863. Anne Bowen's (his former fiance's) father had died and her mother married William Davies of Tredegar, and they were living in her home in Swansea. Mr. Davies had a daughter Martha by a previous marriage. Islwyn met her, courted her, and they were married in Swansea in March 1864. The couple moved in with Islwyn's mother at Green Meadow, Cwmfelinfach, which she had occupied when Islwyn'd father died in 1854. In 1871 Islwyn and Martha moved to Y Glyn ay Ynysddu, in the shadow of Mynyddislwyn Mountain.

From his earliest writing days Islwyn had various poems and articles published in a wide range of periodicals. He also held many posts on the editorial staff of various papers, all of which helped add to his income. He was also an agent for The Liverpool and London Fire and Life Assurance Company. But when Sunday arrived he was away preaching the Gospel.

He supervised the building of Ynysddu School (now demolished) opposite the Black Prince, and was Chairman of the Governors. In July 1877 Islwyn asked the headmaster for the school keys, and he and the children locked themselves inside the school and would not open it again until the headmaster granted a three-month school holiday. They settled for three weeks.

Ralph Caple at Babell Chapel with Islwyn's four Bardic Chairs.

155

His hectic lifestyle took its toll and in his last years he was often ill. He died in bed at Y Glyn on 20th November 1878. A niece of his, present at his death bed, said that his last words were in Welsh - *'Diolch I ti Martha am y cyfan a wnest I mi. Buoest yn garedig iawn. Rwyf yn mynd at Anne nawr'*. (*'Thank you Martha for all you did for me. You have been very kind. I am going to Anne now'*).

He was buried in Babell cemetery at the foot of Mynyddislwyn Mountain, and some years later his brother-in-law, the Minister at Babell, was buried next to him. Islwyn's grave is marked by a marble obelisk.

There were special celebrations at the centenary of Islwyn's birth. They were recorded in the newspaper, as follows

'Bishop's
Tribute to Islwyn.

* * *

Bard's Exceptional
Insight

* * *

Meaning of the Pen-name

All the religious bodies of Ynysddu and district joined on Sunday to render tribute to Islwyn, Gwent's great poet, hymn writer, and preacher. It was regarded as the closing day of the Islwyn centenary celebrations.

In the morning a commemoration service was conducted at St. Theodore's Church, Ynysddu, by the Rev. C.W. Kelly, (vicar), and hymns written by Islwyn took the place of the usual hymns.

The Bishop of Monmouth preached on the words 'Let us now praise famous men'. In that passage, he said, it was remarkable to find that the musician and the poet were bracketed with great Kings and Emperors as those for whom praise was due to God. That was the spirit in which they were met that day. The poet was a man gifted with a peculiar insight, a capacity to find and to show to others the beauty in common things. The poet did more than please the ear, otherwise there would not be much reason for offering praise to God for him.'

Mystery of Hill and Vale

Islwyn possessed in an exceptional degree that gift of insight. He saw in the hills and valleys of Monmouthshire wonder and mystery, and was able to reveal them to others. Islwyn was a minister of the Christian faith, brought daily into touch with the commonplace of human nature, and saw there the mystery of human patience in suffering, loyalty in friendship, and the mixed joy and sorrow of human life. The great danger of these days was that people passed through life half blind, with eyes that did not see the wonders of the commonplace.

The afternoon proceedings were in the open air within a few yards of Ty'Agent, now almost roofless, where Islwyn was born. All the Sunday schools of the area gathered for the service, over which the vicar presided. The Rev. E.L. Evans (Congregational), Ynysddu, and the Rev. Frank Thomas (Presbyterian), Llansamlet, took the devotional part and Mr. Morgan Jones, M. P. was among the speakers.

'Voice of the Wind'

In the evening the Rev. E. J. Edmunds (vicar of St. Catherine's, Caerphilly, and a grandnephew of the bard) gave a number of reminiscences of Islwyn related to him by his mother, who was Islwyn's last surviving niece.

Islwyn, he said, was a shy, retiring man who hated publicity. He loved children and saw beauty in everything. What better nom de plume could the bard have chosen than Islwyn, which meant voice of the wind or voice of the storm. In these days of stress that voice came into their troubled lives to help them.

A commemoration sacred concert was held at the Workmen's-hall, over which Mr. Charles Edwards M.P. presided.

Urdd Celebration

Members of Urdd Gobaith Cymru took part in the celebrations on Saturday, when boys and girls from the secondary schools of Pontllanfraith, Caerphilly, Hengoed, Pengam, Bargoed and Rhymney attended in such numbers that Babell Chapel proved too small to accommodate them and the meeting had to be held at the church-hall. Mr. Islwyn Jones, Pengam, presided, and a varied programme (all in Welsh) was given by the members.

Under the auspices of Adran Gwent Professor W.A. Gruffydd, M.A. gave a lecture on 'Islwyn' (in Welsh) before an appreciative audience. Mr. D.W. Jones, Newport, presided.'

"Mawreddig, Gymru ydwyt, I'r byd bendith ddirith wyt."

ISLWYN'S CENTENARY   NATIONAL CELEBRATIONS
(Canmlwyddiant Islwyn)   *(Dathliad Cenedlaethol)*

JUNE 15th, 18th and 19th, 1932
(Mehefin 15fed, 18fed a'r 19eg, 1932)

The Committee of the above request the pleasure of the Company of

Mrs Stephens

at the Islwyn Centenary Meetings as shown on Programme enclosed.

R.S.V.P.,
   A. W. GAMES,
     Ty Celyn,
      Cwmfelinfach.

157

Ty'r Agent, Ynysddu, birthplace of William Thomas (Islwyn). At the base of the front wall can be seen the top of a stone arch. Was there a cellar under the house, or did the arch accommodate a weigh bridge for passing trams on the Penllwyn Tramroad, for Mr. Thomas to record passing tonnages to charge tolls.

Ty'r Agent, Ynysddu, photographed in 1932, the year that it was pulled down, which was the centenary of Islwyn's birth.

Travelling up the Sirhowy Valley out of Ynysddu, Lily Farm would have been seen between the modern new road and Pontgarn Terrace. In her little booklet, Mrs. Meyrick wrote *'Lily Farm, occupied by two spinster sisters, Misses Margaret and Mary Williams. They knew their work and farmed the holding without any outside help. Their brother lived with them. He was a railwayman and did not interfere with anything in their business. I do not believe they would have welcomed him if he wished to as they were quite capable of managing their own affairs; besides, they were rather independent. They seemed to value their independence as a pearl of great price and there was no gold, silver, or cajoling that could be used to bargain for it. Mary kept a flock of sheep on some rough ground belonging to the farm, while Margaret tended to the cattle, pigs and poultry. I can remember her having a large number of chickens roosting high in the trees and I never heard of trouble with foxes.*

I never met anyone who could dress a chicken or goose as clean and as nice as Margaret the Lily, and the best Christmas cake I ever tasted was made by her. A great friend of Islwyn, she had the honour of administering to him his last needs. She was at his bedside when he died. The proudest hour of her life.

The lives of the Misses Williams the Lily was not solely confined to drudgery, they were very intellectual and were capable of giving advice to others on points of law, agriculture, and religion, they could not be asked the wrong question'.

The Tithe Apportionment Book of 1839 tells us that it was not a farm then, but a cottage and garden with one arable field, with a total area of two roods and thirty three perch. It was part of the Moggridge Estate, and its annual tithe was rated at one shilling and six pence.

Lily Farm was pulled down about 1950 and a modern bungalow now stands in its place.

Mention has already been made of the Penllwyn Tramroad built by John Jones of Llanarth, and opened in 1824. In this part of the valley its route has been covered by the A4048 road, which was opened in 1928. A little way above Lily Farm that tramroad crossed the River Sirhowy by means of Pont Gam (the Crooked Bridge), a beautiful single arch stone built bridge, still standing after all those years. How many tons of coal were trundled over the bridge in horse-drawn trams heading down the valley to Newport?

Just above Pont Gam brings us to the spot where the activities of a hundred years ago were so wonderfully described by Mrs. Meyrick in her booklet. *'A short distance beyond the mill was the scene of the annual sheep washing process. About 500-600 sheep were brought down from the mountain for their annual bath. Big baskets full of food were brought down there; home made loaves of bread and Caerphilly cheese, boiled ham and beef. A nine gallon cask of beer was stalled on the bank. Hurdles were fixed in place for pens, and the noise was deafening; dogs barking, sheep bleating, and the men shouting. Yet it seemed in harmony with the occasion. Seven or eight men would enter the river and would rub and scrub until the job was completed at about 4 o'clock. They would not have a full meal while in the river, only sandwiches, tea brewed in tin cans and buckets, and plenty of beer.*

They would leave the water and they'd go to the wood close by to change their clothes. They were then feeling fit, merry and bright, being warmed on the outside by the sun and on the inside by the beer. They were then ready for a good square meal. When that was over, it was time to gather things together for the homeward journey.

The sheep would then be taken back to the mountain to dry and mature ready for shearing, which was another great day. I can remember a shoulder of veal being roasted in the big bread oven for that day. About 14 men from the neighbouring farms would come and take their places along the shearing benches and would be kept very busy until the late evening. The farmer himself did no shearing on that day, but he was a very busy man. He acted as a kind of veterinary surgeon, barman and home ruler, and he'd see that there was a keen edge on each pair of shears. When the shearing was done the sheep were stamped with the owner's initials in black pitch, and were taken back to the mountain once more to graze contentedly for another twelve months'.

A short distance closer to Pontllanfraith stands today what is left of Cwmalsie Farm. Mrs Meyrick wrote of it *'We reach Cwmalsie, the home of a once well known character John Jenkins. A straw chair and skep maker, a skilled tradesman at such work, his chairs occupied a place of honour in many farmhouse kitchens in the district.*

It was said that he would scent a swarm of bees half a mile away, and if they came within half a mile of Cwmalsie they would surely find a home in one of John Jenkins' skeps.

He managed to educate his son to become a clergyman, the Reverend Jabez Jenkins, Rector of Vaynor, near Merthyr'.

The following letter tells us that at one time this was the home of a mole catcher. The letter was found when the present owners of Cwmalsie, Mr. and Mrs. Doug Thomas, were undertaking renovation work inside the house. A stone came out of the wall, to reveal an earthenware bottle. The letter was inside that bottle - a time capsule at Cwmalsie.

Cwmalsie lost land for the building of Springfield estate about 1950, and the little land that it retained was taken about 1990. When the Pontllanfraith by-pass was built , the remaining part of a field, with cattle barn and pig styes (both much altered for modern use) disappeared under that road, which runs within an arms length of Cwmalsie back door..

Cwmalsie Farm, with the remains of cattle barn and pig styes behind, both of which were pulled down in the late 1980s for the building of the by-pass road.

Cwmnantyrodyn

(Taken from 1846 Tithe Map)

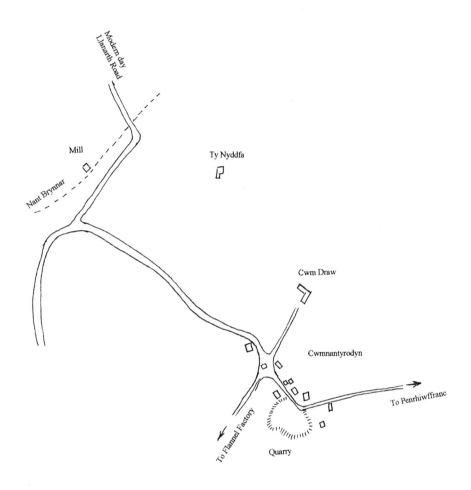

In the introductory chapter to this book mention was made of the Mortarium found here, and the bronze figurine of a horse found about a $^{1}/_{4}$ mile away, also dated to the Roman period. Could these finds be indicative of a possible Roman or later Romano-British settlement in the area?

The name Cwmnantyrodyn suggests a kiln in the valley by the stream. The word Odyn usually refers to a lime kiln, a place where lime was made. Long before cement was used in building work, lime was used to make mortar. Lime was a vital ingredient in building construction. Such lime was made by burning limestone in a specially built kiln to produce quicklime. This quicklime reacts violently when water is added, a process known as slaking. This slaked lime was mixed with sand, soil or river silt to make mortar for building. If water is added to the slaked quicklime it produces a thick paste which was used to make renders and plaster for wall coverings, both inside and outside. If more water is added the white liquid can be brushed on to walls. The limewashing built up over many years of application to waterproof the walls, to give a neat appearance to buildings, but more importantly to act as a disinfectant.

Nothing can be proved, but as all the farms on the Mountain, and the Church itself, would have needed lime in its many forms, can we guess that a small but important industry was centred on Cwmnantyrodyn. The limestone that was needed to go into the kiln could have been quarried at nearby Risca where it outcrops. It could have been carried to the kiln by horse and cart, or in panniers hung on the sides of animals, and locally mined coal from the Mynyddislwyn Seam could have been used as the fuel, or even charcoal, which has been mentioned elsewhere in this book as having been produced on The Mountain.

When Archdeacon Coxe toured Gwent in 1799 he wrote in his book '*It is impossible to travel in Monmouthshire without being struck with the appearance of neatness and cheerfulness which results from the custom of whitewashing the houses; on account of the abundance of lime, this operation is annually performed, both within and without, and greatly contributes to the health of the inhabitants. The white colour of these dwellings, scattered along the summits and sides of the hills, and surrounded with foliage of different hues, considerably heightens the picturesque effect of the diversified landscapes'.*

The drawing on previous page is taken from the 1846 Tithe Map. Not too much has changed in this little community, except that some of the older houses have been pulled down and newer ones built on the same site. The Pennant sandstone quarry was quite extensive at that date, but was to become even bigger over the years. (Cwmnantyrodyn has a mention in the chapter on 'Quarrying' further on in this book).

In her little booklet, Mrs. Meyrick wrote '*A very quiet hamlet and an ideal place for peace and tranquility, there was no one bearing a title (surname) there for many years, everyone was addressed by their Christian names, until a lady came there from across the English border by the name of Mrs. Pitt, and she was the first person who bore the description. Welsh was the only language spoken there, some of the folk could not speak any other language.*

I can remember two profitable industries there, a coal level owned by Mr. Thomas, Tylagwyn, and a quarry owned by Mr. William George of Ynysddu'.

The author has an interest in Cwmnantyrodyn because family history research has shown that an ancestor, John Edwards, born 1776 at Groeswen near Caerphilly, lived here with his wife Elizabeth, maiden name Lewis.

A view over the houses of Springfield Estate, showing Cwm Draw Farm and Cwm Draw Cottage next door. At one time they were owned by two brothers, Bill and Arthur Morris. Bill Morris owned the farm, to be followed by Lawrence Organ, then Ken Harris, then Ron Lloyd. In the early 1980s Ron Lloyd turned the farmhouse into a public house, but after he died, it became subject to a compulsory purchase order and was demolished in 1989 to stop anyone moving in and hindering the building of the new by-pass road.

Next door to the farmhouse was Cwm Draw Cottage, that had once been part of the farm. It had originally been two cottages; as the room layouts with fireplaces and stone spiral stairs at both ends proved. The cottage was last lived in by Mr. Arthur Morris, and was compulsorily purchased.
He was moved out in 1989 to be re-housed by the council, and the cottage was demolished the very next morning.
All that now remains is the big beech tree behind the cottage, which now stands at the top of the bank alongside the new by-pass road.

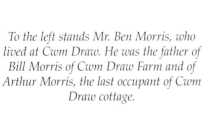

To the left stands Mr. Ben Morris, who lived at Cwm Draw. He was the father of Bill Morris of Cwm Draw Farm and of Arthur Morris, the last occupant of Cwm Draw cottage.

Cwm Draw Farmhouse on the left and Cwm Draw Cottage on the right.

Mynyddislwyn Mountain rising gently above Pontllanfraith. The houses in the foreground form part of Islwyn Terrace in what is today Springfield Estate. Behind them, to right of centre are Cwm Draw Farm and Cwm Draw Cottage. To the extreme left of the photograph is Ty Nyddfa, which still stands today, but much altered. How many children went through that door to have piano lessons off Madam Bayliss? At the top of the photograph is the New Bethel area, with Chapel and graveyard, Yew Tree Cottage, Penrhiwffranc Farm, and Ty Fry Farm. The mass of trees below Penrhiwffranc are covering up an old coal tip, made of waste from the coal level just below the farmhouse. Around 1990 the by-pass road was built which now runs across the centre of the photograph.

At the extreme left of the photograph on the previous page was Glan Brynnar Mill. It was a corn mill situated at the entrance to the modern Welfare Ground, Springfield, and nothing of it now remains. However, I have been told by some of the older generation who grew up in the area that they can remember the big mill stones lying about. The mill wheel was turned by the water in Nant Brynnar which today is piped under part of Springfield, only to emerge at the site of the mill, to run behind the grandstand in the Welfare Ground before joining the river.

The oldest record that I have found is in the Earl of Pembroke's Survey of 1570 (mentioned in the first chapter), when Lewis ap Rosser held a water mill called Melin Brynau on a 99 year lease from the Feast of St. Andrews, 1489, paying the yearly rent of 6 shillings and 8 pence. The Land Tax Assessment Register of 1805 lists 'Brynar Mill' owned by Samuel Glover (Lord of the Manor of Abercarne, and of Abercarne Estate), and occupied by William Abram. Its value was listed as ten shillings, with a Land Tax of two shillings.

The next available Land Tax Register is for 1808 where it is listed as owned by John Hodder Moggridge. The 1811 Register is identical, and the next that survives is for 1828, when the occupant was John Waters.

Although it is clearly marked 'Mill' on the 1846 Tithe Map, the Tithe Apportionment Book of 1839 lists it as 'Houses and Gardens' occupied by William Anthony and others. It covered an area of 1 rood and 6 perches.

The 1880 O.S. Map shows a tenement of two houses with an outbuilding at both ends, which confirms the 1839 listing.

In an agreement of July 1863, Sir Benjamin Hall, Lord of the Manor, allowed Thomas Powell and Sons to work Tyr Filkins Colliery. That agreement lists all lands that such coal workings will work under, and bordering the Brynnar stream is 'Glan Brynnar Mill Lands' at 3 acres and 17 perches.

So although the mill had been converted to houses, its original use was remembered in its name.

The other side of the Brynnar Stream, in what is today the Welfare Ground, was Elim Chapel, built in 1869. It is mentioned in the chapter about Twyn Gwyn Chapel.

The Next Road Up

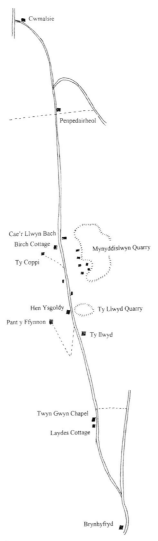

Before the early twentieth century, with the building of Cwmfelinfach and Ynysddu, and of the new road (A4048), the way up the valley beyond Cwmfelinfach was to turn up Twyn Gwyn Hill and travel roughly parallel with the valley bottom, before dropping down again at Cwmalsie Farm. We will now look at some of the history of that route.

Mention has already been made of Twyn Gwyn Hill with the building of a one roomed Mission Church, built in 1905. It doubled up as a school from 1907 until

March 1909, when the children moved into a temporary school at the end of Maindee Road, near the heart of Cwmfelinfach. The following entries from the School Log make interesting reading. Imagine 141 children in one room.

Playtime Cwmfelinfach School.
At the Mission Church, Twyn Gwyn Hill. Handwritten underneath the photograph was 'Presented to Charles F. Thomas for highest jump'.

Outside the corrugated one-room Mission Church on Twyn Gwyn Hill.

168

When the colliery was sunk there was a great influx of people, and a temporary church building was put up for them on Twyn Gwyn Hill. That Mission Church was a corrugated sheet structure with just one room, built in 1905. The children of the new village needed educating and the only school for them was the old school at Ynysddu. In 1907 the Mission Church doubled up as the first school in Cwmfelinfach, opening its doors to the 141 children on 2nd December.

1 1907.
Dec 2nd   This school was opened in temporary
          premises at the Mission Church, Cwm-
          felinfach on Monday December 2nd
          1907. There were present at the
          opening:-
                Mixed.   36 Boys 39 Girls
                Infants   42 Boys 24 Girls
          making a total of. 141.
          The staff consisted of:-
          T. Uppington Head Master
          Miss M.H. James. Uncert. Assistant.
          Miss L.M. Thomas Uncet. Assistant.
          The Head master took the third
          standard. Miss James the first
          and second, while Miss Thomas
          had charge of the Infants.
Dec 3rd   The numbers in the various classes
          are. St. I.   22.
               St. II   32
               St. III.   35
               Infants.   66

Imagine the chaos of having five classes being taught at the same time in one room.

The following entry in the Log for 4th June 1908 is delightful -
'*Sent Standards 1 and 2 out to top of hill before the school in order that they may have a good birds eye view of the village and the valley, to assist their comprehension of the topography of the locality*'.
And what a view they would have had from Twyn Gwyn Hill.

As important as education was, the vicar still had first call on the Mission Church, as this 1908 entry shows.

> Sept 3rd The school having been granted for the afternoon to the vicar for the purpose of holding a tea party school was closed at twelve o'clock for the day.

The following entry in the Log casts doubt over the safety structure of the Mission Church. Imagine five classes of little children being in a corrugated structure that moved a few inches out of the perpendicular. There must have been some frightened children. Such a comment makes it easy to understand the building being destroyed in a storm in 1916, after it ceased to be used as a school.

> Sept 10th The weather today was very wet & stormy, & consequently the registers were not marked all day. In the afternoon the attendance was only 40%. The wind blew so ... that several times the whole building moved two or three inches out of the perpendicular and seemed as if it were going to collapse. In consequence of this and of most of the children being wet, they were all dismissed in the afternoon at half past two.

A comment from the days when school life was less hectic and not so many deadlines had to be met.

> June 13th A half-holiday will be given this afternoon, for Twyn Gwyn Children's Treat, by permission of Managers.

Near the Mission Church was Brynhyfryd, an early 19th century house, two up two down, which has been known as Peacock House for many years. This is because a keen gardener in the past has practised his skills of topiary and shaped two peacocks out of the hedges. Unfortunately, they no longer exist, but they live on in the house name to this day.

Bryn Ivor painted by Obediah Hodges in 1914. It is one half of a pair of semi-detached housed on Twyn Gwyn Hill.

Mynyddislwyn Mountain looking north-east. To the right of the photograph is Draenog Valley, with the reservoir at its top end. Climbing up out of Cwmfelinfach is Twyn Gwyn Hill.

Twyngwyn Baptist Chapel

(Extracted from a work by Reverend David Davies)

About 1780 a difference arose in the Baptist church at Hengoed which caused great grief to the church for months. Owing to that dispute, about 14 members were given letters of transfer. They formed themselves into a religious fellowship at Twyngwyn in 1782. Mr. Watkin Edwards, the assistant minister at Hengoed, accompanied them, but he soon returned to Hengoed. Records show that this first fellowship met *'in an old chapel, not far from the present chapel'* and consisted of *'a few brethren and sisters from Blaenau, Hengoed, Argoed, Bassaleg, and surrounding places.'* It would appear that the 14 who left Hengoed were reinforced by others from the surrounding area. This community continued in the old Twyngwyn meeting house for some years, but that small community was subsequently dispersed. Some of the members joined together to begin the cause at Tonyfelin, Caerphilly; others *'went this way and that'*. Thus, at length, no service was held at Twyngwyn, until *'about 1825 when some brethren and sisters came from Beulah and other places to begin the cause anew.'*

'The History of the Baptists, by David Jones, Carmarthen, published 1839' gives us the following paragraph - *'A monthly meeting was held at Castell y Bwch in the parish of Henllys, and as no church had sent an invitation for the next meeting, Mr. Thomas Jenkins ventured to announce that it would be held at Twyngwyn, namely, the old meeting house, which was then tenanted by a widow named Anne James, a much respected member of the old church, but at that time a member of Beulah. Many ministers met at the appointed time, and the meeting was so successful as to create a thirst in the neighbourhood to revive the cause there. Mr. B. Williams of Maesyberllan, and others, were strenuous to their support of this movement and God prospered the effort, for many were baptised, and the hearers were so increased in number as to lead to the decision to build the Twyngwyn Chapel. Mr. Daniel James, one of the members, gave the site for the building, and an additional plot for a burial ground was bought of him for £10. Their number at that time was 33, who were received by letter of transfer as follows, 27 from Beulah, 4 from Hengoed, and 2 from Bethesda.'*

Entries from old church records entered by William Harris in 1865, secretary at Twyngwyn at that time, show a slight divergence to the above account by David Jones. Mr. Harris, in his account, stated that *'about 1825'*, as already quoted, *'a few brethren and sisters came from Beulah and other places to begin the cause anew'* adds that they continued at the old Twyngwyn for 4 years, and that then, in 1829, they built the present Twyngwyn Chapel. This would seem the more accurate statement. There can be no doubt with regard to the date of building Twyngwyn Chapel, as the date of 1829 is set in stone on the front of the building.

Mr. Harris stated that at that time Mr. T. Jenkins was the pastor of Siloam Chapel, Machen, as well as of Twyngwyn. It appears evident that Mr. Harris was in possession of more facts up to that date than David Jones. But Mr. Harris complained that after that date, and until 1865 when he wrote, the secretaries of the chapel had neglected making records with the result that only a little was known about the period of 35 years, except that Mr. W. Roberts was pastor of the chapel for some time, and that after him, the Rev. Owen Williams was minister for 4 years, when he died.

After a few years of inactivity, the local vandals have left their mark on Twyn Gwyn Baptist Chapel.

In the 1990s Twyn Gwyn Chapel was bought and converted into a private house.

Inside Twyn Gwyn Chapel, showing the pulpit, organ and Sêt Fawr, once used by the mighty Christmas Evans.

Looking down from the balcony inside Twyn Gwyn Chapel, after the vandals had started their destruction in the early 1990s.

It is with regard to this period, concerning which, Mr. Harris confesses he knew little, that David Jones supplies several interesting facts, of which Mr. Harris makes no mention. He stated that the cost of the building was £300, and that towards this amount, £40 was received from London. He also stated that 3 members (Phillip Jones, David Williams and Lewis Walters) contributed between them £100, and that the other members and their neighbours contributed all the rest, with the exception of £40. He stated that it was proposed by the members to clear the balance of debt on the building. This he considered to be a most praiseworthy effort for a chapel so young and so small. He also stated that at that time Mr. William Roberts had succeeded Mr. Thomas Jenkins, and that Mr. Roberts was also then the pastor of the chapel at Coed-duon (Blackwood). He added that Mr. Roberts had not spent his strength for nought at Twyngwyn as the membership of his chapel had considerably increased during his ministry there. At that time there were 3 deacons, David Williams, James Knight and Lewis Walters, while the membership numbered between 60 and 70, and the Sunday School about 50.

A record of the ministry of the Rev. William Haddock is given in the Church Book, written by Mr. James Jones, a former secretary of the Chapel. Mr. Haddock was ordained as pastor in 1867. In 1868 Twyngwyn Chapel decided to build a School Room at Pontllanfraith, The building was completed in August, and was opened on September 14th 1869, on the occasion of the monthly meeting of the district being held there. (This building was very close to the entrance to the Welfare Grounds at Springfield Estate,on the bank of Nant Brynnar, and was later called Elim). In 1871 Mr. Haddock removed to Cwmbwrla, Swansea.

In a few months after the departure of Mr. Haddock, the Rev. W.M. Evans of Tregolwyn became pastor of the Chapel, commencing 8th October 1871. He was pastor for 3 years and 5 months, before removing to Trosnant (Pontypool) in March 1875. Towards the end of 1876 the chapel was re-roofed and otherwise extensively repaired and improved, and 2 years later, the jubilee meetings of the building were held on 14th and 15th May 1879, when the Revs. J. (Gomer) Lewis and R.D. Roberts (Llwynhendy), R. Lloyd (Castleton), and Dan Davies (student at Pontypool) preached.

On 6th June 1882 Mr. Samuel Davies, student at Haverfordwest College, was ordained as pastor. At the close of 4 years ministry he removed to Abercanaid (Merthyr) in May 1886. On 8th February 1891 the members of Twyngwyn who worshiped in the Schoolroom at Pontllanfraith, received letters of transfer and formed a separate church called Elim, on the Schoolroom site. In 1893 the chapel at Twyngwyn was re-seated and refurbished, but the old oak chair (Sêt Fawr) was retained, which was used by Christmas Evans on his visits to Twyngwyn during his ministry at Tonyfelin, Caerphilly.

After Samuel Davies, there was no pastor for 17 years, and Twyngwyn depended upon ministers who visited Sunday by Sunday. On 31st August 1903 Rev. T. Thomas of Brynbank (Laugharne) was recognised as pastor until his death in April 1909.

As the Rev. Thomas arrived, members of Twyngwyn who lived at Cwmfelinfach received letters of transfer, and in August 1903 they formed an English Church in that area. Five years later another section of Twyngwyn, consisting mainly of members who had come from Treorchy expressed their wish to found a Welsh Chapel at Cwmfelinfach to meet the needs of the Welsh inhabitants of the district. (This was as a result of the fact that it had been decided to hold English services at Twyngwyn instead of Welsh services on account of the change of language in the neighbourhood - this was the time of the sinking of the colliery at Cwmfelinfach). Hence, on Saturday 24th October 1908 a service was held in the vestry of the English Baptist Church, Cwmfelinfach, when the Welsh church was formed. The Rev. T. Thomas presided and 49 members were enrolled. In a few years another movement resulted in the transfer of 18 members, who lived at Ynysddu, in order to form an English Church in that area, and the new church was formed in April 1911, meeting at a schoolroom, but on 1st November 1912 the new building of Glyn Church was opened. At this time the Pontllanfraith members of Elim, who were using the old Schoolroom at the entrance to the Welfare Ground, moved into their new Elim Church on Newbridge Road, Pontllanfraith, in 1912.

The date stone from the original Elim Chapel, a daughter Chapel of Twyn Gwyn Baptist, which was built near the entrance to the Welfare Grounds, Springfield Estate.

Twyngwyn has played its part in the spread of Christianity, forming new churches in areas of increased population in the valley bottom. With a change in occupations, and less people living on Mynyddislwyn Mountain, Twyngwyn was left 'high and dry'. After its closure it was locked up and left unoccupied for a number of years, during which time it was sadly vandalised. It was bought privately and changed into a house which has, thankfully, saved its structure from demolition.

A photograph taken in 1946. In the foreground is a little cottage once called Laydes Cottage, while a little further on the walker is approaching Twyn Gwyn Chapel.

Immediately to the south of Twyn Gwyn Chapel was a little cottage. Although it was tiny it still had a chimney at both ends. The Tithe Apportionment Book of 1839 lists it as Cottage and Garden, 3 roods and 32 perches in area, with an annual Tithe payment rated at 1 shilling and 8 pence. It was occupied by Lewis Watkins, a tenant of the Moggridge Estate. The 1881 Census called it 'Laydes Cottage' occupied by George Lewis, a railway signalman, with wife and son. For many years it lay in complete ruin, but in the last years of the 1990s the cottage was lovingly rebuilt and is now occupied once again, while the Chapel has been converted into a private house.

A little further along the road is a rough track up to the right leading to Twyn Gwyn Farm, which will be dealt with in the next chapter.

On the right hand side of the road is Ty Llwyd Farm, one of two farms on the Mountain by that name, the other having been close to the Flannel Factory. This farm was a Welsh Longhouse (Ty Hir) built end-on into the hillside. The 1839 Tithe Apportionment Book lists it with acreage of 29 acres and 33 perches, with an annual Tithe payment rated at £1 11s 5d. The Farm was owned by Thomas Price but tenanted by Thomas Rees. In the early years of the twentieth century this farm was the home of the Jenkins family. Richard Jenkins was friendly with Arty Moore of Gelligroes. Together, they experimented with some of the earliest wireless transmissions. Gelligroes Mill and Ty Llwyd established communication and by 1908 orders for animal feed were passed 'over the air'. Richard Jenkins transmitted from a wooden shed in the garden, his Wireless Telegraph Cabin. Arty went on to greater fame a few years later when his wireless picked up the S.O.S. distress call from the sinking ocean liner Titanic. However, he received that call at Gelligroes Mill which is just outside the area of study set for this book.

Ty Llwyd Farm with living area built uphill into the bank, and beasthouse down hill.

Almost opposite Ty Llwyd was the entrance to the track leading down to Pant y Ffynnon Farm. Unfortunately, this farm was pulled down in 1996 after being compulsorily purchased by the local council. It had suffered from the 'Time Bomb' at Ty Llwyd Quarry immediately uphill. It is listed in the 1839 Tithe Apportionment Book as being 25 acres and 12 perches in area with its Tithe rated at £1 8s 1d per year. It was occupied by Daniel Lewis, a tenant of the Moggridge Estate.

The farm was built into the sloping hillside so that the two bedroom windows at the back were level with the ground. In a field just below the farm was a grass tennis court, built in the 1920s by local people, mainly teachers.

180

The caption on this photograph read 'Mountain Youths as Wireless Telegraphists. A.E. Moore, the miller's son of the Monmouthshire village of Gelligroes, at the door of his wireless telegraph cabin, and his associate, R. Jenkins of Ty Llwyd, leaving to go to his occupation as electrical engineer at the colliery. These youths have been receiving messages of the world's news for some weeks'.

Some of the twenty one children of the Jenkins family of Ty Llwyd in the early 20th century. Richard Jenkins experimented with wireless transmission. Daniel Jenkins was present at the laying of the Foundation Stone for Mynyddislwyn Urban District Council Offices at Pontllanfraith in 1913, and was on the official photograph. One of the girls married and became Mrs. Morris, and lived at Ty Cae Brith, along the top ridge where she raised her 18 children.

181

About 1850 Lewis Lewis of Llanfabon, with his wife and children, came as tenants to the farm. Besides farming, he worked in Cae'rllwyn Quarry, up the hill. About 1900 Lewis Lewis and wife moved up the hill to farm Cae'rllwyn Ganol, leaving his son Alfred and wife Catherine (nee Jenkins of Rhyd y Ffraith, Full Moon) behind at Pant y Ffynnon. Alfred was also a quarryman, and with Catherine he had three daughters.

Catherine had a nephew, William Jenkins, who moved in with her as an 8 year old, and grew up on the farm. Alfred died in 1919, aged 47. Catherine and her three daughters moved up the hill to live with her in-laws at Cae'rllwyn Ganol, where she died in 1953, leaving nephew William as the tenant at Pant y Ffynnon.

A family story goes that Alfred and Catherine had a maid at Pant y Ffynnon who gave Alfred a damp shirt to wear, and he died of pneumonia.

The freehold of the farm was bought by Mr. Harry Davies who farmed there for a number of years before passing it on to his son Ivor, who was the last occupant.

The farm was rented out many times in living memory. At the turn of the 20th century it was leased by the Jenkins family, William and sister Annie. William was an Elder at nearby Twyn Gwyn Chapel. Annie married and became Mrs. Booth. Other occupants included Eddie Symmons, Colwyn Cook, and Mr. Ruff.

Pant y Ffynnon, photographed the day before it was pulled down, September 1996.

182

Pant y Ffynnon Farm, which no longer exists. Above it is the filled-in Ty Llwyd Quarry, while virtually nothing remains of Cae'rllwyn Ganol Farm to the left of the quarry. Ty Llwyd Farm is to the right of the photograph.

Pant y Ffynnon Farm at the bottom of the photograph, with Ty Llwyd Farm above it. To the extreme right can be seen Twyn Gwyn Farm, while the top half of the photo shows Ty Cae Brith, Panty Trwyn and Ty'r Waun Farms. Pant y Ffynnon had a grass tennis court, below the farmhouse and in the left corner of the photograph.

A short distance along the road, on the left hand side, are the ruins of Hen Ysgoldy (Old Schoolhouse) which can easily be passed by without notice. In the 1839 Tithe Apportionment Book it is listed as 'School House' with three perches of land. It was occupied then by Thomas Lewis, who must have been the school master. No doubt, lessons were all taught in Welsh at that time.

In the mid 1950s it was the home of Alf Holly, who was the last person to die there. The previous tenant had been Joe Savage, who died there in 1936. He had worked at Ty Llwyd Farm. Local legend tells us that the School House was built as the result of an endowment by one of the Lewis family of The Van, Caerphilly, but that fact is unproven. One of that family was responsible for the founding of Lewis School, Pengam.

Hen Ysgoldy (old Schoolhouse) had long ceased to be a school and became a private house. The chalked sign beside the road, guarded by the dog, reads 'Gooseberries for sale'.

Ty Llwyd Quarry is the opposite side of the road from Hen Ysgoldy and has caused much anguish on the Mountain. Long after the quarry had become disused, Monmouthshire County Council granted permission in January 1966 for it to become a dump for the tipping of industrial waste. Tipping was carried out in the late 1960s and early 1970s.

As the Monmouthshire County Council was the Planning Authority, the local authority (Mynyddislwyn Council) had little control over the tipping at the site.

The Deposit of Poisonous Waste Act and Control of Pollution Act did not exist at that time. In spite of planning conditions to the contrary a considerable amount of drummed liquid waste, sludges and toxic materials was dumped. All such tipping was completed by the end of 1972 when the site was capped and made to look like a poor quality field, contoured to match the surrounding hillside.

And that was the end of the story as far as the Authority was concerned. However, the site has turned out to be a time bomb, with the saga running on for well over twenty years.

The site of the quarry was located in a 'White' area in the County Development Plan which is reserved for rural and agricultural purposes only, and in which it is not intended to permit general development proposals. From the onset, the dumping of waste in the quarry was out of accord with the County Development Plan.

The ground had not been covered with a lining, so there was nothing to stop seepage into the earth. An objection early on concerned local drinking water. Whilst the quarry site was located outside the direct catchment area of the Nant y Draenog Reservoir, underground percolation could have occurred through geological faults, and particles of obnoxious material could have been carried on the wind onto the reservoir surface.

The tipping of industrial waste was carried out by Purle Waste Disposal Company of Cardiff, to be joined by Monsanto, Coates Paints and Johnson and Johnson, to leave a real cocktail of pollutants. Drums were turning up every day marked with Skull and Crossbones.

From the beginning, local people were angered by the inconsiderate way the operation was carried out, and through the Farmers Union of Wales approaches were made to the Monmouthshire County Planning Authority. In April 1970 the F.U.W. voiced the possibility of seepage of fluid waste through the rock strata to adjoining farm springs and water sources as a possible hazard. The Planning Department's reply said *'An inspection of the site was made immediately on receipt of your letter and no evidence of the tipping of toxic material was found'.*

On the evening of 4th July 1970 the whole site caught fire, resulting in clouds of black toxic smoke, which the fire brigade could not control for over 24 hours. Samples were taken from the quarry to be analysed, and the results were sent to the F.U.W. The deposits varied in colour from grey to black, although a pure white ash was seen, which was identified as Titanium Dioxide. Another sample was found to contain pieces of white fibrous tissue cloth, which also contained Titanium Dioxide. The ash resembled the result when 'J Cloth' is heated. The laboratory conclusion was that the fire was the result of 'dumping of J Cloth' in various stages of manufacture, which subsequently caught fire producing acrid vapours. Unfortunately, no one knew what Johnson and Johnson waste consisted of, since their manufacturing process was secret.

After the site had been capped and landscaped late in 1972, there were problems for Mr. Davies who farmed Pant y Ffynnon, downhill from the quarry site. Surface water ran off the tip area carrying stone dust and earth, which was deposited all around his farm and inside some of the buildings.

Warnings about the danger of tipping toxic waste went unheeded for twenty years despite the disclosure that Purle Waste Disposal had already poisoned two other quarries in South Wales with potentially lethal chemicals. That company had taken over from Industrial Waste (Reclamation) Ltd. in 1968 and continued their tipping operations at Maendy and Brofiskin Quarries in Mid Glamorgan. As early as 1966 residents were complaining about pollution from Maendy Quarry. By 1973 experts from London recorded 16 different poisons at that tip. In their report they accused the Welsh Office of issuing an 'Obstructive and untrue' statement by saying that there was no danger from the tip. Purle Waste Disposal (Wales) Ltd. was voluntarily wound up in 1980. The remnants of this and other companies disclaimed all responsibility for the site.

Back at Ty Llwyd Quarry, further and more serious trouble came to light in 1989 when the contents of the tip were found to be leaking out. The 'Cocktail of chemicals' had probably been leaking for twenty years, and the Islwyn Council's Chief Environment Health Officer was reported in a newspaper as saying *'We are treading on the edges of knowledge. It is completely out of my league. The quarry contained a cocktail of many different chemicals'*. Those included P.C.B.s which do not degrade, causing concern about the contamination of soil, water and animals.

It was decided to put a 'rubber umbrella' over the tip to prevent rain water from entering the tip through the ground, and to prevent airbourne contamination, while completely surrounding the site with a concrete dam. In 1990 three monitoring bore holes were sunk at the tip which will be used to check water levels within the tip.

People living below the quarry had long been warned not to eat the food grown in their gardens, and the Welsh Office banned the movement of cattle and other food products from Pant y Ffynnon Farm in August 1991. A compulsory purchase order was placed on Pant y Ffynnon as the council had decided that the ground was badly contaminated by chemicals from the quarry site, and the farm was bought by Islwyn Council. In September 1996 the farm had been pulled down, so that today all evidence of the farm and its out-buildings have been totally erased from the hillside. But the pollutants were also contaminating areas lower down the hillside near the Pontgam, Caerllwyn and Glenview Terraces.

Lessons should have been learned, but in 1991 Islwyn Council was considering an application for waste disposal at the nearby larger Caerllwyn Quarry (Mynyddislwyn Quarry). Thankfully, nothing has come of that.

Continuing on along the road, the keen-eyed walker will see the remains of a building and garden on the right hand side, now almost lost in the hedge line, and now long forgotten about.

A track up to the right leads to Mynyddislwyn Quarry and the three houses that remain out of the nine that were originally in the quarry area.

Down to the left is the track leading to Ty Coppi, a name that occurs three times on the Mountain, although one is called Tir Coppi. It is the only three-storey house on the Mountain (there have been others with a cellar making up a third storey). As the photograph overleaf shows, it had an attached barn at its northern end until recently, but the barn roof line has now been lowered, and the

barn converted into an extension of the house.

Inside Ty Coppi there are two stone spiral stairs, one leading up to the first floor, and one leading up to the second floor. Recent modernisation revealed an interesting feature inside the house. The old floor covering was removed upstairs to reveal stone flagstones. The new owner feared for the weight of these stones and started to remove them, to find them bedded in three inches of soil. They knew how to build in the old days. The 1839 Tithe Apportionment Book calls it Tyr y Gopi, and its 13 acres and 1 rood was rated at 18s 2d. It was owned and occupied by John Davies.

At the bottom right of the photograph is Ty Coppi with the roofline of the attached barn lowered. Above it to the left is Cae'rllwyn Bach Farm. Above that can be seen Mynyddislwyn Quarry, and on the skyline, to the left, is St. Tudor's Church.

An aerial view looking north, with Mynyddislwyn Quarry to the right of the photograph and Cae'rllwyn Ganol Farm below it. In the centre of the photograph, to the right of the road, is Cae'rllwyn Bach Farm, while almost opposite can be seen Birch Cottage. Down Hill (to the left) is Ty Coppi, while further down is Pont Gam Terrace. Below that can be seen Lily Farm. Across the Sirhowy Valley can be seen Wyllie Village.

An aerial view looking south, with Pont Gam Terrace bottom right, Ty Coppi above it, and Birch Cottage and Cae'rllwyn Bach either side of the 'Next Road Up'. In the distance, the enormous waste tip from Nine Mile Point Colliery looks about to engulf Cwmfelinfach.

A very short distance along the road brings us to the spot where Birch Cottage once stood. Nothing now remains of that house. The 1839 Tithe Apportionment Book lists it as Moggridge Estate, leased by Thomas Lewis, with two fields and garden measuring 2 acres 3 rood and 14 perches. Its Tithe was rated at three shillings and six pence per year. The house was last lived-in about 1970 and quickly fell into disrepair before being demolished in 1975. Mrs. Meyrick's little booklet tells us *'Birch Cottage, the home of Mrs Leah Jones, a lady of outstanding personality, tall and dignified, always well dressed and well spoken, a good neighbour and a firm friend, especially in cases of bereavement. She would help to ease the burden off the shoulders of the bereaved and smooth their path for them'.*

The ruined shell of Birch Cottage in the mid 1970s.

Almost opposite the site of Birch Cottage stands Caerllwyn Bach, once the home of the clock maker on the Mountain. This old farm is covered in the next chapter, so we will move on. The road crosses a small bridge that has long been forgotten, and most people are unaware of its existence, even when passing over it. The bridge carries the road over an old tramroad incline that carried trams of coal from Caerllwyn Colliery down to the valley bottom in the early years of the twentieth century.

A little further on we reach Penpedairheol Cottage, better known as the Pink House, although it is losing its colour these days. It sits at a crossroads where the tarmac road up the valley is crossed by a rough track leading from the river bridge at Gelligroes Mill up to St. Tudor's Church. It is probably a very old Parish

Road, leading the way to marriages, Christenings and funerals at the church. Today this old track is in a deplorable state of preservation.

But back to Penpedairheol. Many years ago it was known as the Travellers, an early sort of pub. The road in front would have been used by travellers going to Newport and the lowland plains from the upland areas to the north of us. They would have needed refreshment and accommodation for themselves and their animals, and here they found both. The beer would have been brewed in the house itself with the cask sat on a tressle, with no bar as we know it today.

Penpedairheol, also known as the Pink House.

A mental picture can be conjured up of life here and other such places from the following description by Archdeacon Coxe following his tour in the area in 1799. Having travelled northwards fringing the western flank of Mynyddislwyn Mountain Coxe wrote *'In visiting the farmhouses, as well in the hilly districts as in other parts of Monmouthshire, I was struck with the enormous quantity of bacon with which they are stored, frequently observing several ranges of flitches suspended from the ceiling in the kitchen. Bacon is almost the only meat served at the tables of the farmers, and with vegetables and the productions of the dairy, forms their diet. Thin oat cakes are a common substitute for bread, and the repass are enlivened by the cwrw, their native liquor, which the classic writers have dignified with the name of cerevitia, and which is immortalised in the songs of the bards; to descend to common language, it is new ale in a turbid state, before it is clarified by fermentation. To persons accustomed to clear and old malt liquor, this beverage is extremely forbidding to the sight and nauseous to the taste; but I had so much of the blood of the ancient Britons in my veins, that I soon became accustomed to their cwrw and preferred it to our Saxon beer'.*

Immediately to the north end of the pink house is an old barn. Legend has it that the lady of the house built the barn herself, walking down the Parish Road to the river side where she collected the stones and carried them up herself, before getting stuck in to her building work.

Today, that barn is part of some boarding kennels.

A short distance along the road we drop down again to the valley bottom at Cwmalsie Farm, which has been mentioned in the previous chapter.

Cae'r Llwyn

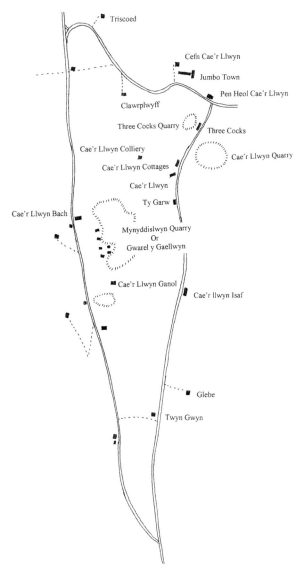

Triscoed

Cefn Cae'r Llwyn

Jumbo Town

Pen Heol Cae'r Llwyn

Clawrplwyff

Three Cocks Quarry

Three Cocks

Cae'r Llwyn Colliery

Cae'r Llwyn Quarry

Cae'r Llwyn Cottages

Cae'r Llwyn

Ty Garw

Cae'r Llwyn Bach

Mynyddislwyn Quarry
Or
Gwarel y Gaellwyn

Cae'r Llwyn Ganol

Cae'r llwyn Isaf

Glebe

Twyn Gwyn

On the western facing slopes of Mynyddislwyn Mountain the name of Cae'r Llwyn·is by far the most common. There were six farms with that name, all old and mostly of the Welsh Longhouse style, with living accommodation and beast house under the same roof, separated from one another by a through-passage. There were also cottages, two quarries and a colliery with the same name.

192

In the last chapter, we started with a journey up Twyn Gwyn Hill, and then headed northwards. In this chapter we will again start at the top of Twyn Gwyn Hill, and follow a circular route taking in all the places mentioned in the first paragraph over page.

At the fork in the road at the top of Twyn Gwyn Hill, we headed off to the left in the last chapter. This time we will head off to the right. After a short distance Twyn Gwyn Farm is to the left. At one time there were three farms of that name within the area covered by this book. One was midway between Ynysddu and Cwmfelinfach, and has now gone. The other became known as Ty Gwyn, between Pennar and Newbridge, and was destroyed about 1990. This particular farm was mentioned in 1839 as being owned by Charles Williams but occupied by Henry Phillips, when it was listed as being 31 acres and 33 perches, with its Tithe rated annually at £1 13s 4d.

William Farr lived in Cwmfelinfach and worked down Nine Mile Point colliery. He had an illness and was not able to continue work down the pit. But he had to make a living somehow. He decided on a milk round. He bought a milk can and collected the surplus milk from farms on Mynyddislwyn to sell in the villages in the valley bottom. He walked up the Mountain every morning to collect his milk. When things were looking up a little, he bought a horse and cart and rented a cottage on the Mountain.

His cottage needed cleaning and he employed a widow lady, and in time they were married. They had a daughter, Olive, born in 1916, who has supplied these facts.

In the meantime, William Farr had rented Twyn Gwyn Farm in 1905. He kept cows and produced his own milk for his milk round. He also grew vegetables to sell. After the Second World War when the Milk Marketing Board was formed, Mr. Farr gave up selling milk as a protest, but he continued with his vegetable growing and selling until he retired in 1950. He moved out of the farm to a villa in nearby Twyn Gwyn Road where he died.

The farm remained empty for two years, then Mrs. Betty Jenkins moved there in 1952. She was a daughter of Eddie Symons, with a background of life on the Mountain, having lived at Ty Coppi, Pant y Ffynnon Farm and Ty Garw. Her grandmother came to stay for her sister's wedding in December 1962. The snow was so bad that she was unable to return home, and sadly, she died at Ty Garw. The doctor was called but the only way up the Mountain was by tractor, because of the snow. Gwyn Robinson (Cae'r llwyn Mawr) used his tractor to get the undertaker, then another journey for the coffin, and the tractor was used to take the coffin to the graveyard at St. Tudor's. The ground was frozen so hard that a tractor tyre was burned on the ground to create a thaw to dig the grave.

On the opposite side of the road is The Glebe, or Glebe Farm. The word Glebe means a property held by a rector or vicar. It was a portion of land going with a clergyman's benefice. It was built by Queen Anne's Bounty. She was Queen from 1702-1714. In 1704 she created the Bounty which restored to the Church, for the augmentation of poorer livings, the Tithes and first fruits taken by Henry VIII. So the Church had financial support to build it. An extension was added in 1855, with a weathered date stone on the wall confirming that date.

The Land Tax Register of 1805 (held in the County Record Office), has the farm listed as 'Clergy Farm', value £20, with a land tax of £4. It was owned at that date by the Hon. Charles Morgan, Bart. (Tredegar Estate). The 1811 Land Tax Register has the name of the farm listed as 'Tithes', valued and taxed as above.

The 1839 Tithe Apportionment Book tells us that it was owned by the Rev. Isaac Hughes (Vicarial Glebe), but occupied by Isiah Edmunds. It covered 35 acres and 32 perches with an annual Tithe rated at £2 10s.

The above named Rev. Isaac Hughes was Vicar of Mynyddislwyn from 1843-1860. If he wasn't living at The Glebe, but renting it out (to supplement his parish income), then the next Vicar of Mynyddislwyn did live there.

Mrs. Meyrick's little booklet tells us *'John Griffiths resided there quite a number of years and several of his children were born there. It was a difficult parish to look after as the majority of the population were illiterate. Owing to this lack of knowledge the people expected Mr. Griffiths to look after them materially as well as spiritually. He was called upon to check their bills and do their letter writing, including getting in touch with relatives overseas.*

I can remember him walking the steep hills of Mynyddislwyn to alleviate the petty grievances and perplexities of those who had an idea that the vicar's time and services were entirely at their disposal. He was also called upon to make people's wills.

Owing to the pressure of his work Mr. Griffiths found the Glebe Vicarage too outlandish, the station and nearest village being several miles away, while his only conveyance was his pony and trap. He built a nice residence at Pontllanfraith, next to St. Augustine's Church, where he also ministered. (He was the first Vicar at St. Augustine's).

He rented out the Glebe and land to a suitable tenant, and it became a farm. He kept a keen eye on the place in case it should be abused. One day the farmer was in the act of pitching hay into the beautiful dining room, through a window. Mr. Griffiths was very annoyed and made him remove it, warning the farmer not to let it happen again'.

Kelly's Directory for 1881 mentions *'The living is a vicarage, tithe rent-charge £582. Glebe, 35 acres, net yearly value £290, with residence, is the gift of the Bishop of Llandaff, and held since 1860 by the Rev. John Griffiths'.*

A snowy day at Cae'rllwyn Isaf Farm.

Further along the road is Cae'r Llwyn Isaf Farm, a Gradel I listed Welsh Longhouse.

The Jones family have lived here since the late 1700s and the present owner, Mr. Trevor Jones, is the fifth generation to farm here. The farm was originally Tredegar Estate. This is the only farm on The Mountain where the dairy cow is still milked in the traditional way in the milking parlour, or byre, attached to the house. It was to this farm that the horses were stabled at night when the Draenog Reservoir was being built.

The 1839 Tithe Apportionment Book lists the farm as owned by Sir Charles Morgan (Tredegar Estate) but leased to Philip Jones. It measured 40 acres and 34 perches, with its annual Tithe rated at £1 19s 4d.

Cadw, who listed the farmhouse in 1982, states that it is probably 17th century, but altered. It was built of rubble and brick, and had a cross-passage entry, with a later porch. The chimney is in the gable end of the house, with a spiral stair in the thickness of that wall. At the back of the old house is a large wing, built about 1900.

Along the road, a lane leads down to the left, to Mynyddislwyn Quarry. At the corner of that lane there used to be an air shaft eighteen yards deep to help ventilate the nearby Caerllwyn Colliery. On the left of the road is Ty Garw. It has all the appearance of a modem house, but was listed in the 1839 records as Cottage and Garden, measuring 8 perches. It was owned by the Moggridge Estate.

A little further on is Cae'r Llwyn Mawr farm. In the autumn of 1799 Archdeacon Coxe was progressing up the Sirhowy Valley and wrote *'We passed under Caerllwyn, or the high place of the encampment, descended to the banks of the Sorwy, crossed over a stone bridge, and went up a steep road leading to Penllwyn'*.

On 14th March 1810, John Llewellin, Agent to Abercame Estate, wrote to Benjamin Hall, Lord of the Manor *'Edward George informed me that the Karllwyn property near Manythysloin Church, belonging to Philip and John Jones, was for sale, and that the latter told him they meant to give you first refusal'*.

The above named Messrs. Jones were of Llanarth Estate. The farm was originally part of Penllwyn Estate but had passed by marriage in 1722 to Llanarth Estate when Florence Morgan married John Jones. In 1810 Benjamin Hall did not buy the farm, which is surprising, because he was enlarging his Abercarne Estate wherever possible. By 1839 the farm was owned by Ann Phillips and tenanted by William Jones. It was listed as 63 acres 1 rood and 37 perches, with an annual Tithe rated at £3 13s 0d. The 1805 Land Tax Register lists the farm as 'Carllwyn' owned by John Jones, but occupied by Edward Morgan. It was valued at £3 15 shillings with a Land Tax of 15 shillings. Rather confusingly, there is another entry in 1805 called 'Carllwyn Tithe Farm' owned by Charles Gore, Esquire, and occupied by James Morris, valued at £2 10 shillings, with a Land Tax of 10 shillings. But which of the Caerllwyn farms was that? It wasn't Cae'rllwyn Isaf.

Cae'rllwyn Mawr, with the Prothero family outside. Annie, born here in 1901, is to the left, with her mother Mrs. Margaret Prothero next to her. The family arrived here from Brecon and settled first in Ty Fry Farm, then moved from here to Ty Glas.

As we have just read, that was a Tredegar Estate Farm. On the 1805 Register, there is no entry for Clawrplwyff Farm, which surprises the author. Could Clawrplwyff have been entered as Carllwyn?

Mrs. Meyrick wrote *'Situated in a very nice spot by the roadside, the house as it stands today was built from the ruins of the old house about 60 years ago (first half of 19th century). It seemed a house of character, large hall with paved floor and whitewashed walls seemed a very cold entrance, but there was always warmth in the welcome that was extended to everyone who made a call upon the inhabitants'.*

In the fields behind Cae'r Llwyn Mawr was Caerllwyn Colliery. It was a series of levels into the hillside rather than a vertical shaft, to work the Top Rider of the Mynyddislwyn Seam of coal. That seam of coal was five feet three inches thick at these workings. The colliery was worked in the last few years of the nineteenth century and up to the 1920s. In 1921 it was listed as 'idle', but owned by the Mynyddislwyn Colliery Company.

In the following chapter, about Quarrying, mention is made of an agreement entered into in 1897 whereby John Lewis would build a tramroad to carry stone from Mynyddislwyn Quarry, and on the way to the valley bottom would also collect coal from Caerllwyn Colliery. John Lewis cancelled that agreement in 1903.

Almost immediately next to Cae'rllwyn Mawr were Cae'rllwyn Cottages, fronting on to the road. They were probably built to house quarry workers from Cae'rllwyn Quarry almost opposite. The cottages were listed in the 1839 Tithe Apportionment Book as being owned by William Lucas and George Yorath, but occupied by Thomas Jones and Owen Davies. No trace of them now remains. They were finally pulled down about 1975.

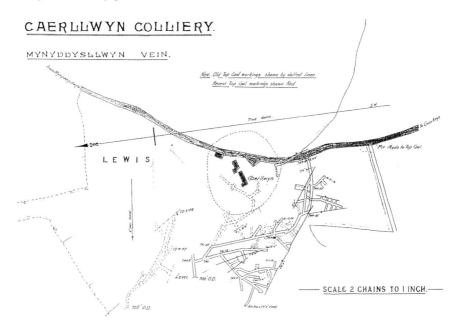

197

In the top right corner can be seen Cae'rllwyn Mawr Farm. Next to it, besides the road, were Cae'rllwyn Cottages, pulled down in 1975. Following along the road and to the left of it were Three Cocks Cottages, home in the late 19th century of this author's great grandparents. At the junction of roads is Penheol Cae'rllwyn Farm (Three Cocks), to which the author has ancestral connections. At the bottom of the photograph can be seen the ruins of Jumbo Town.

Almost opposite the cottages was Cae'rllwyn Quarry, which in 1839 was listed as owned by Ann Phillips, but occupied by William Jones. It measured 3 acres and 25 perches with its annual Tithe rated at three pence. Rubble from here was taken for the foundations of Llanwern steelworks about 1960.

Back to the road, and on the left hand side was Three Cocks Cottages. They were built in 1892 fronting on to the road. The two little houses were joined, or semi-detached, while joined to them on the north end was a stone arch. Entry through that arch was to Three Cocks Quarry, behind the houses. The quarry was shown on the 1880 O.S. map, so it was quite a few years older than the houses. The official name of the quarry was Penyrheol Caerllwyn. It was put up for sale at auction on 17th June 1903, advertised as follows -

'Penyrheol Caerllwyn Quarry
And the ground rent of two cottages which are held under lease for a term of 99 years from the 24th June 1892, at a yearly rent of £9, of which the purchaser will receive the benefit'.

They were sold by the same John Lewis mentioned previously at Cae'rllwyn Colliery. The cottages were abandoned and finally pulled down about 1960. The rubble was carried off to become a very small part of the foundation for the soon-to-be-built Llanwern Steelworks.

The road now reaches a junction, and we will continue our circular route by turning downhill to the left. At the junction is Penheol Cae'rllwyn, an old farmhouse of the Longhouse design. When the present owners bought the house about 1980 from Danny Winnett, they only bought the living accommodation, about half of the building. It was a two-roomed house, one room up and one room down. The attached barn, separated from the house by a cross passage way, was owned and used by a local farmer. This farm has a huge fireplace set into the end wall of the house, where is to be found also the spiral stone stairs. Besides the fire was the bread oven which was too big for the thickness of the wall, so it protruded outside the main end wall. Outside the house and near to the oven bulge can be seen the well for domestic water.

At one time this farm was known as Three Cocks, and it is strongly rumoured that it was a pub of that name, but no proof has come to light. When the present owners were renovating the house, the inside of the front door had writing on it, barely visible, that suggested a pub. Mrs. Meyrick's little booklet mentions 'Three Cocks Cottage'.

The 1839 Tithe Apportionment Book lists it as House and Garden. It was owned by the Rev. John Davies but occupied by John Howells who owned the nearby Flannel Factory. Here we could have a basis for a pub. John Howells would have employed quite a number of workers, who would have needed liquid refreshment after a long hot day at their work. Was he operating a sort of Truck Shop for his workers, by providing the beer and other provisions for the wives? On the photograph overleaf can be seen a stone style leading from the house to the Flannel Factory, a few fields away.

Penheol Cae'rllwyn Farm, as it was in 1980. The two roomed house, one up and one down, is on the right, while the former beast house is to the left, slightly down hill. The porch covers the through-passage.

Travelling down the hill, on the right is the site of Jumbo Town, of which nothing now remains. Jumbo Town is covered in the following chapter in this book.In front of it still stands Cefn Cae'rllwyn, an old farmhouse. In 1839 it was listed as owned and occupied by Henry Williams, and measured 25 acres, 2 rood and 15 perches, with an annual Tithe rated at £1 12s 8d. Today it is a private house.

Cefn Cae'rllwyn in 1973, at that time the home of Mr. and Mrs. Col. Cook.

On the left of the road a lane leads to Clawr Plwyff, a very old farm. That is also the name of one of three Hamlets within the parish of Mynyddislwyn. In fact, the whole of the Mountain fell within the Hamlet of Clawrplwyff. Next to the house was a barn which has now been converted into a house. That barn was where the Tithes for the Hamlet were collected - a Tithe Barn.

The name translates as *'Lid of the Parish, or Boundary of the Parish'*. When the farm was purchased by the present owners, the Downing family, in 1978, the farm was little more than collection of fields, the house being derelict. It was scheduled for demolition and due to be replaced by a bungalow. The new owners did not wish to destroy the 350 year old building. Planning permission for the bungalow was revoked and approval obtained to use as much of the old building as possible.

Implementation of Building Regulations inhibited repair. The exterior walls had to be taken down and rebuilt on new foundations. The core of the farmhouse was retained, and new walls put up in their original positions.

'Boundary of the Parish' seemed inappropriate to a farm that no longer had the status that gave it that name, but as the original house stones were used in rebuilding the exterior walls, 'Ty Cerrig' (Stone House) became the new name for this farm.

The original farmhouse was built about 1600 as a Welsh Longhouse. The existing house copies the plan and layout of the original, and many pieces of old timber have been re-used. It was a downhill sited Longhouse with a right-angled side-wing. The original house contained a single room with a gable fireplace and stone oven, and spiral stair. It was separated from the adjoining cow shed by a cross passage. A deep well lay immediately in front of the cross-passage door.

To this longhouse was added a cross-wing, with a spiral stair leading to a narrow room of one bay. This wing had a large gable fireplace with a brick oven, and a corner stair leading (in a straight flight) to the upper floor. Beyond the fireplace was another set of rooms with another spiral stair backing onto the fireplace.

The surviving timber fragments were analysed and the result suggests that the wing was added in the early 1600s, so the original longhouse must have been even earlier.

The 1839 Tithe Apportionment Book tells us that the farm was owned by the Devisees of the late Edward Blewitt, and occupied by William Thomas. It measured 144 acres and 14 perches with an annual Tithe rated at £5 9s 1d. Of interest is the fact that the farm had two fields on The Lemage, one of which measured over 46 acres, the biggest field up there. As these fields reached the wall of the Common (Mynydd y Lan) the farmers at Clawr Plwyff were Commoners and could turn their animals out onto the common. The farm retained that right well into the twentieth century.

The above named Edward Blewitt lived at Llantarnam Abbey and owned Cwmbran Ironworks, and coal levels at Upper Cwmbran. What was his connection with Mynyddislwyn Mountain?

Throughout this book mention has been made of the little booklet written by Mrs. Ann Meyrick, about her childhood memories on the Mountain. She was born at Clawrplwyff, one of the two daughters and four sons of William and Mary Richards. The census tells us that a female servant, Sarah Rees, also lived there.

Continuing on down the hill, the next farm on the right is Triscoed.

The original Triscoed Farmhouse.

Illtyd David in front of one of his paintings. He was born at Triscoed Farm in the early 20th century. His mother drowned in the farm well, and shortly afterwards, the family emigrated to Canada. Illtyd could not settle there and soon returned home. He became an agent for a feed company. He was an amateur painter, specialising in miniatures. As a youngster he watched Obediah Hodges painting. Illtyd became a member of the Royal Academy and his paintings fetched a high price. He was also a leading member of the Mynyddislwyn Agriculture Society. He died in the 1990s.

Alan James of Triscoed and John Way of Sweet Wells, at Triscoed Farm.

Mrs. Meyrick tells us that Triscoed was at one time the home of Daniel Davies, a boot and shoemaker and repairer. *'One of the finest craftsmen of his day without mistake, he kept the whole parish and a few besides comfortably shod. His workshop was built behind Triscoed House'*. The original house is now a ruin, with the present owners, Mr. and Mrs. Alan James, living in a new bungalow in front of it.

Triscoed was part of the Moggridge Estate, having been bought in 1804 by John Hodder Moggridge, 1839 records list it tenanted by Lewis Watkins. It measured 13 acres, 3 rood and 32 perches, with its annual Tithe rated at £1 2s 3d.

The short lane leading from the road to Triscoed originally continued through the farm, past Sweet Wells, and forked, either down to Cwmnantyrodyn, or up to the Flannel Factory.

Down the road from Triscoed is a junction with the road that was travelled in the last chapter. At this junction was a small triangular area where there was a milk churn stand until quite recently. Turning left we re-trace the route of the last chapter, but in reverse.

On the left stands Cae'rllwyn Bach Farm.

This is an old Welsh Longhouse built end-on into the hillside, with beasthouse on the downhill side. In 1839 it was owned and lived in by Henry Harris. It measured 15 acres 3 rood and 37 perches, with an annual Tithe rated at 15 shillings.

Mrs. Meyrick tells us *'Caerllwyn Bach Farm, the home of the late Mr. Henry Harris. He owned the farm and another one along the lane. Mr. Harris was a clock and watchmaker by trade and his clocks were fine specimens of his work, handsome in appearance and good timekeepers. Caerllwyn Bach was a big rambling house. Several of the rooms were used as workshops and stores for his clocks. Later on they were used in parts for couples and old people'*.

Henry Harris made Long Case clocks, and also gold wedding rings. The main features of his clocks were Swan Neck pediment, reeded columns and a brass eagle on a brass ball. These features, with the style of his work, and the paintings on the enamelled clock face date his clocks from 1770 onwards.

Henry Harris probably assembled his clocks from parts that he bought in. It was typical of that period for a clockmaker to accept a commission, which needed a specific scene to be painted on the face. A travelling rep would call on him at regular intervals, and the order would be taken to the Midlands where parts for the movement would have been manufactured. The rep would visit the site which needed to be painted on to the clock face, and he would make a rough sketch of it, or would accept Henry Harris's sketch, ready for it to be passed on to the Midlands factory where the enamelled face would be made. The artist concerned would probably never have seen the original scene and much artistic licence would have been involved.

The face and movement of the clock would be delivered to Henry Harris who must have had some engineering skill to partly machine the parts before assembling them. He usually used local oak for his cases, which he would have made himself. He made a copy of the style popular throughout Britain at that time.

Henry Harris died at Cae'rllwyn 6th January 1838 aged 72 years. This would give him a date of birth about 1766, which would fit in nicely with the dates of his clock style. His dates, 1766-1838 fit in with a 1960 National Museum publication by Iorwerth Peate about Welsh Clockmakers, which lists Henry Harris as late 18th - early 19th century, but he did not quote his source.

The records at Eglwysilan Parish Church show that Henry Harris, Cae'rllwyn Bach, married Mary Davies of that parish in 1840. He must have been the son of the afore named clockmaker. But the 1841 census shows that the son was also a watchmaker.

Henry Harris
age 35
Watchmaker
Caerllwyn Bach

Mary
age 40
wife

William Davies
age 69
father in law

Cae'rllwyn Bach has been the home of John and Rita Purnell since 1967. Since living there they have tried many different projects. At first they rented out the land until they could afford to buy stock. They kept chickens for eggs and for the table. After a few years they bought sheep and still farm their small Welsh Mountain flock. They grew mushrooms in the sheds for about 18 months, then ran a boarding kennel for about nine years.

The couple were very active with the Sheep Dog Society, where Rita became part of the ladies committee (formed in 1973). She organised the catering for sixteen years after Mrs. Roberts of the Blacksmith's gave up that job. John joined the trials and the first job that the committee gave him was to build a ladies toilet. That was really starting from the bottom up. He was chairman of the Society for two years.

Before the Purnell family moved in to Cae'rllwyn Bach, the contour of the land behind the house had recently been much altered. Stone was taken by lorry from the big quarry behind the house to be used as foundation for Llanwern Steelworks. Part of that quarry was on Cae'rllwyn Bach land, and two pillars of rock remain standing in the field behind the house. The land would have gone to the top of those pillars, and there was a style on top of one of the pillars, so the footpath had to be diverted.

One of the contractors was Don Symons whose parents lived at Cae'rllwyn Cottages. He lived with his wife Ivy at Birch Cottage, almost opposite Cae'rllwyn Bach.

Behind Cae'rllwyn Bach was Mynyddislwyn Quarry or Gwerel y Gaellwyn as it was known in 1846. This quarry is mentioned more fully in the chapter on Quarries later in this book. Mrs. Meyrick wrote *'The quarry has been responsible for many huge and important buildings throughout the principality, including the docks at Newport and other large buildings in the town. I can remember the stones being hauled in carts to a truck at the tramroad at Ynysddu. The truck was then drawn by horses to the nearest siding to be put on rail for Newport. Many times I ate my lunch in the truck followed by a drink of water from Islwyn's well on my way back to school, until it was rumoured that pins had been seen floating in the water from the clothing of the corpses at Twyn Gwyn Chapel. I never enjoyed a drink from the Glyn spout any more.*

At one time they had got very short of labourers in working the quarry so they got immigrants from Ireland to fill the vacancies. They built what they called barracks in those days in readiness for them. The time of their arrival was approaching so the farmer at Clawrplwyff of that day went around before hand to find if everything was in readiness for their comfort. He found that the place was not quite finished off but would be alright in a few days. He kept watch for them coming, and then he explained the circumstances and told them, after greeting them into their new surroundings, that he had plenty of clean straw in the barn, plenty of blankets and plenty of food, and if the menfolk would care to take it, he would give them a few days work on the potatoes. The answer was "Sure Sir, give us the tools and show us the fields and the work will be done". *They were given a few meals and went to rest. They were up next morning with the dawn, women and men, and they were as good as their word, the work was done. They were very reluctant to receive payment but the farmer insisted, as they were pilgrims in a strange land. Those Irish people always seemed to owe a debt of gratitude for those incidents, typical of the Irish people. But that never entered anyone else's mind, as it was a pleasurable duty helping the traveller on his way, especially the wanderers and the lost'.*

At the southern edge of the quarry was the last 'Cae'rllwyn' on this circular route, Cae'rllwyn Ganol. It was an old Welsh Longhouse, built end-on to the hillside, with a cross-wing forming a letter L. Nothing of it now remains. About 1900 the Lewis family moved there from Pant y Ffynnon, Lewis Lewis and wife Catherine, leaving his son Alfred and his wife Catherine or Kate and their three daughters to farm Pant y Ffynnon. When Alfred died in 1919 his wife and daughters moved up to Cae'rllwyn Ganol. The story goes that Kate would take her cattle at night to another farm's field and take them out again before morning.

The daughters were Elizabeth Ann, born 1909, who became a nurse and emigrated to Australia after World War II, where she married John McNeilage whose job was managing incoming migrants. Next was Margaretta (1910-1982) who also became a nurse and married John Bryn Roberts, a schoolteacher of Cardiff. They had one daughter, Janet (who has supplied this information), born 1941. Next was Gwynneth or Gwyn (1914-1955). She had a son Brian who sadly died, aged 7 years, after an accident in the nearby quarry.

The farm house was burnt down in 1985, and the last owner, the above named Mrs. Gwynneth James, then left the area. She lived in Ynysddu for a time before moving to Australia to live with her sister, where she died in 1995.

In 1839 Cae'rllwyn Ganol was listed as part of the Moggridge Estate leased to James Gardner. It measured 29 acres and 3 perches with its annual Tithe rated at £1 6s 5d.

Having made mention of several old farms and small houses, it is worth recording the observations of Archdeacon Coxe when he travelled this way in 1799. *'The principal articles of diet among the labourers are oat cakes, potatoes, milk and cheese, with an inferior species of cwrw (beer). Almost every cottage is provided with a small garden, and the greater part are even abled to keep a cow, which ranges the common for subsistence. The comforts of the cottager are increased by the abundance of fuel, either coal or wood, which prevails in every part of the country; and the price of labour being the same as in most of the counties in England, with these additional comforts, the condition of the peasantry in Monmouthshire is very advantageous'.*

Quarrying

All stone quarries on Mynyddislwyn Mountain worked Pennant sandstone, which is the main rock of our area. But it does not go down continuously to unknown depths in the earth's crust. There are seams of coal not too deep below the surface (the Mynyddislwyn Seam) and also seams of softer mudstone and clays. But where the earth covering has been removed on a sloping hillside the sandstone slabs that form a rock face can be quite high.

Pennant sandstone is a hard rock which wears away slowly. It has been the main building material of the South Wales valleys since stone was first used. Look at any old farmhouse and outbuildings and it was built from Pennant, while the roof was made from stone tiles that had been split thinly. The walls to enclose fields were from the same rock. When industry came to the valley bottoms it was Pennant that was used to build the long snaking rows of workers houses to form the ribbon developments so characteristic of our surrounding villages and towns. When tramroads were first built to carry coal off the Mountain, Pennant sleeper blocks were laid down every three feet under the rails, or tramplates. How much Mynyddislwyn stone went down to Newport for the building of the town, and for its dock, it is impossible to say. It has been 'dressed' to form countless miles of many-coloured flagstones to form pavements in so many towns, which have been edged with kerbstones from the same quarries. They gave character to a place, but sadly few now remain, having been replaced with soul-less colourless concrete kerbs and paving slabs. The Pennant flagstones were used to form the floor downstairs in farms and houses before the days of more readily available concrete. (In at least one building on the Mountain flagstones formed the upstairs floor as well), while animal carcasses were prepared and salted on long, very flat, salting slabs of the same stone. In more recent times Pennant sandstone has been crushed to form small chippings for road surfaces, as an aggregate in concrete, and as a sewage media.

Farms have existed on the Mountain for hundreds of years so it is fair to assume that there were small quarries here from those times. The earliest mention of quarries on the Mountain is the Earl of Pembroke's Survey of 1653, listing 'Quarries of slate and tile stone'. The 1846 Tithe Map shows a number of quarries.

There follows information on some of the quarries on the Mountain. Not all quarries are mentioned because information about them is not available.

COX'S QUARRY - John Cox and his wife Emily were both born in Mangotsfield in Gloucestershire in about 1825. Their first son, William, was born in Bristol in the mid 1850s and soon afterwards the family moved to Crosskeys.

A document of 31st December 1857 between Sir Benjamin Hall (Lord of the Manor) and John Cox, Quarryman, allowed Cox to lease for 99 years from 25th March 1857, at an annual rent of £3 8s, land and buildings lately erected by John Cox. That house later became numbers 97, 99 and 101 High Street.

Just across the River Ebbw from that property was a short section of the Monmouthshire Railway and Canal Company's tramroad which had been built in 1829, but which had been by-passed when the tramroad was converted to a railway in 1848. John Cox used that abandoned section of tramroad as a siding on which he could load quarry stone from his new quarry on the hill above.

The Tithe Map of 1846 shows that what was to become Cox's Quarry did not exist at that date. The Ordnance Survey map of 1880 shows a small quarry immediately above Cox's railway siding. That was his first quarry in the area which started work in 1856-57. A larger quarry was shown higher up the hillside.

John Cox's second son, James, was born in 1860 and his first daughter, Ellen, in 1861. Both were baptised at St. Mary's Church, Risca. The baptism register describes John as a quarryman, while the 1861 Census Report lists him as Grocer and Quarryman, employing twelve men and boys. By the time of the 1871 Census, John is listed as a Stonemerchant, suggesting that the business had progressed to 'dressing' the quarried stone as well as marketing it. The Census also showed three year old Emily Emma and a 16 year old Ynysddu girl as a live-in general servant.

The sinking of North Risca Colliery in the mid 1870s, with the associated colliery buildings, and the colliers' houses at Newtown, created a massive new demand for building stone. It was probably at that time that Cox started the quarry higher up the hillside that now bears his name.

On the 1880 Ordnance Survey map Cox's Quarry was shown to be a very large undertaking with an internal tramroad system for moving stone around the quarry and a tramroad incline to take the stone down to his railway sidings. It was a balanced incline, with the weight of full trams going down bringing the empty trams on the other track back up, controlled by a brake mechanism on a large dium at the top of the incline. The stone wall that held that brake drum still exists. The incline was also the route to and from the quarry for the men and boys who worked there.

In January 1879 John Cox used his house as security for a loan from Evan Phillips of Risca Manor. That was certainly linked to the great expansion in Cox's quarrying operations.

An explosion at Risca Colliery in July 1880 resulted in 120 deaths. Such was his status by that time that John Cox was a juryman at the subsequent inquest.

John Cox died on 10th June 1889 and was buried at St. Mary's Risca. In his will dated 9th July 1887, he left his house and associated land to his wife for her lifetime, and then to be split between his daughters, whilst the business side and the residue of the estate was left to his sons. The total estate was valued at £2,122 16s 1d. That was a huge sum at that time for this area.

William and James carried on the business although both married and left the family home. The large amount of house building in the area in the last quarter of the 19th Century and first decade of the 20th Century (the whole of Wattsville and most of the lower part of Crosskeys) made for a profitable concern. They subsequently transferred the business into a limited company, but trade suffered during the period of the First World War, by which time the local building boom had ended.

The quarry is said to have ceased operation at around the time of the General Strike, but by then it was run by another company, the Cox family having sold out.

Around the corner of Mynyddislwyn Mountain from Cox's Quarry, and just in the Sirhowy Valley, was another quarry with an incline tramroad to send stone down to North Risca Colliery. Both quarry and route of tramroad can be clearly seen today.

CWMNANTYRODYN QUARRY - This quarry is shown on the 1846 Tithe Map and no doubt the many houses forming the little settlement there were for quarry workers. The Tithe Apportionment Book of 1839 lists the quarry owner as Henry Lewis of Gelly Gynnas Farm (Oakdale), and the quarry covered 2 roods and 16 perches in area. He also owned some of the houses there, but most of them were freehold and occupied by the owners (Thomas Jones, Thomas Thomas, Eleanor Morgan, and Isaac Williams).

In January 1950 Robert Evans and Sons had planning permission to extend the stone quarry workings. In 1953 the production was 10,000 tons a year with a maximum possible estimated at 30,000 tons a year, while its estimated approved life was 20 years. At that date 21 persons were employed there.

The quarry was worked until about 1962, producing stone for masonry. The Blue Pennant was cut and dressed by hand to produce a range of items including kerbing stones, walling, fireplaces, cladding and finished stone. Approx. 800 tons of stone were quarried a month at that date, employing 12 men.

In the 1950s the Birmingham Corporation ordered dressed stone for reservoirs in the Elan Valley. Stone dressers were brought in from Italy because of a shortage of suitably skilled stone masons locally.

Part of the site was leased to another Company for coal stocking from about 1960, and a car dismantlers yard was later established. Permission was granted in August 1996 for inert tipping and a waste transfer station, but that hasn't happened yet.

GELLIGROES - Across the river from Gelligroes there is a high faced quarry alongside the road that today has a pond in its bottom. This was used for buildings and shaft linings at the Gelligroes Colliery immediately opposite, across the river. A bridge over the river to carry a tramroad has long gone. That colliery site is now covered by the car park of Hawker Siddeley Switchgear.

The author can remember this quarry site permanently dry when it was used as a stop-off place on the annual migration of a family of gypsies with their horse drawn caravans.

MYNYDDISLWYN QUARRY or CAERLLWYN QUARRY - This was shown to be an extensive operation on the 1846 Tithe Map when it was called Gwarel y Gaellwyn. Houses were also shown on that map, which would have been for workers in the quarry. The 1839 Tithe Apportionment Book lists part of the quarry owned by Henry Harris of Caerllwyn Bach, measuring 2 acres and 3 perch, and part of it owned by Mathew Moggridge and Co. measuring 6 acres, 1 rood and 5 perch. Also shown was another small quarry, now filled in, between the main quarry and Caerllwyn Ganol Farm, which covered 1 rood and 10 perches.

Planning permission was granted in December 1948 to Caerllwyn Quarries Ltd. for the continuation of quarrying and stone crushing here.

In the early 1950s Italian workers were brought to work in this quarry as well as at Cwmnantyrodyn, when this quarry also had a contract to supply stone for the building of the Elan Valley dams in mid Wales.

In 1953 the production at this quarry was 20,000 tons a year, with an estimated maximum production of 50,000 tons a year. At that date the estimated approved life of the quarry was 40 years. The quarry was operating in 1956/57 producing Blue Pennant for paving and walls. Blasting was carried out once every 4-6 months.

In the late 1950s and early 1960s the ground was being prepared for the massive Llanwern Steelworks on marshland. Millions of tons of hardcore were needed. Some of that came from Mynyddislwyn Quarry and the upper ground of Caerllwyn Bach Farm, where two pillars of rock are left standing. The land would have gone up to the top of these pillars, and there was a style on the top of one of them, so the footpath has had to be diverted.

In the last years of the 19th Century, Mynyddislwyn Quarry was operated by John Lewis, a timber and stone merchant, of Pontypridd. He also ran the nearby Caerllwyn Colliery. He entered into an agreement with I.J.C. Herbert of Llanarth Estate to lease land off the Estate to build a tramroad from the quarry to remove the stone. That tramroad would also pick up coal from Caerllwyn Colliery. The agreement took effect from 25th, December 1897, for 42 years, and gave John Lewis power to build an *'Incline Railway or tramway, with sidings, connections, stationary engines, machinery, plant, and all other works necessary thereto, and to go and repass over and along the same with or without waggons, horses, locomotive, steam or other engines or winding ropes'*. As the map on the following page shows, the tramroad would leave the quarry and pass by the mouth of two coal levels before dropping steeply down hill to cross the River Sirhowy on the Pont Gam (Crooked Bridge) and then run northwards on the Penllwyn Tramroad, before climbing steeply up hill to join the railway running from Tredegar to Newport between the Halfway and Bluebell pubs at Gelligroes.

John Lewis would pay a fixed yearly rent of £4 16s 3d for the land, and also a wayleave rent of one half penny for every ton of coal, stone, and other minerals carried down the tramroad. The minimum royalty was £15 a year, so if tonnages carried each year did not amount to £15 worth of half pennies, John Lewis had to pay the difference. (This amounted to a minimum of 7,200 tons being carried each year).

However, something went wrong for John Lewis, because on the 1st December 1903 he surrendered the lease and cancelled the agreement, having to pay a rent amounting to £108 19s 4d in respect of the land in the agreement. From that date he had no rights to the tramroad down the mountain, and probably not to the quarry or colliery either. He must have overstretched himself financially and become bankrupt. It is an interesting speculation as to whether he bought Jumbo Town and gave it its new name of Lewis Town, because as the following advertisements show not only was John Lewis selling houses in Mynyddislwyn Quarry, 'someone' was also selling the nine houses of Jumbo Town (Lewis Terrace). It seems too much of a coincidence. That sale was advertised to take place on 17th June 1903, six months before he surrendered his lease. Was it a desperate last act to try to raise enough capital to keep his quarry and colliery open?

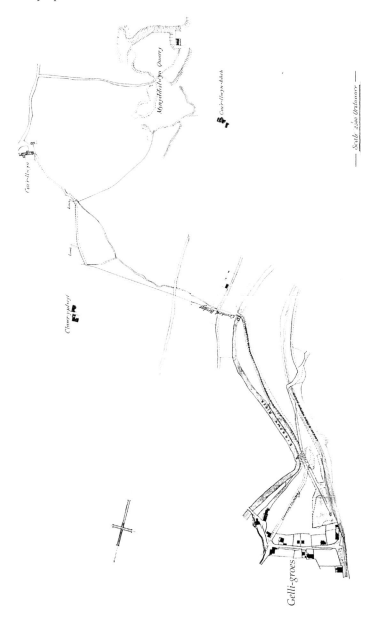

LOT 11

'All those 4 Copyhold Dwelling Houses and Gardens situate near Caerllwyn (generally known as 'Mynyddislwyn') Quarry in the hamlet of Clawrplwyf in the parish of Mynyddislwyn in the Manor of Abercarn, in the county of Monmouth, containing 1 rood 19 perches, or thereabouts. These houses and premises known as No.1 Quarry Cottages are situate close to the Mynyddislwyn Quarry in the Sirhowy Valley and are let at rents varying from 6/6d to 5/6d per fortnight, bringing in a total of £31 4s 0d per annum.

Sufficient land is attached to this lot to enable the Purchaser to erect several more dwelling houses thereon'.

LOT 12

'All that Copyhold Messuage or Dwelling House and Garden thereto belonging, and also the Piece or Parcel of land adjoining thereto, situate in the parish of Mynyddislwyn and in the Manor of Abercarn in the county of Monmouth, containing 105 square yards.

This property is also situate close to the Mynyddislwyn Quarry, known as No.5 Quarry Cottage. It is let at the extremely low rental of 4 shillings per week. There is sufficient land attached to this lot to enable the purchaser to build several more houses'.

Today all that is left of all the houses that were in the quarry are three houses in a short row, Nos. 7,8 and 9 Quarry Cottages.

Mynyddislwyn Quarry. Date unknown, but style of clothing would suggest the end of the 19th century.

214

Trevor Cullis dressing stone for paving slabs in Mynyddislwyn Quarry.

Mynyddislwyn Quarry. Beautiful Pennant Sandstone being dressed by a skilled stonemason.

CAERLLWYN QUARRY - Another quarry of the same name is situated almost opposite Caerllwyn Mawr Farm. This quarry is also shown on the 1846 Tithe Map, along with Caerllwyn Cottages across the road from the quarry, no doubt the homes of quarry workers. In the 1839 Tithe Apportionment Book the quarry was listed as being 3 acres and 25 perches, while its Tithe was rated at three pence a year.

THREE COCKS QUARRY - This quarry was shown on the 1880 Ordnance Survey map. It was almost opposite the above named Caerllwyn Quarry, and was alongside the road, but below road level. In 1892 two workers houses were built between the quarry and the road, the houses also being known as Three Cocks. The two little houses were joined, or semi-detached while joined to them on the north end was a stone arch. Entry through the arch led down into the quarry.

The official name of the quarry was Penyrheol Caerllwyn. At the auction on 17th June 1903 (mentioned earlier) the following advertisement appeared *'Penyrheol Caerllwyn Quarry - and the ground rent of two cottages which are held under lease for a term of 99 years from the 24th June 1892, at a yearly rent of £9, of which the purchaser will receive the benefit'*. The author's great grandparents lived here in the 1890s.

It seems likely that this was also John Lewis's.

Workers in Mynyddislwyn Quarry. In the distance can be seen a corrugated lean-to, the only protection against the weather for the stone-dressers.

CRAIG Y TRWYN (or ADAMS) QUARRY - This quarry was behind Brynawel. In the 1920s it employed about seven men. The stone was of a poor quality and was used mainly undressed for rough walls, and was also crushed down for road stone. From this quarry poorer quality waste was used to in-fill during the construction of Newport Docks. Also from here came the rough stone for the walls of Wattsville and Ynysddu Schools. This quarry has now gone, having been infilled as a waste dump. It was once called Thorne's Quarry.

THORNE'S QUARRY - John Thorne of Toneiddon Farm had a quarry just below Pen Top (Penrhiwarwydd Farm), just off the road up the Rhiw. The area is now covered with forestry but it is still possible to see the stone walls that held the brake drum that controlled the descent of trams of stone down the steep hillside in the direction of Cwmfelinfach.

Just around the corner of the hill was another quarry which supplied stone for Cwmfelinfach. That also had an inclined tramroad running down the hillside and the large cast iron wheel to control the brake mechanism, and the stone walled housing for the wheel are still in-situ. This was probably built by Burnyeat Brown & Co. who started to sink the colliery in 1902.

A steam crane in Mynyddislwyn Quarry. A very dangerous place for children. The photograph was taken either on a Sunday, or at a holiday shut-down.

DRAENOG - Mention is made earlier in this book of the Nant y Draenog Reservoir. Many years before that was built, two small quarries existed nearby, one either side of the Draenog dingle. Both were mentioned in the 1839 Tithe Apportionment Book. One was on Cae'rllwyn Isaf land, the field listed as arable

217

and stone quarry. The other, across the dingle, was much larger, and was on Pant Glas land. Both quarries are still visible, and no doubt both supplied stone for the dam wall and filter bed houses of the reservoir many years later.

CWMALSIE - Behind Cwmalsie Farm was a sizeable quarry, with indications that a tramroad had run out of it, down past the farm. The quarry was filled in when the by-pass road was built about 1990, that road cutting off access to the quarry site from Cwmalsie Farm.

TY LLWYD QUARRY - This 'Time Bomb' has been mentioned in the 'Next Road Up' chapter.

Numerous smaller quarries existed, some probably to provide stone for enclosing farm fields. In 1839 a quarry was listed two fields up from Triscoed Farm. Small stone workings can still be seen on Toneiddon Farm. A quarry existed overlooking the Ebbw Valley in Cwm Llwch, close to the seven-arch stone bridge that Benjamin Hall built to carry his tramroad across the valley in 1828. Another small quarry, now much overgrown, was uphill above Spiteful, while another was in Tilla Cox (or Cocks) Wood, opposite Celynen South Colliery, and probably supplied stone in the building of that colliery.

At the end of the Second World War there was a shortage of skilled stone masons to work in our local quarries, so Italians were brought in to do the job. The gang of Italians in this photo were employed for a contract to supply Mynyddislwyn dressed stone to a reservoir in Mid Wales. At the time of the photograph Mynyddislwyn Quarry was owned by Eddie Rees, who owned the lorry.

One of the many Pennant sandstone quarries on The Mountain. At the bottom of the photograph can be seen all that remains of the large cast iron wheels (with rim broken off) with wrought iron shaft that provided the brake mechanism to lower trams full of stone to the valley bottom below. Originally, the wheels would have been covered with thick wooden boards around which was wound a thick wire rope. The wheels were held in place between strong stone walls, known as a wheel pit. Stone from the quarry in this photograph was used in the early years of the 20th century at the sinking of Nine Mile Point Colliery and in the building of Cwmfelinfach village.

Jumbo Town

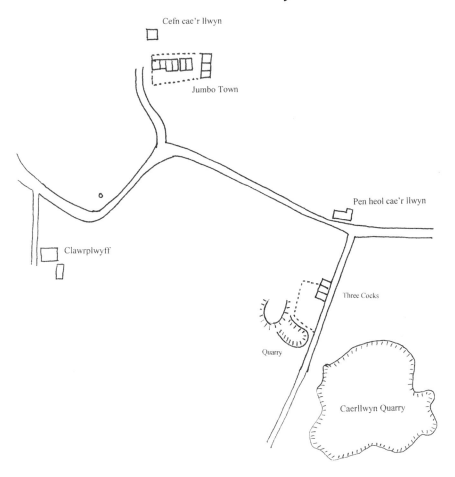

Cefn cae'r llwyn

Jumbo Town

Pen heol cae'r llwyn

Clawrplwyff

Three Cocks

Quarry

Caerllwyn Quarry

This was a small community very close to Cefn Caerllwyn Farm. Sadly, absolutely all trace of it has disappeared off the Mountain. Mrs. Meyrick's small booklet about her childhood memories about 1880 mentions '*Charles Williams came here from the Forest of Dean. Being a big man he was called Jumbo. He bought a cottage and about half an acre of land. He opened an old quarry nearby and commenced raising wall and paving stones. He built pig styes there. He bought horses and carts and kept travelling to Newport to purchase second hand doors, timber, and everything he needed in his building business. He drew his own plans and commenced building houses. He had a good many sons and stepsons who all worked in Abercarn Colliery by night. They would come straight home from the coal face and mount the scaffolding. Jumbo himself did all the walling. He built eight or ten houses on that small plot of land. The first tenant I remember there was a watch and clock repairer.*

The tenants were usually a coming and going type of people that lived in many places before, and when they were displeased they would pack up their troubles and make a move. When they got tired of Jumbo Town they would suddenly leave, sometimes without honouring their obligations as tenants and forgetting to leave their rent behind.

The men were good workers and the women kept their homes neat and tidy. Things worked well through the week until Saturday night. The men would have had their week's wages and a few drinks. The women would have done their shopping. They would then commence to air their grievances. We could hear them from my home (Clawrplwyff) and we would sometimes predict a murder in Jumbo Town before morning'.

As Mrs. Meyrick"s memoirs refer to the years about 1880, they give us valuable information as to the date of the building of Jumbo Town. It appears that the community was built by Charles Williams about 1880. However, the 1879 O.S. map does not show it, while the next survey of 1900 shows it completed.

But the origins of Jumbo Town could go back many years before that date. The Tithe Map of 1846 shows two buildings with the surrounding land enclosed, covering the area that was to become Jumbo Town. The 1879 O.S. map shows it almost identical. The Tithe Apportionment Book of 1839 lists these buildings and enclosed land as belonging to William Williams. Although Williams is a common surname, could there have been a family link between William and Charles Williams ? Did Charles leave this area to work the Pennant sandstone of the Forest of Dean and return years later to claim his inheritance? We will probably never know the answer.

Whatever their origin, there were nine houses at Jumbo Town, built close to Cefn Cae'rllwyn Farm. There was a terrace of three across the top with six houses going down the hillside, (a pair then a terrace of four). The houses were of different sizes.

Mrs. Meyrick mentions Jumbo working the sandstone quarry. There was no shortage of these in a short walking distance from the hamlet. There was the large Caerllwyn Quarry, Three Cocks Quarry, a small quarry downhill from Jumbo Town towards Triscoed Farm (now filled in), the large Cwm Nant yr Odyn quarry, and the even larger Mynyddislwyn Quarry was within easy reach.

The Electoral Register for the year 1900 (an official document) lists residents at 'Jumbo Town'. The O.S. map of 1901 calls it 'Lewis Terrace'. Information received tells us that at one time the community was owned by Mrs. Blanche Lewis, but this is unproven. In 1898 John Lewis entered into a lease for forty two years with the Landowner to open up nearby Caerllwyn Colliery. Was he the 'Lewis' of 'Lewis Terrace'? That lease was surrendered in December 1903, a date that is   very coincidental with the following advertisement. Did John Lewis overstretch himself and run into financial difficulties? If so, he could have tried to offload Jumbo Town, and if that didn't satisfy his creditors, then he had to back out of his colliery venture as well. But this is all guess work by the author.

On Wednesday 17th June 1903 Jumbo Town was put up for sale, at auction in Newport. Lot 10 lists -

'ALL THOSE NINE COPYHOLD MESSUAGES OR DWELLING -HOUSES Outbuildings and Gardens containing about 1 rood and 11 perches, situate in the Hamlet of Clawrplwyf in the Parish of Mynyddislwyn, in the Manor of Abercarn, in the County of Monmouth, numbered 1121 on the Tithe Map of the said Parish.

These Dwelling-houses which are known as Lewis Terrace have recently been placed in a good state of repair, and are situate near Tredegar Junction, near Mynyddislwyn Quarry, and near Messrs. Burnyeat, Brown & Company's new pits.

The houses are let at a rental of three shillings and six pence per week each, bringing in a total of £81-18 shillings per annum'.

By the mid twentieth century Jumbo Town was heading the same way as so many other houses on The Mountain. People were more interested in the new developments which were a result of immediate post-war boom, Springfield and Penllwyn Estates, with running water, indoor toilet, bathroom, etc. and on a bus route, and older more inaccessible properties like Jumbo Town fell into decay. Parts of it were knocked down in the 1940s, as an aerial photo of 1947 shows, and what was left was finally demolished in the late 1970s.

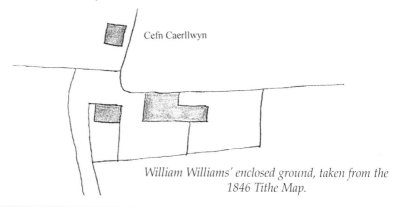

Cefn Caerllwyn

William Williams' enclosed ground, taken from the 1846 Tithe Map.

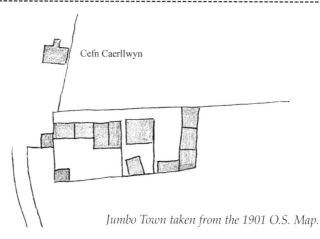

Cefn Caerllwyn

Jumbo Town taken from the 1901 O.S. Map.

n Division of Monmouthshire.   Pontllanfraith Polling District.   District **W**

Part of the Parish of Mynyddislwyn—continued.

PONTLLANFRAITH ELECTORAL DIVISION.

South Ward for Election of Rural District Councillors.

OCCUPATION ELECTORS (other than Lodgers).

DIVISION ONE—Persons entitled to vote as Parliamentary Electors, County Electors, and Parochial Electors.

Name of each Elector at full length, the Surname being first.	Place of Abode.	Nature of Qualification.	Description of Qualifying Property.
Jenkins, William	Ynysddu, near Pontllanfraith, Mon.	dwelling house	Ynysddu
Jinks, Thomas	Jumbo Town, Pontllanfraith, Mon.	dwelling house	Jumbo Town
John, Samuel	Three Cocks, Pontllanfraith, Mon.	dwelling house—successive	Factory and Three Cocks
John, Daniel	Caerllwyn Isaf, Pontllanfraith, Mon.	land and tenement	Caerllwyn Isaf
Johns, Jones	Tynyllwyn, Pontllanfraith, Mon.	land and tenement	Tynyllwyn
Jones, Alfred	Glanyrafon, near Pontllanfraith, Mon.	land and tenement	Glanyrafon
Jones, Benjamin	Panty-ty-trwyn, Pontllanfraith, Mon.	land and tenement	Panty-ty-trwyn
Jones, Edward	Gellygroes, near Pontllanfraith, Mon.	land and tenement	Gellygroes
Jones, John	Sweet Well, Pontllanfraith, Mon.	dwelling house	Sweet Well
Jones, John	Tonymoch, near Pontllanfraith, Mon.	land and tenement	Tonymoch
Jones, Daniel	Caerllwyn Isaf, Pontllanfraith, Mon.	dwelling house	Caerllwyn
Jones, Edwin	Pontllanfraith, Mon.	dwelling house	Pontllanfraith
King, William Henry	Pontllanfraith, Mon.	land and tenement	Pontllanfraith
Lambert, James	Pontllanfraith, Mon.	land and tenement.	Pontllanfraith
Leng, John	Ynysddu, Pontllanfraith, Mon.	land and tenement	Ynysddu
Lewis, Edward	Pontllanfraith, Mon.	dwelling house—successive	Woodland terrace and Pontllanfraith
Lewis, George	Nine Mile Point, Cross Keys, Mon.	dwelling house	Nine Mile Point
Lewis, John	near Elim, Pontllanfraith, Mon.	dwelling house	Pontllanfraith
Lewis, Lewis	Pantyffynon, Pontllanfraith, Mon.	land and tenement	Pantyffynon
Lewis, William	Twyn Gwyn, Pontllanfraith, Mon.	land and tenement	Twyn Gwyn
Lewis, Thomas	Pontllanfraith, Mon.	dwelling house	Pontllanfraith
Lewis, Thomas	Bontgam, Pontllanfraith, Mon.	dwelling house	Bontgam
Llewellyn, George	Factory, Pontllanfraith, Mon.	dwelling house	Factory
Long, Henry	Pontllanfraith, Mon.	dwelling house	Pontllanfraith
Lloyd, Thomas	Vicarage, near Pontllanfraith, Mon.	dwelling house—successive	Globe Farm, Vicarage and Pontllan- [fraith
Lloyd, Thomas	Caegarw, near Pontllanfraith, Mon. [Mon.	dwelling house—successive	Penmain and Caegarw
Mansfield, Herbert	Quarry, Mynyddislwyn, Pontllanfraith,	dwelling house—successive	Cwmshingrig and Quarry
Macarthy, Charles	Cwmfelyn Fach, Pontllanfraith, Mon.	dwelling house	Cwmfelyn Fach
Macarthy, Florence	Cwmfelyn Fach, Pontllanfraith, Mon.	dwelling house	Cwmfelyn Fach
Masters, Isaac	Ynysddu, Pontllanfraith, Mon. [Mon.	dwelling house—successive	Ynysddu and Veintree
Matthews, William	Ynysddu, Black Prince, Pontllanfraith,	dwelling house	Ynysddu
Miller, John	Quarry, Mynyddislwyn, Pontllanfraith,	dwelling house —successive	Factory and Quarry

The ruins of Jumbo Town in the 1970s. To the left of the photograph is Cefn Cae'rllwyn.

Jumbo Town as it would have looked, drawn with information from people who lived there long ago.

Drawing by Jean Burland

Sweet Wells

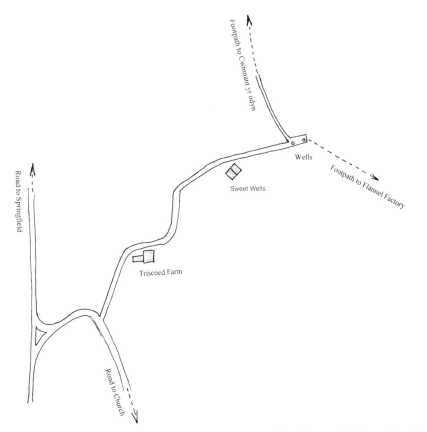

A pair of semi-detached stone built houses with Welsh slate roofs. The old sash windows were replaced in the late 1950s. Each house had two rooms downstairs, living room and front room, with a walk-in pantry. A door beside the fire was access to the stone spiral stairs leading to two bedrooms upstairs. The stairs went into one bedroom, which you walked through to get to the other bedroom.

Water was collected from the wells up the lane, and when they ran dry water had to be carried from Triscoed Farm or from Cwmnantyrodyn. There was also a spring up the fields. A pair of toilets (Tai Bach) were outside, at the end of the side gardens. These had no flush water. They were emptied manually, with the soil dug out and buried.

The only thing delivered to Sweet Wells was the daily post. Everything else had to be collected by the tenants. Coal was dumped at Triscoed and had to be carried up the untarred lane to Sweet Wells. The last ton of coal to be delivered was carried by Gwyn Little, who drove his lorry through the fields and dumped it on the lane in front of the houses, and said *'I told you I'd do it one day'*.

Into the mid twentieth century the houses were owned by Mrs. Lawrence of Aberbeeg who rented them out. In the early 1960s the Way and the Jones families moved out. A family from Abertillery moved into one of them for a short time, but when they left, Sweet Wells became uninhabited, and vandals burned them down.

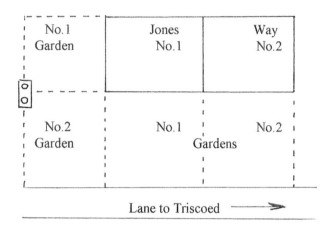

Toilets
Manually cleaned
Dug out and buried

| No.1 Garden | Jones No.1 | Way No.2 |
| No.2 Garden | No.1 Gardens | No.2 |

Lane to Triscoed ⟶

Mr. Ernie Way at the back of Sweet Wells, leaning over a tree stump. The tree was cut down in 1957 to make way for an overhead powerline to allow electricity to be installed at Sweet Wells for the first time.

Mr. Ernie Way and wife Cissie with son John on the front path at Sweet Wells.

Barbara Way and Valerie James (Triscoed Farm) inside the front gate of Sweet Wells.

Ellis Brasington and John Way inside the front gate at Sweet Wells.

Bob and Hariet Gregory of Coedyridder Cottage, with their four children. Another four were to be born later. Hariet's father was Charles Withers, Sexton to St. Tudor's Church. The little girl to the bottom right in the photo is Mrs. Cissie Way, later of Sweet Wells, who was aged in her ninetees when this book was researched, and could still remember this photograph being taken. The family went to a studio, carrying her new dress and shoes (shown in the photograph) in a bag. At the studio she was dressed, the photograph was taken, and the dress and shoes went back into the bag for the journey home, which upset little Cissie.

Flannel Factory Area

The following is taken from the 'Employment of Children' Act of Parliament of 1842 - *'In general, the Welsh women are remarkable for attention to warm clothing, which they secure for themselves in woollens, flannels etc.; nor are they less anxious for their husbands and children - the men and children are always well defended against the general inclemency of the mountain country'.*

The Flannel Factory and its pond are listed in the Tithe Apportionment Book of 1839, but putting an earlier date to it is impossible. In her little booklet describing the years 1880-90, Mrs. Meyrick wrote - *'We now cross the fields to the factory, first coming to a small hamlet of about four houses tenanted by people who knew the way to live in harmony with one another, avoiding gossip and evil tongue.*

Then about one hundred yards below we'll reach the real factory. All I can remember of it was the mill pond storing the water that turned the mill wheel and a rusty looking object that was once the mill wheel. The factory was once a very prosperous business run by Mr. John Howells.

He bought all the wool from the farmers of the district and manufactured it into flannel, blankets, cloth, and all kinds of woollen goods. He employed several men, a number of girls, and Mr. Howells was a weaver himself. John Howells was no believer in sparing the rod and spoiling the child.

If he caught the girls away from their work he would put the yardstick across them and drive them back to their work. But one day they found a subject for a piece of gossip at John Howell's expense. The day before he had been in a tight corner with two bags of coal - I never heard the details - when they were sure J.H's back was turned they gathered together in one of the workrooms to discuss the matter and to exact as much fun as they could out of it; when who should walk in but John Howells, yardstick and all, he surely did lash it into them this time muttering as he moved from one to another that this is not

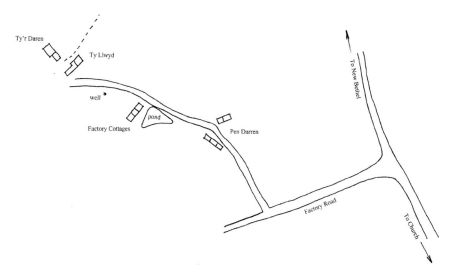

the place for gossip and play, wherever I was yesterday I'm here today. I'm sure he didn't hurt them too much as they laughed more than they cried over it, and it was a standard joke for a long time.

Well, as time went on for some reason John Howells wound up the business and moved away from the district.

He turned the old workshops into tenements and rented them to local people. They were not very hygienic, but if they fell ill they had the best doctors in the land to attend them'.

The Tithe Apportionment Book of 1839 lists the above named John Howells. The 'Woollen Factory' was occupied by John Howells but the landowner was Joseph Phillips. Mr. Howells was a tenant, and although he worked the Factory, he did not live there. He lived a short walk away at Pen Heol Caerllwyn (also called Three Cocks), in the old farm that was owned by the Rev. John Davies.

The little community around the Factory was approached down a lane from Factory Road. On the left hand side was a tenement of three houses. The northernmost one was one up one down; the middle one was two up one down, and the southernmost house was three up two down. Almost opposite was the old Pendarren House, a house with stables underneath, with outside steps up to

The Flannel Factory and Jumbo Town area of The Mountain. At the top left corner of the photograph is Factory Lane, and to the right of the junction can be seen Pen Heol Cae'rllwyn (Three Cocks). To the extreme right lie the ruins of Jumbo Town and Cefn Cae'rllwyn. At the bottom left of the photograph is the Factory area. On the extreme left is Pen Darren. Down the lane can be seen the pond, water from which turned the Factory wheel. Below that again can be seen Ty Llwyd and Ty'r Daren Farms.

the house. Attached to it was the beast house in Long House fashion. A little further along the lane, and slightly down hill, was the pond which collected water from a small stream, and was used to drive the water wheel of the Flannel Factory. This wheel in turn drove a shaft off which leather drive belts turned various pieces of machinery upstairs in the workshop. The Factory was immediately below the pond. As Mrs. Meyrick wrote, it had ceased life as a factory by her childhood, about 1880, and had since been turned into tenements, a row of three houses. One of them had inside stairs up to a bedroom, while the other two had outside steps to the upper story. The mill gear was underneath the three. It was here in Old Factory Cottages that Obediah Hodges lived, in the northernmost end house.

At the back of Pen Darren House were Ben Lewis and Bill Symons, with baby Myfanwy Lewis (Mrs. Les Carpenter). Leading up to the building of New Bethel Chapel, its members met at this house from 1760 to 1765.

Continuing on down the lane, on the right hand side was the entrance to a coal level sunk in the 1920s by '*Eppy*'. A short distance further brought you to Ty Llwyd farmhouse, last lived-in in the 1950s by an ex-teacher Miss Williams, who came here from Dinas Powis, and who is remembered for her goats. These goats gave milk which Miss Williams turned into cheese. She also kept geese which terrorised the children in the neighbourhood. It has been remembered by a few of those children (now senior citizens) how her table was always laid out as for high tea, but sadly she had few callers. In her little booklet, Mrs. Meyrick recalled how it had been the home of Mr. and Mrs. Henry Rees, *'Very reserved people, good farmers, kind, and very much respected. Mrs. Rees was an expert in Caerphilly Cheese making'*. Finally there was another farm house, Ty'r Darren, an old Long House with beast house attached. From the front it looked similar to how Caerllwyn Isaf looks today, The old farm house had a reputation for being haunted. In the main room downstairs were exposed oak beams, and one was carved with the date 1605, which sadly has not survived. The house was last lived in by the Harris family in 1938. Mrs. Meyrick's little booklet tells how she remembered it as the home of Mr. and Mrs. Daniel Davies. *'They had farmed Triscoed Farm before coming here to Ty'r Darren in semi-retirement. Mr. Davies was a boot and shoemaker and repairer. One of the finest craftsmen of his day without mistake, he kept the whole parish and a few besides comfortably shod. They brought up two very clever children, their son Tom Davies was headmaster of Danygraig School, Risca, for many years, and he was joint secretary of the Bedwellty Show'*.

A number of the houses above described were last occupied in the 1950s, then all were abandoned before being demolished in the early 1980s.

George and Gertrude Suter with sons Jack and George and grandson Gary Waters, outside Factory Cottages.

Gary and Graham Waters with Raymond Bowden outside Factory Cottages.

A sunny day outside Factory Cottages as Trevor Waters seeks some shade.

233

John Lewis standing on his front bailey outside Ty Llwyd Farmhouse (close to the Factory). He came to this area from mid-Wales to become a pit sinker at Nine Mile Point Colliery. He was a founder member of the English Baptist Church at Cwmfelinfach, and was known as John the Baptist. He moved into Ty Llwyd in 1914, became the publican of the Blacksmith's in 1928, and moved to Ty Glas (near New Bethel) in 1936.

			WOOLLEN FACTORY, &c.											
Phillips, Joseph	Howells, John	1125			Arable	3	0	13	0	1	0	0	4	10
		1126			"	2	3	5	0	0	11	0	4	5
		1128			"	3	2	28	0	1	1	0	5	10
		1129			"	3	0	9	0	1	0	0	4	10
		1142			Garden	0	1	33						
		1142a			Brake	0	0	24						
		1143	Factory and		Yard	0	0	26						
		1144			Pond	0	0	18						
		1145			Waste	0	0	25						
		1146			Pasture	0	2	37	0	0	4	0	0	2
		1147			Arable	3	0	16	0	1	0	0	4	11
		1149			Pasture	2	1	7	0	1	0	0	0	6
		1149a	Barn and		Fold	0	0	21						
						19	3	22	0	6	4	1	5	6
Phillips, Mark	Griffiths, John	4847	House and		Garden	0	0	20						

234

Obediah Hodges

Obediah Hodges was born on the 15th December 1873 at No.9 Graham Street, Newport. He was one of six children born to James William and Mary Ann Hodges. The children were William John Hodges, born 1870; Obediah 1873; Henry 1876; Alfred Ernest 1877; Sydney 1879 and Charles 1881. The 1881 census shows the family at 22 St. Julian's Street, Newport. Obediah was christened at St. Woolos Church, Newport, where the family worshipped.

Nothing is known of his formative years, but between the ages of 18 and 27 (1892-1900) he worked as a merchant seaman, sailing to many parts of the world from various ports, including Newport, Cardiff, Penarth and Barry.

During this period his home was Turnpike Cottages, Iron Acton, Gloucestershire, and it was there that he met and later married Sarah Ann Blake, the daughter of Charles and Elizabeth Blake.

Obediah was of a serious disposition and a strict disciplinarian. He was a small man, standing 5 feet 3 inches tall, with light coloured hair, fair complexion, and grey eyes. On his left arm was tattooed a female head, an anchor and a ship.

Between 1900 and 1902 Obediah moved to Bristol Road, Iron Acton. Whether this was due to his marriage or not isn't known, but the couple are believed to have married during that period.

Sometime between 1902 and 1909 Obediah and Sarah moved to the old Woollen Factory Cottages at Mynyddislwyn where they brought up their three children, Vera Irene, born 1909, Obediah, born 1912, and Rembrandt Oswald, born 1920. It was there that Obediah and Sarah spent the rest of their lives.

The family was very poor. The boom in colliery and railway development that occurred in the area during his early years at Mynyddislwyn failed to attract Obediah, and he was insistent that his sons would not become colliers. Instead, he relied upon his talent with brush and easel to eke out a living. He painted all the local scenes and must have relied upon memories of his foreign travels for his paintings of Highland Cattle and Oriental scenes, as well as ships, flowers, birds and animals.

Worshippers leaving Mynyddislwyn Church on a Sunday would be confronted by an array of his work on the grass bank, and he never missed the opportunity afforded by the sheep dog trials, which in those days were attended by hundreds of people. He travelled many miles to sell his paintings and more than once settled the account of a local trader in kind.

Illtyd David, himself a celebrated artist, remembered how as a child he would creep up behind Obediah to sit and watch him paint. Obediah, without looking up or slowing his stroke, would say to Illtyd *And what do you want?'*

Obediah died during 1937 aged 64, and he was buried in the graveyard at Mynyddislwyn.

Obediah Hodges 1873-1937.

St. Tudor's Church, Mynyddislwyn, painted by Obediah Hodges.

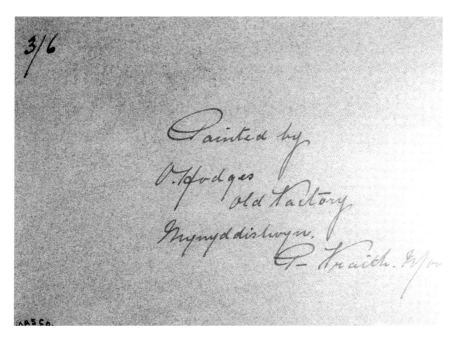

On the back of an Obediah painting, written by the artist. The painting was priced at 3 shillings and 6pence (17$^{1}/_{2}$ pence).

Obediah's painting of New Bethel Chapel.

237

Coal

Coal in this area must have been known about for centuries, because where the seams of coal are not too far below the surface, they outcrop on the hillsides, and have been worked relatively easily. One such seam of coal not too deep is the Mynyddislwyn Seam. It underlies a much bigger area than that covered by this book, and probably got its name because it was worked almost everywhere within the parish. To call it a seam of coal is inaccurate, because the Mynyddislwyn Seam is in fact four separate seams of coal, the Lower and Upper Mynyddislwyn, and the Small Rider and the Big Rider, separated from one another by other rocks, clays, etc.

The Lower Mynyddislwyn Seam varied between 22 and 26 inches in thickness and was generally unworked because the thicker and better quality Upper Mynyddislwyn Seam, some distance above it, proved to be much more profitable. The Upper Seam varied between 28 and 54 inches in thickness and has been largely worked out because of its high quality.

The Lower and Upper Mynyddislwyn Seams are separated by as little as nine inches to the north (in the Manmoel area) but southwards, they are separated by as much as 32 feet at Cwmnantyrodyn.

The coal was mined from many levels going into the hillside, but near the A472 road to Newbridge, where the coal seam is thicker, it was also worked from collieries with vertical shafts. In fact, it was the northern slopes of The Mountain, dropping down to the A472 road, that proved to be the most productive area of coal mining in our area, (until the big deep coal mines were sunk down to the Steam Coal).

Above the Lower and Upper Seams were the Small Rider with generally only a 12 inch thickness of coal, and above that again was the Big Rider with about 30 inches thickness, generally. However, although the thicknesses above are generalised, they can often be wrong. One such example occurred in the late 1960s when the former Islwyn Colliery, near Penrhiwffranc, was sampled with a view to opencasting, and the seam of coal was unusually thick. But the local authority refused permission for the work to go ahead because of the congestion that heavy lorries would have caused on the narrow road off The Mountain.

Two hundred years ago coal mining became an important local industry, coinciding with the opening of the canal from Crumlin to Newport, and a number of tramroads that were built about the same time. The coal could he taken to Newport where it was loaded on to boats at the riverside, to be shipped up, down, or across the channel.

One of the great difficulties of looking back to those early days of coal mining in our area is that when a coal level or colliery opened, it had a particular name. Market fluctuations often closed them down, to be opened again under a new name when economic conditions improved. An example is the level below Penrhiwffranc Farm, which has been called Penrhiwffranc, Churchlands, Church Farm Colliery, New Pennar, Islwyn Colliery, and finally Penrhiwffranc Level again. Also, a particular name has been used by different coal levels at different times, so reading a name on an old report makes it difficult to pin point the exact location.

Those old reports make the most interesting and informative reading. One such report is the affidavit of David Davies, sworn for a Court of Chancery law case in 1877 (which the author has found in Chancery Archive, London). He was 83 years old at the time, which would give his date of birth as 1794.

David Davies of Incline Cottage, Pentwynmawr, in the parish of 'Mynyddyslwyn' in the county of Monmouth, collier, cross examined on his affidavit sworn the 12th day of March 1877, stated *'I am 83 years of age I believe. I worked underground with my brother at Pennar Colliery when I was 8 years old (1802). I cannot say when I was born but I am 83 years old. I worked at Pennar when I was eight and I was hauling after that. William Phillips was the owner of the land and Jenkins and Vaughan were the owners of the coal when I was there. Jenkins paid me for working. Perhaps 40 or 50 men were there at the same time with me. The 40 or 50 men I have mentioned all worked at once and all the week except when they were ill. The coal came down this way to the canal here. There was a tramway from the Pennar levels to the canal at Newbridge and I can show it to you now. There were two levels at Pennar called the Upper Level and the Lower Level. Both were called Pennar because they were not far from one another. One might have been called Vaughan's Level. I worked there for 6 or 7 years. I was haulier when I became big enough. I was hauling when I was about 9 years old and I continued hauling till I was twelve. There were four horses. There were from 30 to 40 trams employed altogether. I knew Church Farm. No coal was worked under there at that time. I cannot say when coal was worked from under Church Farm. The coal from Church Farm did not come out of these levels. It came out from another above the rubbish. I cannot say when that was. It was after I worked at Vaughan's Level. After I was fifteen (1809) Mr. Vaughan did not open the level in the Church Farm but he did open the one I worked in. That was opened 75 years ago (1802). There was also Phillips' Levels besides Church Farm, but they were both entered by one mouth. The level on the right brought coal from Church Farm. The other on the left bought coal from Pant yr Esg and other lands. The Pennar Levels were nearly worked out when the others were opened. There were three levels at Pennar in my time, that is from the time I was eight till I was fifteen. The level above the rubbish was under Pencoedcae. The owner of Pencoedcae in old times was Harry John Harry. He was brother to Jenkin John Harry who lived at Penrhiw Darren, that was the name of his farm. I don't know where Penrhiwffranc is. I do know a level called Penrhiwrfranc. It was I who opened it. I do know a farm called by the name of Pennar Ganol. Edward Shon y Gof had a pit between Pennar and Pant yr Esg. I don't know to whom Pant yr Esg belonged. I don't know anything about Pentremawr Colliery. I never worked there. There is a level called Cwmcaedee. I did not work there. It had been worked out before I commenced working. Harry Thomas Lewis was the owner of the farm. I went into Cwmcaedee Colliery when I was a boy after rabbits. I do not know whether that belonged to Abercarne Estate. Adjoining Harry's land was a field belonging to Lady Llanover. I was not under that. There is a mouth there now but there was not one then.*

I remember very well when the Battle of Waterloo was fought. I was cutting coal then at Pennar Level. Edward Shon y Gof's pit was 24 yards deep, and he had another not far off 17 yards deep. It was worked by a windlass drawing half a hundredweight at a time. The coal was sold about the country as Country Coal. Edward Shon y Gof was the owner of the land. There was no level there, only two pits. The second pit was sunk when the first was exhausted. I have been down in the pit cutting coal when I was 21 years of age. When we got to the bottom of the pit we could not go anywhere else. Only one man worked in the pit at a time. We got as much out of the pit in one day as we could sell. I could have cut three tons per day in that pit. Whenever there was a call for coal I went to work. The demand came sometimes only once a week. I was working underground driving a level at that time when I was not working the coal. When they wanted coal they came and fetched me.

I knew the land on which Edward Shon y Gof's pits were sunk. I do not know the name of it now. When I was working there I was 21 years of age. I can't recollect but I think when I was working there that it was called Pennar Ganol, or the Middle Pennar. There was an old house there which has been since rebuilt. I may say it was the works that undermined the old house. The old house was not down entirely when I went to work there but it was leaning over. I recollect going into some old works under Edmund's land when I was working at Edward Shon y Gof's. I don't think that people knew in those days how to prop properly. Small stumps of coal held up the roof in those old workings'.

At the same court case, another affidavit was read out, that of Edward Morgan of Pentwynmawr, sworn on the 12th March 1877 - *'I cannot speak English. I do not understand English much and therefore I shall not attempt to speak it. I am about 86 years of age (born 1791). I remember my age since I was a boy, I have remembered it all the time. I have been a collier since I was a boy. I can remember since I was 6 or 7 years of age and be certain about it. I first worked in the pit of Thomas Johnes down by Ton y Pistyll. I was between 6 and 7 years old. Ton y Pistyll belonged to Glover, the gentleman that was there long before Mr. Hall. I worked in a pit of Country Coal. The pit was about 15 yards deep, as far as I can recollect. I and another boy were carting coal to the bottom of the pit. It was a cart to convey half a hundredweight. We did not work every day. The people took the coal away on the backs of horses, about the houses, everywhere where they sold it. I worked at Pennar a little during Vaughan's time when I was about 12 years of age, I think. There were two levels there at that time. Perhaps 20 tons of coal, perhaps more, came out per day. The coal went over the tramroad down to the canal. I ought to know Pentwynmawr Farm, it is down close by here. Pentwynmawr is what they call the Pennar Works. I know the Church Farm very well, it was thereabouts I was brought up. They did not work coal so far under that farm at that time. They had not nearly reached the coal there at that time. There was no level mouth on Church Farm, it was opened on Pennar land. I know the farmhouse called Penrhiwffranc, it is on top of the hill there. It is Williams' farm. There is a level a little way beyond there. It was opened a long time ago, but I cannot say when. I have seen Pant yr Esg. There was a level there long ago but it has stopped working now. The level was stopped 9 or 10 years ago so far as I can recollect. I know a farm called Pentre near the Church. Philip Jones was the owner of that farm. There is no level there'.*

Both of these affidavits mention a tramroad running from Pennar to the canal. Such a tramroad is shown on Thomas Dadford's map, of 1793, for the building of the canal, but he drew it running beyond Pennar. He was planning long term.

In Archdeacon Coxe's book 'A Historical Tour in Monmouthshire' he wrote in 1799 *'At Newbridge, so called from a bridge which crosses the Ebwy, large quantities of coal are brought down a railroad from the mines of Mynyddyslwyn and conveyed by the canal to Newport'.* That tramroad ran from the area of the Nailers public house,

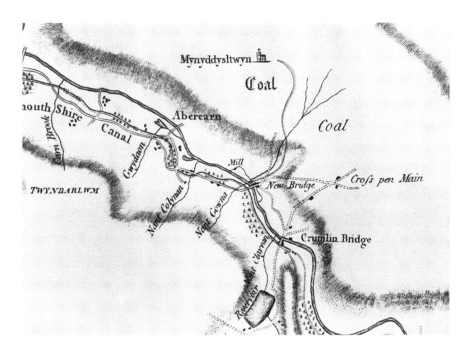

A small part of Thomas Dadford's map of the Monmouthshire Canal and its Crumlin Branch, dated 1793. It clearly shows a tramroad from Mynyddislwyn Mountain joining the canal at Newbridge. This was the Pennar Branch Tramroad. He was using artistic licence, because the tramroad did not get so close to the Church as Dadford suggests. This was the tramroad seen and described by Archdeacon Coxe in 1799.

through Tonypistyll, and down into Newbridge via Tynewydd Terrace, behind Beulah Chapel, across the river by a bridge that no longer exists, to join the canal by Newbridge rugby club. (This is shown on a map dated 1807 in a private collection).

When Benjamin Hall became Lord of the Manor of Abercarne in 1808 he immediately set about planning a tramroad that has become known as Hall's Road. With his agent, he did a feasibility study to see how many collieries then opened, or intended soon to be, could possibly carry their coal on his new tramroad. Part of a letter dated January 1809, written by Hall to his agent, reads

'Probable Tonnages - Pontymister Company 8,000 tons say 2½ miles
From Pennar   at 5 pence $\Big\}$ £166 13s 4d

Uncertain Tonnages - Church Farm may be expected to
*   Produce 10,000 tons at 6 pence   £250'.*

The above named Pontymister Colliery was situated alongside the above named tramroad, a little way behind the Three Horseshoes public house.

The Pennar Branch Tramroad is shown on a map of January 1810 (in Chancery Archives, London) when Benjamin Hall, Lord of the Manor of Abercarne, entered into a court case against Sir Henry Protheroe (mentioned earlier in this

241

book in the 'Ebbw Valley' chapter). But its route has by then been altered. Instead of running down to Newbridge it skirted around Tylla Cocks Wood and ran down into Abercarne. Mention is again made of this tramroad further ahead in this book under 'Penrhiwffranc'.

The two sworn affidavits tell us that David Davies and Edward Morgan started work underground as young children. Up until the 1840s it was common practice for young children, boys and girls, and women, to work long hours in the collieries and iron works throughout Britain.

Government Commissioners toured the industrial areas of Britain, interviewing child workers, and in December 1841 presented to Parliament their 'Report on the Employment of Children and Young Persons in the Collieries and Ironworks, and on the State, Condition and Treatment of such Children and Young Persons'.

It made appalling reading. They didn't visit every colliery and coal level, which would have been impossible, but in the parish of 'Mynyodduslwyn' they reported on seven collieries, which provided employment for 514 male adults, 169 males under 18, and 91 males under 13 years of age. Unlike neighbouring Glamorgan, they found no young girls employed in our area. The Report read *'An exact total of children employed could not be obtained as several (Collieries) have not made their returns and others have objected to do so'.*

At nearby Argoed, the mineral agent said *'Young boys are taken down as soon as they can stand on their legs'.* In another case, the medical assistant said *'They (the people) certainly had a bad practice here in taking children down as soon as they can creep about, many as early as 5 or 6 years of age'.* The cashier of the Waterloo Colliery (Oakdale) said *'Fathers carry their children below at 4 or 5 years of age'.*

The above are reported from our neighbourhood, so must have been identical on Mynyddislwyn Mountain.

The Report tells us that the youngest children worked as air-door boys. *'The airdoor boy is generally from 5 to 11 years of age; his post is in the mine at the side of the air-door, and his business is to open it for the haulier, with his horse and tram, to pass, and then to close the door after them. In some pits the situation of these poor things is distressing. With his solitary candle, cramped with cold, wet, and not half fed, the poor child, deprived of light and air, passes his silent day; his or her wages 6 or 8 pence per day. Surely one would suppose nothing but hard poverty could induce a parent so to sacrifice the physical and moral existence of his child!'*

'The hours of work are generally from 6 in the morning until 6 at night the labour of children and young persons accompanies the labour of the adult workmen, their hours of labour are of the same duration as the labour of the men'.

'The children and young persons employed in collieries generally take to their work bread and cheese for their meal in the day-time. The haulier eats his food as he drives his horse along; the little air-door boy may take his meal when he pleases; and as the colliers are paid per ton for their work, they too choose their own time. A supper, however, is generally provided for the colliers' return, of bacon and vegetables, most usually, for the colliers rarely eat fresh meat during the week.'

'On the subject of ventilation in the workings of a particular vein of coal, being a Red Ash coal, extending from Mammoel in the parish of Bedwelty to Church Farm in the

parish of Mynyodduslwyn; and to this subject my attention was more particularly drawn by the fact of the frequent stoppages of the works in consequence of choke-damp'.

A mineral surveyor of Newport reported *'The principal seam at present in work for the supply of the export trade of Newport is a Red Ash coal, in which fire-damp is not found. The absence of fire-damp in this vein, the Mynyodduslwyn, has operated very prejudicially throughout the district, by creating a confidence in the minds of the parties engaged, that whatever the state of the ventilation may be, no explosion of fire-damp can possibly occur; consequently the ventilation of the collieries is much neglected. It is a common occurrence for colliers to be obliged to leave their work from not being able to keep their lights in, and, in some cases, when the wind is in an opposite point to the level, the ventilation is so bad as to stop the work; the colliers work as long as they can keep a light in, but the small quantity of air necessary barely to maintain combustion must be a very unhealthy atmosphere for respiration'.*

The same 1841 Report listed schools open to the Working Classes.

'Newbridge - one day school; average attendance 60 to 70. If the people can get employment for their children at any age, if it were only two shillings a week, they will immediately take them from the school and put them to work'. - the Schoolmaster.

'Mynyodduslwyn - one day school, principally supported by colliers; average attendance 40, average fees 4 pence per week. Nine Sunday-schools; two belonging to the Established Church, two to the Baptists, two to the Independents, two to the Welsh Methodists, and one to the Wesleyans. There is also an evening-school held in the vestry-room on Friday evenings, for reading and psalm-singing. There is neither a National nor a free-school in the parish. This parish is 10 miles by 8 and full of collieries, and yet there is but one church and one school room'. - Rev. J. Evans, Rector.

(The above report is for the whole of the parish, and not just the Mountain).

In another part of the Report, the Rev. J. Evans said *'Children are not overworked in our collieries, but they are often idle at home when they ought to be at school; and the general excuse of parents is that they cannot afford to send them. We want more schools in the Welsh hills; in fact, we have neither schools nor churches to answer the population.'*

'The school is attended principally by quarry men and farm labourers; average fee 4 pence to 6 pence a week. I built the school-room; have been there twelve months'.

Thomas Lewis, Master.

Was that Hen Ysgoldy which has been mentioned in the chapter 'Next Road Up', and which was mentioned in the 1839 Tithe Apportionment Book?

At the nearby Penllwyn Colliery, sited just across the river, alongside the Tramroad in Pontllanfraith, the following statements were taken for the Report. Sixteen youngsters under 13 years of age were employed.

'William Crew, aged 10, air-door boy.

Works 12 hours; been down 3½ years. Been to Sunday-school 12 months; when in full work gets 4 shillings a week. Likes daylight work best. Does not know a letter'.

'Charles Cobley, aged 11, collier.

Began to work when 7 years old; never was hurt; cannot read; father cannot read; gets bread and cheese, but very seldom gets meat as the work is not regular; potatoes and salt nearly every day'.

243

'John Treasure, aged 18, collier.

Been 12 years below; has always worked at Panllwyn; the work is very hard, particularly for young boys who do work; had my legs crushed 3 years ago and was off 5 weeks; we don't often get meat when work is on; boys sometimes labour 15 to 16 hours'.

'Mrs. Sarah Tobay, village of Pontllynfright.

I have 8 children, 4 at work; my husband's wages, taking all things together, have not been 10 shillings all the year through; my husband gets his pay in cash as he is favoured; but where one receives cash 30 are compelled to deal at 'The Shop'; we have frequently been obliged to do so; I am sure I can save 3 shillings in the pound by buying my own goods where I like; but those who are discontented are marked'.

As a result of the Report, Parliament passed an Act in 1842 ending child labour in the collieries.

As mentioned at the beginning of this chapter, coal mining in this area goes back a long way. The Earl of Pembroke's Survey of 1653 mentioned Mines of Coal in the Manor of Abercarne. Coxe mentioned coal, and a tramroad off the Mountain, in 1799. An agreement dated 5th Nov. 1804, from the author's collection, reads *'Memorandum of Agreement made this day between Thomas Lewis Richards and Samuel Glover, both of the parish of Monythusloyn, and county of Monmouth - that is to say the said Thomas Lewis Richards agrees to grant a lease of 21 years to the said Samuel Glover for liberty to drive a Horse Coal Level, or levels, in and through his lands, called Cauia yr Ffynnon, near Monythusloyn Church. Also for the coal under said lands for same term, the said Samuel Glover paying for the former £2 per annum, and 8 pence per ton gallage or Royalty for the latter. And whereas the said intended lease will not be valid without the said Samuel Glover (as Lord of the Manor) granting a licence to the said Thomas Lewis Richards for so doing. The said Samuel Glover agrees to grant a licence for that purpose'.*

Thomas Lewis Richards was a freeholder, and as such owned the minerals below his land. However the law of the day dictated that he had to get permission from the Lord of the Manor to lease out his minerals. Coincidentally, it was that same Lord of the Manor who wanted to work the coal.

P.S. Samuel Glover was Lord of the Manor of Abercarne before Benjamin Hall.

Other agreements read *'Memorandum of Agreement made between Benjamin Hall of Lincolns Inn, London, Esquire, and William Edmunds of the parish of Monydysloyn in the county of Monmouth, Gentleman. Whereas the said William Edmunds is possessed of certain Copyhold lands and premises called Cae Penheol, Skin Kin, Y Tair Erw, Cae Fynnon and Caya Glase, part of the Manor of Abercarne, situate near Church Farm in the parish of Monydysloyn. And whereas there is coal under the said lands and premises and the said Benjamin Hall is Lord of the said Manor. The said Benjamin Hall, in consideration of the sum of 21 shillings yearly paid by the said William Edmunds, on the first day of January every year, agrees to grant him Full Licence and Authority to work coal... As Witness our hands the twenty fifth day of March, 1809'.*

'Memorandum of Agreement made the twenty first day of September 1811 between Benjamin Hall, Esquire, Lord of the Manor of Abercarne, of the one part, and Thomas Davies of Bedwas, Gentleman, and John Edmunds of the parish of Monydysloyn, Farmer, for himself and Thomas Edmunds and William Edmunds, his brothers, of the other part. The said Benjamin Hall hereby agrees to let to the said Thomas Davies, John Edmunds,

244

Thomas Edmunds and William Edmunds, all that Vein of Coal now about to be worked lying under a certain Copyhold Farm of them the said Thomas Davies, John Edmunds, Thomas Edmunds and William Edmunds called Pant yr Hesk, part and parcel of the Manor of Abercarne, at the rent of £25 per annum, for 17 years, from the 1st day of January next. And the said Thomas Davies, John Edmunds, Thomas Edmunds and William Edmunds agree to surrender to the said Benjamin Hall sufficient land to continue his Level, late Mr, Thomas' of Pontymister, to the Church Farm. And the said Benjamin Hall agrees to permit all the Coal now leased, as above, to come out through his land and down his Incline Plane as agreed with Mr. John Thomas'.

N.B. Benjamin Hall has realised the true earning power of coal licences having increased the rent from 21 shillings to £25 per annum in just two years.

'Memorandum of Agreement made the 10th day of September 1835 Between Benjamin Hall of Abercarne, Esquire, of the one part and Martin Morrison of Crumlin, Coal Master, of the other part. The said Benjamin Hall hereby agrees to let to the said Martin Morrison the vein of coal commonly called the Mynyddyslwyn Upper Vein (now opened upon in the lands adjoining) which lies under the Penycoedcae Farm, save and except on Range in the coal of the width of 120 yards under and across the said farm already included in the lease to Moses Moses, at and for the Galeage or Royalty of 10 pence for the weight of 2,500 lbs. (commonly called the Ton Long Weight) and for all other the said veins (now let) according to that weight of the usual good and marketable quality which can or may be worked or gotten under the same Penycoedcae Farm.'

A letter of December 1844 (from the author's collection) tells us that Mr. Rosser Williams of Penrhiwffranc Farm was robbing the pillars of coal from Pennar Colliery. These had been left to support the roof and to stop the whole works collapsing. The letter was from the agent of Abercarne Estate.

'Mr. Rosser Williams,
Dear Sir,
I have just been informed that you are drawing back the pillars that support the main level heading of the Pennar Colliery. You are perfectly aware, as well as myself, that a considerable quantity of Pillar Coal has been left unworked in a heading formerly belonging to Mr. Richard Jenkins' Colliery, called No.8 Heading, and you must also know that it is still standing, and can be opened at a very trifling expense, from the above main level heading. I have looked at the Pillars in No.8 and believe that there is about Three Thousand Tons of good sound Coal within, and my object in now writing to you is to request that you and your partners will immediately discontinue drawing back the main level heading and take the necessary steps for working this Pillar Coal in No.8 heading. I have no hesitation making Messrs. Latch & Co. the same abatement of 9 pence per ton, the original galeage for this Pillar Coal, as my father allowed them for Pillar and Sparry Coal they have latterly been working from Church Farm. I should be glad you would lay this letter before them and let me know your sentiments in a day or two, and a line from you by the bearer stating you will immediately stop any further drawing back of the Pennar Colliery main level heading will oblige.
I remain etc
William Llewellin'.

The late 1870s saw a depression in the local coal mining industry when many of the smaller collieries and levels were being closed down. This coincided with a migration of local colliers to the deeper pits being opened in the Rhondda Valleys and the Aberdare area, as well the newly opening local deep pits at Risca and Celynen.

But coal continued to be worked in some of the small levels on Mynyddislwyn Mountain well into the 20th century, but on a much smaller scale, employing far fewer colliers. In fact, the last coal to be removed from our area was when the new by-pass road was being built in 1990. When the overburden of soil and rock was removed in the Pentwynmawr area, there were countless tons of the Mynyddislwyn Seam that had to be taken away before laying the foundation to that road.

The Northern Edge

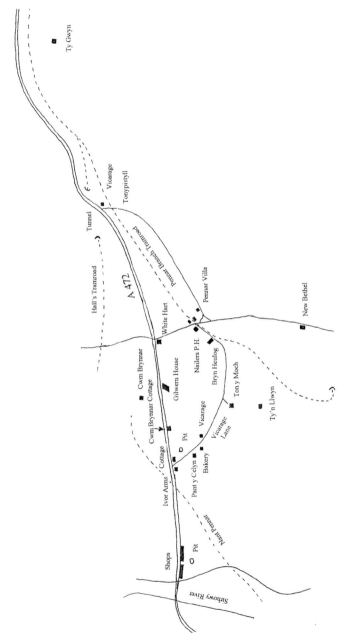

The Northern Edge (before the by-pass road).

247

The area covered by this book must have a boundary, and the natural one for the northern edge of Mynyddislwyn Mountain is the A472 road, from Plough Corner, Pontllanfraith, to Newbridge. This road has been in existence a long time. On a 1750 document it was listed as the road from Pontypool to Ystrad Mynach. That old road must have had a very rough surface. In 1810 there was an Act of Parliament to establish Trustees for a Turnpike Road along this route. The Act starts *'Whereas the Road leading from a certain place called Ystrad Mynach, to a place called Pontymoil near the Town of Pontypool, through the several Parishes of Lanfabon and Gellygare in the county of Glamorgan, and Bedwas, Monythusloin, Panteague and Trevethin, in the county of Monmouth, are very much out of repair, and in many parts thereof narrow, circuitous, and inconvenient to Travellers and Carriages, and the same cannot be effectually amended, widened, diverted, altered, repaired and kept in repair by the ordinary Course of Law. And whereas if the said road were amended, widened, diverted and repaired, and the Course thereof in some places varied and altered and a bridge built over the River Sirhowy near Penllwyn, it would be of great advantage, and attended with much convenience to the owners of Estates, and other inhabitants near the same, and would be of great public utility'.*

The lengthy Act was accompanied by a map, which unfortunately showed no detail either side of the road, but named the many landowners through whose land it was to pass. Above, is the spelling of the parish as it was written in the Act. On the accompanying map, the parish was spelt *'Myniddyslwn'*.

When the Turnpike Road was built, travellers along it had to pay a fee or toll for passing through gates along each section of its length. However, by 1840 it was in need of repair, and a traveller put a letter in the Monmouthshire Merlin newspaper describing its condition as being so bad that he saw no justification for making travellers pay charges for its use, unless they be considered as payment for the beauty of the scenery along its course.

The Act of Parliament empowered the Trustees to set up Gates or Turnpikes across the road, with Toll-houses. Tolls were charged at each of the gates *'before any horse, beast, cattle or carriage shall be permitted to pass through the same.*

For every horse, mare, gelding, or other beast of burthen, laden or unladen, any sum not exceeding two pence. For any horse, mare, gelding, drawing any waggon, wain, cart, with wheels of less than 6 inches breadth, any sum not exceeding six pence, and with wheels of 6 inches and upwards, any sum not exceeding 4 pence.

For every horse, mare, etc. drawing any waggon etc. loaded with timber, between the first day of November and the first day of March, any sum not exceeding one shilling.

For any horse etc. drawing any coach, chariot, chaise, landau, gig, car of pleasure, or for travelling, any sum not exceeding 6 pence.

For every score of oxen or other neat cattle, any sum not exceeding one shilling and eight pence. For every score of calves, swine, goats, sheep or lambs, any sum not exceeding 10 pence.

248

On each and every Sunday, to be computed from 12 of the clock on Saturday night to 12 of the clock on Sunday night, the Toll-gatherers or Collectors shall demand of each and every carriage, horse, beast, etc. passing through any Gate, Double the Toll demanded on any other day of the week'.

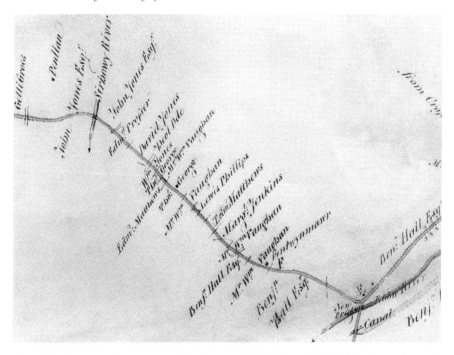

A part of the map that accompanied the 1810 Act of Parliament to build the Turnpike Road from Ystrad to Pontymoil. This has become the A472 road, part of which runs from Pontllanfraith through Pentwynmawr to Newbridge. To the left of the map the road crossed the River Sirhowy by a bridge near the Greyhound Pub, Pontllanfraith. Just beyond that, the road is intercepted by the road from Penmaen at Plough Corner. A road is marked crossing at Heol ddu. Today, this is a narrow footpath opposite the Ivor Arms. Thomas George's Cwm Brynnar Farm is marked. Below the name Mr. Wm. Vaughan is the road crossing at Tonypistyll.

The north-western corner of our area has altered much over the years. Gone is Pantycelyn Row. Many alterations have been made to the shops in Newbridge Road. What is now Waites Spa shop used to be two shops, Mr. and Mrs. Abbotts wool and ladies fashions, and Miss Flowers gift shop. Next was Fords general store. The present double glazing showroom used to be Lewis Lewis and Son bread shop and café. Next was Mr. and Mrs. Henry Harry's hardware shop, while the present hairdressers used to be Hilditch greengrocers, and before that Vi Newmas had a greengrocer's shop. Finally, the present Sirhowy Tiles used to be Stevens the butcher, and before that Tuckers butchers.

A cast iron Parish Marker from beside the Turnpike Road. It has been moved a short distance from its original position for security reasons.

As already mentioned in the last chapter, coal played an important part in the history of this area. Behind the above shops on Newbridge Road, once stood New Tir Philkins Colliery. The single shaft was sunk in 1874, and was 221 feet deep to the Mynyddislwyn Seam of coal. To assist with ventilation it was linked underground to the workings of Old Tir Philkins Colliery (near Woodfieldside) and New Penllwyn Pit (alongside the Tramroad, now under the Ready Mix concrete site). At sinking, the owners were Walter and Henry St. John Powell, sons of the famous (or infamous) Thomas Powell (whose name lives on in the Powell Duffryn Company).

A flood occurred at New Tir Philkins in June 1877 which put in excess of 150 men and boys out of work. Water was thought to have come from the Old Penllwyn Pit. The colliery manager at the time was Lieut. Temple Stroud.

In 1891 the manager was Edward Beddoe who was charged with neglecting to examine the interior of the boiler at the colliery. He was fined £2. The colliery finally closed in January 1892.

The author has childhood memories of visiting the annual travelling shows and circus on this site, and always going home black from the coal waste in the ground.

Opening of the New Pits at Tyr Philkins
(Monmouthshire Merlin, June 1874)

'The Messrs H. and W. Powell celebrated this event "Big with Blessings" to the neighbourhood, by a grand dinner to all the sinkers, mechanics and engineers connected with the works, at the Royal Oak, Blackwood, on Saturday.

The chair was taken by the Manager, Lieut. Temple Stroud, and Mr. J. Jeremiah, Manager of the Company's collieries at New Tredegar, occupied the vice-chair. A number of gentlemen connected with the works were present, among whom were Mr. D. Phillips, the Chief Engineer, Mr. Jacob Thomas, Newport, Mr. David Thomas and Mr. Williams, Manager of the Company's collieries at Aberbeeg and Llanhilleth.

An excellent spread was provided by the hostess, Mrs Coggins, who was complimented upon the getting of the dinner. The usual loyal and patriotic toasts having been duly honoured, the toast of the evening "Success to the New Pit" was drunk with tremendous applause. A very pleasant evening was spent and the Company are to be congratulated upon having won coal so soon'.

Flooding of a Colliery
(Monmouthshire Merlin, June 1877)

'A serious mishap has occurred at the Lower Tir Philkins Colliery belonging to Messrs. W. and H. Powell, owing to a rather sudden influx of water into the workings in a part where the men were driving a hard heading. The workings have all been stopped, and upwards of one hundred and fifty men and boys thrown out of employment. It was at first thought that the water had come from Old Penllwyn Pit and a float was put down, but the water in the pit does not shrink, and it is generally feared that the water from the Sirhowy River is finding its way through a fault'.

Breach of Mines Act
(South Wales Times, August 1891)

'Mr. Edward Beddoe, New Tyr-Philkins Colliery, Pontllanfraith, was charged by Mr. Martin, H.M. Inspector, with neglecting to examine the interior of the boiler at the colliery from 29th May to 5th June.

Mr. J. Plews, solicitor, Merthyr, appeared to prosecute and stated the particulars, to which he pleaded guilty, and the Magistrates imposed a fine of £2 including costs'.

Behind the shops and houses in Newbridge Road, Pontllanfraith, was the site of New Tir Philkins Colliery. Elim Chapel, opened in 1912, can be seen, so the photograph was taken after that date.

Mrs Annie Lewis inside her bread shop and café on Newbridge Road near Plough Corner. She was the wife of Mr. Lewis Lewis, the baker from Windy Ridge. Today the premises is a double glazing window showroom.

After passing the site of Tommy Williams' garage (today a carpet showroom), the next place of interest is the Ivor Arms public house. The 1871 census lists the Ivor Arms, with Anthony Lewis the publican, a coalminer. The 1881 census lists 70-year-old Catherine Lewis, widow, as Inn Keeper. So the pub was built some time between the 1861 census, when it was not listed, and 1871.

The pub was taken over by the Barnfield family in 1921, who can be seen on the photograph overleaf. The landlord and landlady were Mr. and Mrs. George and Ann Barnfield. Mrs. Barnfield ran the pub from the time George died in 1931 until her death in 1948. The photograph shows the family standing by the front door. That is now altered to a window, with the door at the end of the building, through an extension. In the photograph both windows are advertising Bass in bottles.

But who was Ivor? The land on which the pub was built was part of Benjamin Hall's Abercarne Estate. Hall's two sons had died before him, so his grandson by his daughter, Ivor John Caradoc Herbert, was his heir, but Ivor had to wait. After Hall died, the Estate was held by his widow, Lady Llanover, and after her death it all passed to Ivor.

However, it is possible that Ivor was given some land during his grandparents' lifetime, held in trust, from which he could have an income from rents and mineral royalties, and the trustees could have negotiated the lease of the ground for the building of the pub. The same man is remembered in nearby Sir Ivor's Road, and also his own family home on his father's side, Llanarth, has given us a few local names.

Tommy Williams' garage on the A472 road. Today it is a carpet showroom.

The Ivor Arms in the mid 1920s. To the left, with umbrella, is George (Barny) Barnfield. Next to him is John Williams (Sionni Bricks), then the landlord's two daughters, Maggie and Violet. The landlady, Mrs. Ann Barnfield, was not keen on posing for photographs.

A road leads up Vicarage Lane. Until 1990 it continued past Ton y Moch, to the former Nailers pub, and on up past New Bethel Chapel. But when the new by-pass road was built, the road was cut short; no fly-over was built. At the end of this short road today is the Mynyddislwyn Vicarage. The first occupant was Canon B. Jones Evans in the First World War. In those early days, his wife ran a small private school from a galvanised sheeting building in the grounds.

Also on this road was a small independent bakery. It had been purpose-built as a bakehouse. Sometime before the outbreak of the Second World War, Mr. Lewis Lewis bought it from Mr. Heales, who lived in the bungalow opposite. The company traded as Lewis Lewis and Son. His wife was Mrs. Annie Lewis, formerly Prothero, who was born at Cae'rllwyn Farm (see photograph in Cae'rllwyn chapter). The bread was baked overnight by Mr. Smith, the night-time baker, and delivered door to door next day. In the early days of the business, deliveries were made by horse and covered cart.

The ovens were heated with solid fuel. Sunday was a busy morning, cleaning out the ashes and re-lighting the fire, which was kept alight throughout the week.

Mr. Roy Fox recalled the snow and ice of 1947. His father had working horses, and during that time they were used for transporting anything and everything. He had a specially adapted sleigh to move 140 lb. bags of flour up to the bakery.

The flour was brought in by rail, and delivered from Pontllanfraith station to the bakery by lorry.

Mr. Lewis Lewis, in white coat, with his van, delivering bread in Pentwynmawr.

Mr. and Mrs. Lewis opened a bread and cake shop, with groceries and light refreshments, on Newbridge Road. As Mr. Lewis's health was not very good, Mrs. Lewis ran the shop. Son Gwynmor delivered bread and daughter Margaret worked in the bakehouse during the day making the cakes, and also birthday, wedding and Christmas cakes.

Mr. Lewis closed the bakehouse in the late 1950s and the building was converted into the bungalow that stands on the site today. The delivery round was sold to John Walker, but he got his bread elsewhere.

Standing in front of Lewis Lewis' delivery van are Gwynmor Lewis (son), Margaret Lewis (daughter), Peggy Grifiths and John Barnes. The two men did the deliveries.

Inside Lewis Lewis' Bakery.

Beside the Bakery was an old house, Pantycelyn House, which still stands today. At one time Jones Biscuits lived there. It was shown on the first Ordnance Survey Map published in January 1833, and was mentioned in the 1839 Tithe Apportionment Book as being part of Benjamin Hall's Abercarne Estate, leased to John Morgan.

Back down to the A472, and today there is a bus shelter and bus pull-in. At that spot was a little house, the home of Mr. and Mrs. Herbert Mansfield. Off the pavement you had to step down into the house. It had two rooms only, a living room and bedroom downstairs. There was no upstairs. Sadly, the house was destroyed in February 1948, and Mrs. Mansfield died in the accident. The Argus reported the accident, as follows

Widow Killed As She Sat By Fire At Home - Cottage Is Wrecked By Lorry

'An Elderly woman was killed while sitting by her own fireside, when a heavy lorry carrying an armoured car crashed through the walls of her cottage at Pontllanfraith.

She was seventy-year-old Mrs. Margaret Mansfield, a widow, who lived alone at Pantycelyn Cottage, Newbridge Road, Pontllanfraith.

The lorry, a former Army troop-carrier, was being towed by another lorry to a car-breaking yard at Pengam when, it is believed, the tow bar became disconnected as the vehicles were descending a slight gradient in the Newbridge Road, near the Ivor Arms Inn.

The troop carrier, loaded with a five ton armoured car, swerved on to the pavement, ran about twenty yards, crashed into the pine end of the cottage, and more than half its length was buried inside the living room. The gun turret of the armoured car held up the roof, which otherwise would have collapsed.

Rescuers were quickly on the scene, and when they reached Mrs. Mansfield after half an hour of desperate work, they found her buried under a heavy stone. Neighbours had seen Mrs. Mansfield in her garden feeding the chickens shortly before the accident. It appeared she had been sitting by the fire when the lorry crashed through the fireplace and carried her back to the wall partitioning off the bedroom.

The crashed vehicles had to be left wedged in the cottage overnight, and the work of extricating them was started at mid-day today'.

This house was also shown on the first O.S. map of 1833. The 1839 Tithe Apportionment Book tells us that this little house was a Nailer's Shop, occupied by John Morgan. Nails would have been handmade there. Probably, the actual nailers manufactory was a small workshop behind the house. This would be confirmed by the 1881 census which lists 'Cottage near Ivor Arms' and separately, 'Old Nailers Shop'.

Immediately behind the Nailer's Shop was the vertical shaft of Diamond Colliery, or Black Diamond Colliery as it is marked on one document. It was owned by William and Edward Beddoe, colliery proprietors of Llanfabon (near Nelson). On a later colliery plan, it is called New Winding Pit, so it was obviously connected underground to the workings a little further to the east.

The next building up the road still stands, Cwmbrynnar Cottage. This is an early to mid 19th C. two-storey house. It is thought to have been built for the manager of one of the many local collieries or levels. It is now a listed building, a rare example of an early to mid 19th century 'valleys' cottage that has retained all

its important character. These
include centre cross-passage, two
end chimneys, spiral stone stairs
beside the stepped chimney breast,
and beamed ceilings. Upstairs, the
two rooms lead directly one from
the other in the traditional manner.

*Mr. and Mrs. Herbert Mansfield.
A few years after the death of Mr.
Mansfield, Mrs. Mansfield was killed
in February 1948 when her little
cottage was destroyed in a lorry
accident.*

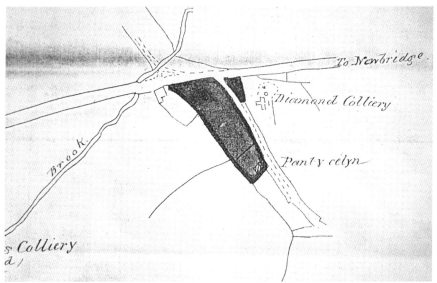

*Diamond Colliery was behind Mr. and Mrs. Mansfield's Pantycelyn Cottage. This part
of an old map shows the A472 road, with Pantycelyn House alongside Vicarage Lane.
Today, immediately above the words 'to Newbridge' is the site of Leo's/Pioneer foodstore.*

257

Just beyond the back garden of Cwmbrynnar Cottage was a shaft 72 feet deep down to the Upper Mynyddislwyn Seam of coal, which is shown on the Coal Authority's Abandonment Plan, but has not been located on the land. When the house changed hands a few years ago, this shaft, being 25 metres from the property, could have given problems over the purchase, but the Coal Authority consider that a mine shaft may pose a threat to a property if it lies within a 20 metre radius of that property. This is intended to protect the property from any emissions of gas or water from the mine workings that could threaten the property or the persons living within it. There is also a risk of collapse or subsidence. This house was found to be safely beyond that 20 metre zone, and the purchase went ahead.

Cwmbrynnar Cottage.

The next building along is Gilwern House. A date outside of 1853 suggests the date of building. Inside, the same date is carved in one of the stone fire places. The house is not shown on the 1846 Tithe Map, so the date would seem correct. Confusingly, the 1805 Land Tax Assessment Register for this area lists a 'Gilwain' farm, owned by William Jones and leased to John Jenkins, with a valuation of five shillings, and a tax of one shilling. But it is impossible to say where that farm was. An old colliery plan shows 'Gilwain' level to the south, near Ton y Moch. The similarity between the old and modern spellings is too close to be a coincidence. Did an old farm exist on this site, to be pulled down before 1846, hence its omission off the Tithe Map?

Surprisingly, Gilwern House is not named on the 1861 or 1871 census returns. Those records list many properties in the immediate area without names, so without knowing the occupants at those dates, it is almost impossible to say which of the entries is for the house. The 1881 census tells us that the occupier was Daniel Davies, a Commercial Traveller in Tea. In 1891 it was occupied by Edmund John James and family, *'living on their own means'*.

At the south end of the house a coal level went into the hillside, but it had ceased working before the Lovell family moved into the house in the 1920s. They knew it as a former Siams (James) Thomas's level. Very close by was an air shaft down to the Upper Mynyddislwyn, probably to the same depth as that behind Cwmbrynnar Cottage. That air shaft was out of sight, behind the stone built Coach House, where the carriages were kept. Next to that was the stable. In front of Gilwern House, a late 19th century colliery map shows a line of coke ovens, which must have made it unpleasant for the occupants of the house, with nasty emissions. The arches in front of the row of ovens existed until a few years ago.

Whoever had the house built, he must have been a rich man. The main stairway in the house was a straight flight made of stone, with ornate cast iron sides and wooden hand rails. High up on the north end-wall are the openings for dove cots, an important food supply for the well off in winter time. Inside are the remains of the numerous bellpull ropes to summon the servants. The servants had their own spiral stone stairs, which were hidden from view behind a wooden door in the end downstairs room, which looked like a cupboard door. Local legend has it that the house was built by the family of James Thomas, whose monument dominates the graveyard at New Bethel. In the north end wall, there is a blocked-up wide doorway. Another local legend has it that the colliers who worked for the Thomas family were paid through here, so the end room probably doubled up as an office.

Gilwern House had its own piped water supply long before such a thing arrived in the area. There was a well in the woods below New Bethel Chapel, and a metal pipe ran from the well to Gilwern House. The house was at a lower level than the bottom of the well, so the water flowed naturally, without having to be pumped. But they only had cold water!

During the First World War, this was the home for a short time of the Vicar, Canon B. Jones Evans, while the Vicarage was being built. It then became the home of Dr. Armstrong, who bought it to convert to a nursing home, but those plans fell through. In the 1920s it became home to the Lovell family. It is now a private residential home for the elderly.

The photo of Gilwern House on the following page shows that it was built at a strange angle to the A472 road, and the north west corner of the building was not square. Parallel to the front of-the house, but a short distance away, was the line of a tramroad carrying coal from the Ty'n Llwyn Colliery to Hall's Tramroad near Pennar Crossing, and at one time another tramroad joined it coming down from Windy Ridge, and possibly extended towards Cwmnantyrodyn. Along the line of that tramroad there still stands a large stone gate post with the date 1843 carved into it. The tramroad was there first, before Gilwern House was built, and the house was built with its front garden wall being a common wall with the tramroad boundary.

The opposite side of the road from Gilwern House stood Cwmbrynar Farm. Although the farmhouse and most of its lands were situated just to the north of the Newbridge Road (the boundary set for this book) some of its fields were to the south of that road, on the slopes of Mynyddislwyn Mountain, so the farm deserves a mention in this book.

The earliest record found is for 24th March 1829 when George Williams of the parish of Monythusloin, Gentleman, bought the farm from six equal shareholders - from

George George of the parish of Monythusloin, Yeoman
Henry George of the parish of St. Hilary, County Glamorgan, Yeoman
Daniel George of the parish of St. Hilary, County Glamorgan, Yeoman
William George of the parish of Newcastle, Bridgend, County Glamorgan, Yeoman
Lewis George of the parish of Landough, County Glamorgan, Yeoman
Thomas George of the parish of St. Melons, County Monmouth, Yeoman.

Gilwern House, photographed before 1990, at which date building work was carried out, with an extension added to the right hand (south) end, and the massive chimney in the centre of the roof was removed.

The date stone outside Gilwern House.

In the yard in front of Gilwern House, at that time owned by Mr. Lovell. Holding the horse is Mr. Fred Fox, an employee of the Lovell family. On the horse's back were June Lovell, Odette Lovell and Glythin Belcher.

Each of the above was paid £183 6s 8d for his share, a total of £1,100. For his money, George Williams bought *'one customary messuage or tenement (Farm-house), one barn, two gardens, one curtillage and twelve pieces or parcels of customary land commonly called or known by the names of Cae Skibbor, Cae Bach, Wain Bont, Wern Cae yr Twyn, Cae Pen Hwnt, Yr Cae Twyn, Bryn Dy, Caer Bryn Ysha, Caer Bryn Ycha, Gwain Vain and Cae Dan y Wain, containing by estimation ten acres of Welsh measure.'*

Although he bought the freehold, the farm was in the Manor or Lordship of Abercarne, and in order to take possession of his property he had to be admitted Tenant of the Manor, for which he had to pay a yearly rent of eleven pence farthing to the Lord of the Manor (Benjamin Hall) as a Fine for his Estate and entry into the Manor.

His son William Williams followed him at the farm, and he made his Will in August 1839, which was proved in November 1839, when Cwmbrynar was left to his brother Lewis Williams.

However, the Tithe Apportionment Book for the parish, of April 1839, shows Lewis Williams owning the property, which measured 35 acres, 2 roods and 10 perches. The Tithe payable was £2 8s 6d.

In 1849 Cwmbrynar passed to Lewis Williams' nephew David Saunders. In September 1849 David Sanders (spellings as per documents) appeared before the Court Baron and Customary Court of Sir Benjamin Hall, Lord of the Manor of Abercarne, when he 'Prayed to be Admitted' tenant of the Manor, for which he had to pay the annual rent or fine of eleven pence farthing.

The Western Mail of March 1875 had the following article

'Love Plough'

'Lieut. Temple Stroud of the Blackwood Volunteers was manager of Tyr Philkins Colliery, owned by Thomas Powell and his sons, and in 1875 he retired. He took over the tenancy of Cwmbrynar Farm. For five years he had been President of the Mynyddislwyn Agricultural Society, and the members of the Society decided to revive the ancient ceremony of the "Love Plough" to launch him as a farmer. On the appointed day 25 plough teams, gaily decorated, turned up at Cwmbrynar to plough any land the new tenant required.

There was a large number of spectators present including many of the local gentry and visitors from Newport. After the ploughing was over they adjourned to a large room, prepared and decorated for the occasion, where an excellent dinner had been prepared, to which 150 persons sat down. The toast of the day was "Success to Lieut. Stroud as tenant farmer" *which was received with tremendous cheering'.*

The Will of William Williams

This is the last Will and Testament of me William Williams of Cwmbrynar in the parish of Mynyddislwyn in the County of Monmouth, Farmer, that is to say; First I will and desire that all my just debts, funeral expenses and the charges that will be incurred in the execution of this my last Will and Testament be first duly paid and discharged by my Executors herein after named. I give and devise to my brother Lewis Williams of Gelly Have the several Farms of Coed y Cefn and Gilfach Fargoed Faen in the parish of Gellygaer in the County of Glamorgan during his natural life only; and after his decease I give and devise the same to my nephew William Howells of Pentoynon and to his heirs for ever. And when my said nephew William Howells will have come to possession of the said Farms, I charge the same with the annuity of Twenty pounds per annum to be paid by my said nephew William Howells to his brother Howell Howells during his natural life only. Also I give and devise to my said Brother Lewis Williams my farm of Cwmbrynar with all the stock and crop and all the household furniture, with the exception of what belongs to my beloved wife Margaret Williams during her natural life only; and after his decease, I give and devise the same to my nephew David Saunders together with all the stock and crop and all the household furniture except as before excepted and to his heirs. But should my nephew David Saunders die without issue, then in that case, I give and devise my said farm of Cwmbrynar to my nephew William Saunders with all the stock and crop and all the household furniture except as before excepted, and to his heirs for ever; but I charge my said Farm of Cwmbrynar with the annuity of Twenty pounds per annum to be paid annually by the devisee in possession to my beloved wife Margaret Williams during her natural life in addition to all her own property which she had in her own right before I married her. I further charge my said Farm of Cwmbrynar with the annuity of Ten pounds per annum to be paid by the devisee in possession to my grand niece Mary Richards during her natural life annually. Also I give and devise to my said niece Mary Richards and her heirs the further sum of Five pounds per annum to be paid her in three years after my decease, out of the produce of the Coaliery at Gilfach Fargoed Fach in the said parish of Gellygaer during the time there will be there coals to be worked. Also, I give and devise to my sister Joan Powell of Gelly Have all my leasehold cottages situate at Gelly Have immediately after my decease. Also I give and devise to my said sister Joan Powell and her heirs the further sum of Twenty pounds per annum to be paid her in three years after my decease out of the produce of the said Coaliery during the time there will be there Coals to be worked. Also I give and devise to my sister Amelia Saunders of Bedwellty and her heirs the sum of Twenty pounds per annum to be paid her in three years after my decease out of the produce of the said Coaliery during the time there will be there coals to be worked. Also I give and devise to my sister Margaret Howells and her heirs the sum of fifteen pounds per annum to be paid her in three years after my decease out of the produce of the said Coaliery during the time there will be there coals to be worked. Also, I give and devise to my niece Jane Treasure and her heirs the sum of Ten pounds per annum to be paid her in three years after my decease out of the produce of the said Coaliery during the time there will be there coals to be worked. Also, I give and devise to my grand niece Mary Treasure and her heirs the sum of Ten pounds per annum to be paid her in three years after my decease out of the produce of the said Coaliery during the time there will be there coals to be worked. Also I give and devise to my nephew Edward Saunders the sum of ten pounds per annum and to his heirs to be paid him in three years after my decease out of the produce of the said Coaliery during the time there will be coals there to be worked. Also I charge my Executors with the bringing up of my nephew Howell George Howell in a manner corresponding with his Rank in life, until he arrives to the age of eighteen years, and when he will be of that age I give to him the *sum of Twenty pounds to be paid him by my Executors after paying the several annuities and fulfilling all other obligations already specified in this my last Will and testament. I give all the residue and remainder of my property to my brother Lewis Williams and my nephew William Howells share and share alike, whom I nominate and appoint my joint Executors, and I constitute this as my last Will and testament. In witness whereof I have this sixteenth day of August set my hand and seal in the year of our Lord one thousand eight hundred and thirty nine.*

Signed sealed published and delivered by the said testator William Williams as his last Will and testament in the presence of us, who at his request, in his presence and in the presence of each other have subscribed our names as witnesses thereto.

William Williams.

David Thomas, Clerk   Edward Gratrex, Senior
Edward Gratrex, Junior

Cwmbrynar Farm no longer exists. It now lies under industrial development between Pontllanfraith and Pentwynmawr, under Cooperative Pioneer, Frontier Plastics and Linde Lansing. All that remains to be seen are two tall yew trees that were on the lane leading up to the farmhouse.

Manor of Abercarne } The Court Baron and Customary Court of Sir
Manor on Wednesday the twelfth day of September One
Llewellin Gentleman Steward of the said Manor.
To this Court came David Sanders of Cwmbrynar in the parish of
the last Will of William Williams late of the same place Farmer deceas
ty nine and prayed to be admitted Tenant of and to All that One C
parcels of Customary Land commonly called & known by the several names
divided into three pieces Brun dy, Cae Brun Isha, Cae Brun Ucha, Gwain
same more or less which lying and being in the parish of Mynyddislwyn
ished And which said Premises respectively constitute and are commonly
ty seven acres and nine Perches (more or less) And the Reversion and
said David Sanders hath granted seizin thereof To have and to hold the
stomary Heirs according to the custom of the said Manor To the intent
me Hereditaments and Premises subject to and in such manner as the
will of his late Uncle the said William Williams late of Cwmbrynar afore
ght hundred and thirty nine By and under the yearly Rent of Eleven Pence Fa
be paid and performed And the said David Sanders hath given the
ven Pence Farthing and his fealty to the Lord having been respited is admitted
A true copy of the Records of the said M

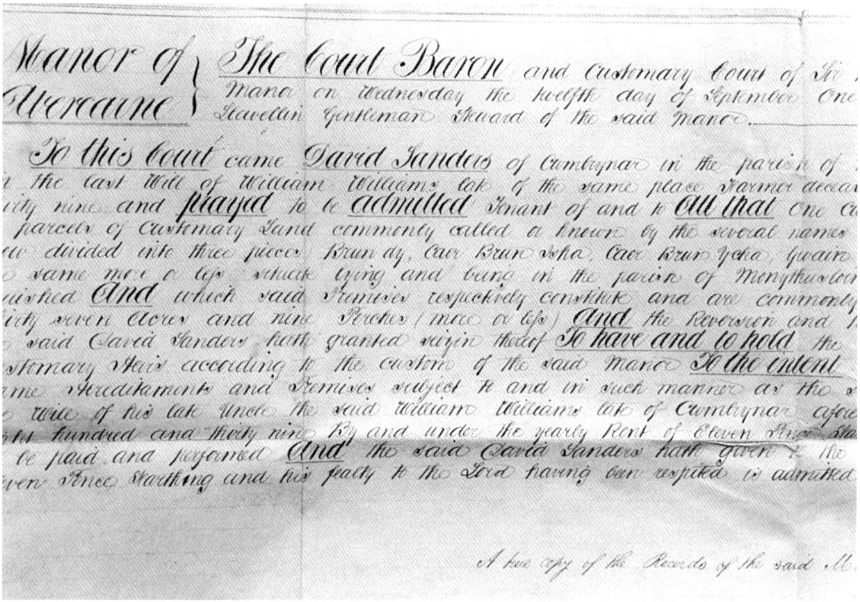

David Saunders of Cwm Brynar Farm prayed to be Admitted a Tenant of the Manor of Abercarne, for which he paid an annual rent or fine of eleven pence farthing.

Further along the A472 takes us to an old crossroads, where the main road was crossed by a road leading from the ancient settlement of Croespenmaen, and beyond. At that corner stood the old White Hart public house, and two short

terraces of houses, one fronting on to the main road and the other built up the lane. Strangely, they did not meet at a right angle. Pub and houses were pulled down about 1960, and the pub was replaced by a new one with the same name, but its external architectural design leaves a lot to be desired.

Thirteen year old John Williams (now of Penrhiwffranc) at the wheel of the tractor, while his father, Mr. Albert Williams tends to the plough. This photograph was taken in the early 1960s at Cwmbrynar Farm. Today, that field is under Leos/Pioneer foodstore. Although it is just outside the boundary set for this book, it has been included because in the background can be seen Cwmbrynar Cottage and the Ivor Arms public house, both of which are on the other side of the A472 road.

The outline of the pub is shown on the 1846 Tithe Map, with the attached houses along the main road, but not the ones up the hill. The 1851 census lists the White Hart, occupied by Ann Williams, Victualler. The census entries immediately before were Sgybor Fach, then another Sgybor Fach, while the entry immediately after the White Hart was Sgybor Fach, occupied by a collier, a retired farmer, and a woollen weaver. This means 'Little Barn', and three entries would suggest the houses either side of the pub. Such an entry suggests the pub started life as a small farm with attached barns, which could have been used for stabling when the pub first opened, but were converted into houses before 1851. The 1839 Tithe Apportionment Book lists the buildings as Cottages and Gardens leased to Thomas Davies and others. They could have been built when the Turnpike Road was built soon after 1810.

Artiss and Muriel Williams, with Margaret and Mair inside the White Hart in 1958.

Grace Hutchings with Margaret and Mair Williams, with the end wall of the old White Hart behind them, photographed in 1955. The sign was advertising Webbs Welsh Ales, brewed at Aberbeeg.

Margaret and Mair Williams outside the front door of the White Hart, in 1954.

Miss Margaret Williams of the White Hart Inn with Mr. Albert Williams of Cwmbrynnar Farm (later of Penrhiwffranc Farm) in a field behind the White Hart, discussing the storm damaged bad harvest of 1957.

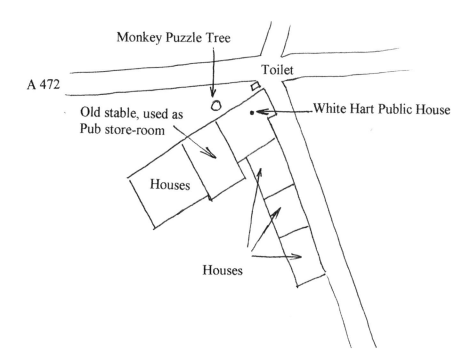

Monkey Puzzle Tree

A 472

Toilet

Old stable, used as
Pub store-room

White Hart Public House

Houses

Houses

Up the lane besides the White Hart leads to an interesting little area. The lane was crossed by the Pennar Branch Tramroad running down from the coal level below Penrhiwffranc, and another from Ty'n Llwyn, to join Hall's Road. The large building to the right hand side was the Nailers public house. The 1839 Tithe Apportionment Book lists it as House and Garden occupied by Gwenllian Phillips, but does not list it as a pub. The 1841 census lists Gwenllian Phillips, Victualler, while the 1851 census names the Nailers Arms, still occupied by Gwenllian Phillips, aged 76, Publican. As it stands today, the front of the building has been altered. A few people have recalled how you had to go down a few steps to go into the pub. The pub closed in 1965, and today is a private house.

Rev. David Tipper told a lovely story about the Nailers. *'Coffins used to be carried up the mountain (to St. Tudor's) from the Sirhowy valley by two teams of bearers - it's a long pull - and the custom was to stop at the Nailers Inn for a drink and to change teams. The corpse was left outside the pub while the bearers met inside, but a new landlord did not like this custom and, meeting it for the first time, promptly had the coffin moved out of sight. Meanwhile both teams of bearers went on refreshing themselves inside. This led to terrible confusion because they emerged separately and saw the coffin "gone". Each thought the other team had done the bearing. The relief team was particularly agitated, believing that the first team would claim all the fee money. Both teams met at the churchyard where the vicar and funeral party were waiting. The confused and excited Welshmen tried to explain the incident, but all the clergyman wanted was the COFFIN. where was THAT? Back they trooped to find it and staggered up the hill again making what speed they could, but they were very late indeed. To cap it all, when the coffin was finally lowered into the ground an onlooker was heard to say* "There goes poor old Harry *'Man'*, but he won't go any further"'.

Just above the Pennar Branch Tramroad stands a very old house, Pennar Cottage. It is shown on the 1846 Tithe Map, so its age and close proximity to the tramroad would suggest some connection with that tramroad. Were tramroad horses stabled alongside? Was this the home of a tramroad workman? Another possibility is to be found in the 1861 census, where the Nailers Arms is listed, and the next entry is 'Nailors House', occupied by 85-year-old John Morgan, Farmer and Nailor, with 60 year old lodger Joseph Owens, a Nailmaker. That nailers house could have been the present Pennar Cottage.

Immediately opposite the front door of the cottage is a small stone built ruin, big enough to have been a 19th century nail-making manufactory. At that time, handmade nails were manufactured in two different ways. Most were worked from wire, which was cut to length, heated in a blacksmith's forge, and hammer shaped. A suitable supplier of such wire was Abercarne Ironworks, which had an Osmond Forge to produce top quality wire from the mid 1700s. That wire could have arrived at this spot via the Pennar Branch Tramroad, which ran past the door. And there was no shortage of coal for fuel, with so many coal levels in near proximity.

The Nailers Arms public house, and to the right of the photograph, the little stone built building that is believed to have been the Nailers Manufactory that gave the pub its name.

Outside the Nailers Arms public house in the early part of the twentieth century.

The other means of producing nails was by casting. Most of the mining community wore boots which were shod with tips and hob nails. The hob nails had to be made from malleable iron. A mould was made in sand, containing the impression of hundreds of nails, with a runner system for feeding molten iron to the nail impressions. The metal used for filling the mould was cast iron, which was produced by melting scrap and pig iron in a small cupola furnace. The molten iron was poured into the moulds, and allowed to cool until the iron was solid.

The mould was broken up and the nails and runners removed, the runner ready to be used as scrap in the next melt. The nails were coated with burnt sand, so were put into a scouring barrel with iron shot or sand, and rotated for a period of time, so that the nails were polished by removing the burnt sand.

Clay pots, which could be sealed, were filled with the cleaned nails and mill scale or iron oxide, i.e. haematite, (from Abercarne Ironworks) and put into a small furnace to be heated to red heat. The pots remained in that heat for a period of time which allowed the carbon in the cast iron nails to combine with the oxide in the mill scale or haematite, causing the structure of the nails to become malleable, like mild steel.

After removing the pots from the furnace, they and their contents were allowed to cool. The nails were removed from the pots and again put into the scouring barrel for a final polishing before being offered for sale.

This process allowed nails to be manufactured on a small scale, in quantity, cheaply. The resultant hob nails were hard wearing and protected the leather sole of a boot, giving good grip in adverse conditions.

There is evidence for such a process, to be found in the ground today. The garden of Pennar Cottage has been a nightmare for the present owner to dig. Everywhere he has been digging up iron slag. That can only have been dumped from a smelting furnace, such as the small cupola described overleaf. The other evidence lies in he name of the public house alongside.

The other side of the Nailers Pub, towards Vicarage Lane, are to be found two houses, Brynheulog, which are of early 20th century origin. But alongside, there were two other houses called Brynheulog, of which no trace now remains. They were built end-on to the road, and were semi-detached. They were mentioned in the 1839 Tithe Apportionment Book as Cottages, being owned and occupied by Edward Morgan. However, on the 1851 census, near the Nailors Arms, was Ton Tyr Garw, occupied by Edward Morgan, a 65 year old Collier. This could well be the same Edward Morgan whose sworn affidavit is included in the previous chapter, and Ton Tyr Garw could be the original name, changed at an unknown date to Brynheulog.

As mentioned, they were end-on to the road, behind a stone wall. That wall had a coal hole in it to feed a load of coal from the road in to the coal cots. From the road you stepped down to the front of the houses. Each house had one room and a pantry downstairs, with two bedrooms upstairs. The last occupants were Mrs. Ford and Mrs. Haines. They were pulled down in the late 1960s when Mrs. Haines left. Before those two ladies, the occupant of the lower house was Mrs. Beacham, whose photograph is on the following page, remembered as usually having a clay pipe in her mouth. The occupants of the upper house were the Morgan family. Joseph, photographed on the right, was born there. He grew up to be the occupant, and his son Bert Morgan was born there, before Joseph moved a very short distance to Pennar Villa, where daughter Betty was born.

Outside Brynheulog Cottages. On the right stands 14 year old Joseph Morgan, just after he had returned home from a shift at Bedwas Colliery, to which he walked both ways each day.

271

Walking away from the Nailers pub, past Brynheulog, the road was originally much narrower, and alongside the road was a tramroad, which can still be traced between the double hedgerow, leading to Ton y Moch. Opposite Brynheulog, that tramroad was joined by another one leading down from Penrhiwffranc, to become the Pennar Branch Tramroad, mentioned in the previous chapter on Coal.

The road mentioned above originally ran down Vicarage Lane, but was cut off in 1990 when the new by-pass road was built. Today it leads to Ton y Moch and Ty'n Llwyn Farm. Ton y Moch was four houses, two pairs of two each. They were mentioned in the 1839 Tithe Apportionment Book as being owned by Henry Jones, who also owned Ty'n Llwyn Farm.

Numbers 1 and 2 have been converted recently into one house by Neil James, while numbers 3 and 4

Mrs. Beecham outside the lower of the two Brynheulog Cottages.

remain as a pair. Between 1 and 2, and Tyn Llwyn Farm, was a coal level. Maps date it back to at least the 1830s. At one time the coal from the level was carried on a tramroad past the front of Gilwern House, then alongside Cwmbrynnar Farm, to join Hall's Road near Pennar Crossing. At another time the coal was carried on a tramroad as described above, past the Nailers. The 1851 census lists the four houses, each occupied by a collier as head of family, so they were probably built as collier's houses and not as farm workers cottages.

Because of the slope of the land down towards the A472 road, a coal level driven horizontally into a coal seam near Gilwern House could only be reached by a vertical shaft a short distance up the hillside. One such shaft behind 1 and 2 Ton y Moch was 56 feet deep.

A short distance uphill from Ton y Moch lies the very old Ty'n Llwyn Farm. It was a down-hill sited Longhouse, with beast house attached to the home. The beasthouse was re-built some years ago after a fire. Some of the house walls have also been rebuilt in brick, whereas they were originally stone. At the rear is an early cross-wing which is now ruinous, and has a gable fire place and spiral stone stairs. This wing is believed to have been the parlour where the Nonconformists met while nearby New Bethel Chapel was being built.

Alongside, were two small houses, which were mentioned in the 1851 census as being built then. By the 1861 census they were occupied by a Colliery Contractor and a Collier. This was common for the area, showing that more homes were occupied by coal workers than by farm labourers. The same census showed Ty'n Llwyn Farm occupied by Thomas Thomas, a Colliery Proprietor.

The Star of Gwent newspaper tells us something about this Thomas Thomas in 1862.

'Penner Colliery, near Newbridge,
Mynyddislwyn.
To Coal Proprietors, Contractors and Others.

Messrs. Cornelius Evans and Son are instructed to sell by AUCTION (by order of the Court of Bankruptcy) on the premises as above, on Thursday the 10th day of July 1862.

All the remainder of the Stock and Colliery Plant, with other Effects, belonging to the Estate of Mr. Thomas Thomas, Coal Merchant, in which are comprised

In the yard - a large waterwheel, with standards and fixings; water trough for the same; blowing fan for smiths' shop; lot of old iron and various sorts; lot of chairs; 10 truck springs; grindstone and frame; large quantity of smiths' and colliers' tools, including anvil, vice, lathe etc.; cart shafts and wheels; planks; 110 yards of rails, with sleepers; 135 yards of tramplates with sleepers; 26 wood level trams; 4 iron level trams; 184 yards of block plates; 2 partings; 1 cross; 1 wing; 1 weighing machine; 15 coke ovens with brick and iron work as fixed; lamp pillar in front of house and shop; about 295 yards of double rails, and sleepers, from yard gate, on siding adjacent to the West Midland Railway; and 2 trucks of coke on the said siding.

At Tynal Colliery, (close adjoining), 6 coke ovens, with brick and iron work as fixed; 11 level trams; 1 carting tram; 603 yards of tram and block plates; 8 pair of rails, 42 yards; 5 sets of tools; 13 partings; 1 wing; 2 crosses; and several tons of coke.

The tram plates, rails, level trams, coke ovens, etc. etc. may be viewed the day previous or on the morning of the sale.

Approved bills at two months' date will be taken for all purchases exceeding £20 in amount'.

The list continued by including the stock at Barcella and Cwmdows Collieries (Behind the present Newbridge Caravan Centre), and Ty Mawr Colliery, Kendon. He had been quite a colliery proprietor.

The bill of sale did not mention the colliery itself. That can only mean that he did not own it, he was leasing the land on which it was sunk. When he became bankrupt, Thomas Thomas ceased to have any interest in the colliery, so it reverted back to the ground landlord, Benjamin Hall, who was able re-lease it at a future date.

The list above mentioned 15 coke ovens. Those were alongside the railway between Pennar Crossing and the Tunnel, behind Pentwynmawr. The West Midland Railway later became Great Western, and ran over Crumlin Viaduct, Pontllanfraith Bottom Station, Bryn Tunnel, Maesycwmmer Viaduct, and on westwards. But the most interesting thing in the list is Tynal Colliery 'close adjoining', with 6 coke ovens. They had to be the coke ovens alongside Gilwern House, so presumably in 1862, Tynal Colliery was the name of the coal level alongside Gilwern House.

The above named Thomas Thomas was also involved in Energlyn (Caerphilly) Colliery, and one at Bedwas. His son married Ellen Tydfil Davies of Bedwas, and was the founder of the Thomas Davies Estates.

Continuing our journey along the northern edge, the next place of interest is Ton y Pistyll. The name is shown on the first map produced by the Ordnance Survey in 1833, along with some houses. The 1841 census has a number of dwellings listed as Ton y Pistyll, with occupants, children and lodgers adding up to the following - 32 colliers, 1 tailor and draper, 2 tailors' apprentices, 1 smith, 3 agricultural labourers, 1 haulier, 4 shoemakers, 1 schoolmaster, and 2 shoemakers' apprentices.

By the time of the 1851 census, things had changed a little, with 3 hauliers, 1 sinker, 2 dressmakers, 12 colliers, 6 cordwainers (shoe and boot makers) 1 accountant, 5 scholars, 1 master cordwainer, 2 coal tippers, 2 sawyers, and many labourers.

The houses that form Ton y Pistyll today are of a later date than those mentioned above, but the area is an old one. It is intriguing to note the number of cordwainers. The number of workmen in this tiny area alone shows how many boots were needed. Could there have been a link between those cordwainers and the nailers about a mile away?

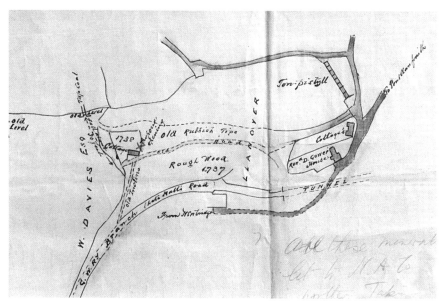

A map showing the amount of coal working in small levels to the east of Tonypistyll.

A little further to the east, as we approach the Ebbw Valley, was Ty Gwyn Farm. As a following chapter on The Edmunds Family shows, this was once a much larger farm, the largest on The Mountain. Unfortunately, the farm was pulled down about 1990 when the new by-pass road was built. Very close by was a coal level, with a tramroad incline running down to Hall's Road. At the head of that incline still stands the ruin of a small building, which until recently had massive cruck-truss roof timbers.

274

Sheep shearing at Ty Gwyn Farm in 1956.
From the left - Harold Collins, Robert Collins, Bob Phillips, Charlie Llewellin, Jack
Bobbart, Tom Watkins, John Davies, Rees Collins.
Bob Phillips was a former captain of the Welsh Sheepdog Trial team.

Edward Waters at Ty Gwyn Farm, in the 1920s.

Edward Waters haymaking at Ty Gwyn Farm, in the 1920s.

New Bethel Area

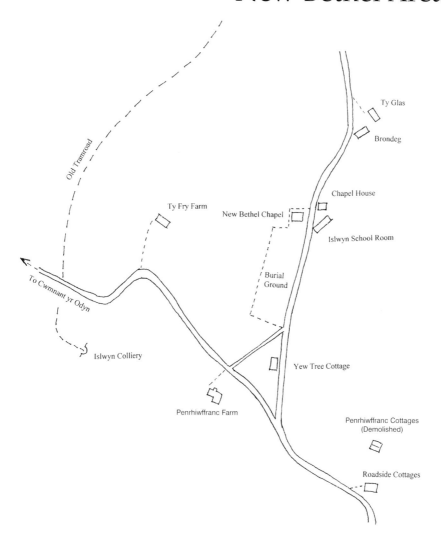

The area around New Bethel has had its connections with the Williams family for a long time (but no connection with the Williams family who farm Penrhiwffranc today). Rosser Williams, a farmer of Penrhiwffranc, died in 1860. He is mentioned overleaf for leaving the Islwyn Schoolroom in his will to the Trustees of New Bethel. Rosser left his estate to his wife, then after her death, to his six nephews. One of his nephews, Thomas Williams, was left Ty Glas, situated alongside the roadside near New Bethel. Today that small cottage has been greatly increased in size, but it retains its old features inside the original cottage.

In 1886 Edmund Thomas of Tyla Gwyn (James Thomas' nephew) and John Thomas Davies purchased the entire Rosser Williams' estate for £2,450, comprising

a) A homestead called Tyr Cross Fach, with garden, stable and barn called Sgubor Ganol, cowhouse, and fields known as Caid duon bach, and Gwain fach, alongside the highway from Croespenmean towards Mynyddislwyn Church.

b) Cottages, gardens, stables, outbuildings and fields known as Tir William Lawrence, situated near Penrhiwffranc.

c) Homestead, beasthouse, stable, two barns, two gardens and sixteen fields known as Penrhiwffranc.

In September 1890 Edmund Thomas bought out John Thomas Davies' half share in the above and became sole owner, until he died in 1922.

In 1928 James William Cooke bought the 54 acres 1 rood and 24 perches of Penrhiwrffranc.

However, the mystery thickens, because in 1913 Thomas Williams 'of Penrhiwffranc' bequeathed in his will Brondeg to his son George, Ty Glas to his son Rosser, and a house at Williams Terrace, Cwmdows, to his daughter-in-law, widow of his son Ellis. Were the Williams family leasing back Penrhiwffranc from Edmund Thomas?

The above mentioned Brondeg was originally two cottages, Brondeg and Arfryn, which in the late 1970s were merged into one house. They were built in what had been the front garden of Ty Glas. The photograph of Ty Glas overleaf could not be taken today because the photographer was standing where Brondeg is now situated. This puts a relative age to the two houses with Ty Glas being much older, Brondeg having been built in 1882.

In b) above, the part of the sale named as Tir William Lawrence was in fact the house that is today called Roadside Cottage, and the now demolished Penrhiwffranc Cottages alongside, and three fields.

Extracts from the Will of Rosser Williams, Deceased

This is the last Will and Testament of me, Rosser Williams, of Penrhiwffranc in the parish of Mynyddislwyn, in the County of Monmouth, Farmer. I nominate, constitute and appoint my beloved wife Louisa Williams sole Executrix of this my Will. I give, devise and bequeath unto Louisa my said beloved wife the said Penrhiwfranc dwelling house, out houses and land on the west side of the Parish Road situate lying and being in the said parish of Mynyddislwyn, to be freely enjoyed by her during her natural life. Also I give and bequeath unto Louisa my said wife an annuity or annual sum of Two hundred pounds from the rent, interest and annual produce of my other copyhold houses and land, and my leasehold houses, and my interest in the Collieries in the Counties of Monmouth and Glamorgan, during her natural life, free from any deduction whatsoever. I give, devise and bequeath unto the Trustees of New Bethel Independent Chapel, for the time being, and their successor Trustees for ever the new Schoolroom near the said Chapel, and the ground under the Stable, and the House in the yard, to be freely enjoyed by them, and at their discretion for the use of the said Connection for ever, subject to the payment of Ten shillings a year unto my executors. Also, after the decease of my said wife, I give, devise and bequeath my property in form and manner following, that is to say, unto my six nephews, Philip, Thomas, Lewis, Rosser, David and Daniel Williams, the male children of my brother Henry Williams, the within named houses and land called Penrhiwfranc, and Cefn Crib Colliery in the Parish of Llanhilleth, in the County of Monmouth, and also my share and interest in Gilfach Colliery and of the Black land at Gilfach Bargoed Colliery, in the Parish of Gellygaer, in the County of Glamorgan, and all my right, title and interest to and in the same and every part thereof, to be equally divided to and amongst my said six nephews, share and share alike, and their issue after them, to and for their heirs, executors, administrators and assigns. Also I give and bequeath unto my nephew the above named Thomas Williams, a dwelling house and premises situate lying and being at or near New Bethel, and all my estate, right, title and interest therein, to have and to hold the same unto my said nephew Thomas Williams, his executors, administrators and assigns, to and for his and their absolute use, benefit and disposal. Also, after the decease of my said wife, I give, devise and bequeath unto my nephew John George, my copyhold houses and land called Twyn College in the said parish of Mynyddislwyn, his heirs, executors, administrators and assigns. I nominate and appoint my friends Thomas Thomas of Tyr Llwyn, Coal Merchant, and William J. Davies of Pentwynmawr, Surgeon, both of the parish of Mynyddislwyn, in the County of Monmouth, joint Trustees to see this my Will properly executed, and to act under the same during the natural life of my said beloved wife. In Witness whereof I have hereunto set my hand this seventh day of June in the year one thousand eight hundred and sixty.

Ty Glas, below New Bethel Chapel, with Mrs. Elizabeth Williams and her son William Henry Williams (of Ty Nyddfa, Pontllanfraith). He was the father of Margarette Williams Bayliss (Madam Bayliss) of Ty Nyddfa.

John Lewis of Ty Glas, known locally as John the Baptist. He was grandfather of Mrs. Myfanwy Carpenter and Mr. Lionel Davies, both still living on The Mountain. He was a founder member of the English Baptist Church, Cwmfeiinfach.

"TY-GLAS," NEW BETHEL,

PONTLLANFRAITH, Mon.

.... 19 ....

M ....

DR. TO

JOHN LEWIS

MILK RETAILER.

New Bethel

About 1617 there came into existence a document known as the Book of Sports, which specified that divine service should be held on Sunday Mornings only, and that Sunday afternoons were to be devoted to games, such as leaping, quoit throwing, and dancing, with the important proviso that only those who had attended Church in the morning could take part in those games. The Book of Sports was issued to counteract the strict sabbatarian views of the Puritans, and all Parish clergy were expected to read this document aloud in church every Sunday. The non-reading of this Book was not, however punishable at first, and there were many clergymen with stricter views as to the proper use of the Sunday who believed that it was wholly wrong that the Lord's Day should be desecrated, as they felt, by giving the sanction of the church to Sunday games, and who consequently refused to read this Book of Sports at their services.

After the accession of Charles I to the throne, the non-reading of this Book of Sports came to be treated as a serious matter so far as the Established Church was concerned, and in 1638 William Wroth, the Rector of Llanvaches (between Newport and Chepstow) was deprived of his living for his refusal to read the Book of Sports and to conform in other ecclesiastical matters. Several of Wroth's parishioners left with him, and in November 1639 the first Independent Church in Wales was established at Llanvaches.

At that time the Curate of Mynyddislwyn was Rev. Henry Walter, who was born in 1611 near Chepstow. About the same time that William Wroth was deprived of his living at Llanvaches, Henry Walter was ejected for the same reasons and, like Wroth, he too was accompanied by many of his parishioners, who thus became Independents. Henry Walter and the Mynyddislwyn Independents met first as a branch of the Church at Llanvaches, but soon they were strong enough to form a Church of their own, and early in 1640 there was established the Free Church of Mynyddislwyn, which was thus the second non-conformist Church in Wales. There was no church building and meetings were held in the farmhouses scattered around the hillsides. At the outset Baptists and Independents met and joined together in common worship, but the Baptists from Mynyddislwyn eventually joined with a group meeting at Blaenau Gwent, while the Independents fixed their headquarters at Penmean, where they built a chapel in 1694.

In the years that followed the Restoration of Charles II in 1660, the religious life of the district, and indeed of Wales, fell into a slate of sleep, which did not alter much until well into the eighteenth century. At that time when Welsh was the language of the people, the Bible used at services in the Church would have been an English translation, and the prayers read would have been in a language that few could understand.

It was against such a background that Howell Harris, Daniel Rowlands and many others began their tours of preaching and evangelising which resulted in the Methodist Revival in Wales, a movement which filled the needs of the people for a living religion, and as in so many places the Church of England refused to recognise this, nonconformist chapels sprang up in every direction to shelter those who felt bound to leave the Established Church.

In the events leading up to the formation of New Bethel Chapel, six persons were (according to legend) the principal pioneers, but only one name has survived - Thomas Waters. He is referred to as Thomas Watters and also Thomas Walters.

It would seem that he, with the other five, left the Parish Church at Mynyddislwyn and commenced the movement which led to the formation of New Bethel. Thomas Waters was chosen to be the Minister of the new Church, which was established in 1758 at a building called Migyn-y-bwlch, near Sych Pant. Thomas Waters had been born 1729 at Pantyresk in the Parish of Mynyddislwyn. The Church worshipped at Migyn-yn-bwlch for two years, and in 1760 moved to a house near the Flannel Factory at a place called Pendarren, where the new Church worshipped until 1765. By that year the members had obtained funds with which to build their own Chapel. To permit the building of the Chapel two members, Henry and Ann Jones, granted a lease dated the 13th May 1765, for a term of nine hundred and ninety-nine years at a yearly rent of two shillings and six pence (12$\frac{1}{2}$ pence). It would appear that the lease was for the plot of land on which the Chapel now stands, the small surrounding graveyard, and the land on which is built the caretaker's house.

By that deed there was leased

One quarter of a rood in Welsh measure, more or less, enclosed out of the upper corner towards the south of a field called Eno We..... With liberty to raise and dig stones out of the said property, and to build thereon a meeting house and stable for the service of the small congregation of Protestant Dissenters which then met at a place called Pendarren in the said Parish of Monythusloyne... to perform Divine Worship in the said meeting house, when built, or to keep school, or for any other purpose, use or uses which the said Thomas Waters, William Thomas, Henry William, John William Harry, Jeremiah Jones and Philip Jones, and their successors, with the consent of the major part of the said Congregation, shall think fit, necessary or convenient.

Reverend Thomas Waters and the others above named were the first Trustees of New Bethel. Within seven years of its formation in 1758, New Bethel was firmly established.

For over one hundred and thirty years, all services at New Bethel were conducted in the Welsh language.

Inside New Bethel is a memorial tablet to Thomas Waters which reads

> Thomas Watters, addfwyn o'dd - ei ddoniau
> I Ddynion gyfranodd;
> Mwyn, merrus mewn ynadrodd,
> Gwledd I'n gwlad yn rhad a rodd.

Translated as

> Thomas Watters, was gentle, his gifts
> He shared with men;
> Gentle, skilful in speech,
> He freely gave a feast to our country.

Thomas Waters remained at New Bethel until he died, on 25th May 1794, at the age of 65.

In these early years some great names preached from the pulpit, among them William Williams, Pantycelyn.

A document with the records of New Bethel state that the building was first registered for the solemnisation of marriages on the 21st November 1837, and in the Certificate of registration the Chapel is described as *'Bethel, situate at Penrhiwffrange in the Parish of Mynyddislwyn in the County of Monmouth'*.

In 1855, to accommodate an ever increasing congregation, the original Chapel was re-built by the present structure to provide a larger seating capacity. The old records refer to the Chapel as 'Bethel' and it can only be assumed that the name 'New Bethel' came into use following the re-building.

In 1872 the Chapel acquired land to extend the cemetery. Hitherto, the only facilities for burial had been in the small plot surrounding the Chapel, and the land now acquired measured two roods *'forming part of a field... called Cae tyr porth'*. Under a Lease dated 19th March 1872 the land was leased for a term of 893 years from the 13th May 1871, at a yearly ground rent of one shilling (5 pence); thus the leases of both plots expire on the same date. By that deed it was declared that the land then acquired was

> To be used as and for a burial ground in connection with the said New Bethel Chapel or in such other manner as the... Trustees or their successors, with the consent of the major part of the congregation of the said Chapel, shall think fit, necessary or convenient.

Between 1896 and 1899 the Minister was Mr. T. Mardy Rees. During his three year ministry it was decided to conduct evening services in English. On 15th July 1899 New Bethel leased a further one half acre of land to provide additional facilities for burial.

In 1928 the Chapel incurred considerable expenditure in extending the electricity supply from Pentwynmawr to New Bethel, in providing road lighting between those points, and in installing electric lighting in the Chapel. This was followed by the metalling by the local authority of the old parish road from Pentwynmawr.

In 1936 a water supply was installed at the Chapel. Prior to that date, all water for the Chapel, the school-room opposite, and the Chapel-house opposite, had to be carried from two water supplies, a well at the entrance to Ty Glas, and a spout near Ty Fry.

In September 1949 a new Manse was opened for the Minister, by Mr. Granville West, M.P. for Pontypool, assisted by the widow of Sir William James Thomas (grandson of James Thomas whose memorial is the greatest land-mark at New Bethel).

The Will of Thomas Waters

In the name of God, Amen. I, Thomas Waters, of the Parish of Monythusloyne, in the County of Monmouth, and Diocese of Llandaff, Protestant dissenting Minister, do make and ordain this my last Will and Testament, in writing, in manner and form following.

First of all I Will that all my lawful debts and funeral charges to be paid and discharges by my Executrix hereafter named. Also I give and devise Henry's Expositions on the Bible, six volumes, Gill on the Canticles, Burkit's Exposition of the New Testament, and Manton's sermons, five volumes, unto the congregation of Protestant Dissenters meeting at New Bethel in the parish of Monythusloyne and County of Monmouth (to be delivered immediately after my Decease into the hands of Philip Jones and Thomas Evans, Deacons in the said Congregation), as Trustees for the said Congregation, and the said Trustees are to deliver the said Books unto such regular Gospel Minister as will take the charges of the said Congregation, to preach the Gospel and to administer all the Ordinances thereof unto them. To be perused by the said Minister while he remains and acts the part of a faithful Minister of Jesus Christ with them, and no longer. The property of the said Books is the said Congregation forever.

Also I give and devise unto my four nieces, the daughters of John Waters, my brother (deceased), the sum of Ten Guineas (which the said John Waters was indebted unto me by a Note of Demand bearing date 30th September 1788), to be equally divided between them.

Also I give unto Pegi Waters, my niece, my great Welsh Bible, after the death of my wife.

Also I give my best suit, coat, waistcoat, and breeches unto John David Harry. Also I give my second suit, coat, waistcoat, and breeches unto Rees John of the Parish of Bedwas. Also I give my third suit, coat, waistcoat and leather breeches unto William Morgan, Tiler. Also I give my best great coat unto Phillip Thomas. Also I give my old great coat unto Thomas Rees. Also I give my boots and best hat unto the Rev. Daniel James.

Also I give to Anne Thomas, my maid servant, the sum of Twenty Shillings. Also I give unto Thomas Waters, my nephew, my watch and the three books he has borrowed of me - viz: - a Welsh Bible, Dr. Owen's work, and Bernard on Revelation. Also I give unto William George, carpenter, Romapre's Walk of Faith, two volumes. Also I give my small Welsh Bible unto Anna Jones, the wife of William Jones. Also I give Byfield's Exposition on the Colossians unto Phillip Jones. Also I give Bishop Usher's Body of Divinity unto Thomas Evans. Also I give Caryl on Job unto Henry Jones. Also I give Henry's Meditations, two volumes, unto Henry the son of William Jones. Also I give Anna Phillips, the wife of Thomas William, Boston's fourfold State.

Lastly I nominate Mary my beloved wife to be sole Executrix of this my last Will and Testament, unto whom I give all my Goods and Chattels not herein given or devised, subject to the payment of all my Debts, Legacies and Funeral Charges.

Now I declare this to be my last Will and Testament. In witness whereof I have hereunto set my hand and seal this 29th day of June, in the year of our Lord, one thousand seven hundred and ninety two.

Signed, Sealed and Delivered by the said Thomas Waters for to be his last Will and Testament, in the presence of us -

Thomas Waters

Lewis Williams   William Morgan

Henry Walter

When Civil War broke out between King and Parliament in 1642, Henry Walter (the former Curate of Mynyddislwyn) took refuge in Bristol, and afterwards in London. Upon the victory of the Parliamentary troops, Oliver Cromwell (himself a Nonconformist) became ruler of Great Britain. One of his first measures was an Act for the Better Propagation of the Gospel. This Act specified that all clergymen who neglected their duties, or led immoral lives, should be replaced by ministers more fitted for spiritual work. 'Approvers' were sent down from London to make investigations. In the list of Approvers for Wales, the name of Henry Walter is at the top. With them went a number of Commissioners, who were empowered to enforce the necessary changes.

The Commissioners suspended Henry Rees, the Anglican curate of Mynyddislwyn, because he was *'not Godly enough for such a famous stronghold'*. They seized the parish tithes, which came to £364 8s 10d. That sum was divided between *'seventeen Godly Gospellers of the Churches of Mynyddislwyn and Llanvaches, who went forth to exercise their gifts and to promote the work of the Lord, mostly among the Welsh in the mountains'*. The Commissioners removed the bells from Mynyddislwyn parish church, and sold them. (The Puritans believed in a simple form of worship, and were strongly opposed to bell-ringing).

During the Commonwealth (Cromwell's rule) Henry Walter was vicar of St. Woollos, Newport. His pastoral oversight included Bedwas and Mynyddislwyn. In the absence of Henry Walter, the parochial duties of Mynyddislwyn were performed by Watkin Jones of Sychpant, who was described as *'a man of substance and learning, and of a creditable family'*. According to his Anglican detractors, Jones committed sacrilege at Bedwas. They state that *'he, in conjunction with another Mynyddislwyn preacher of the name of Reese John David, removed out of Bedwas Church a very fine old font of stone, taking pious objections to some old carvings on the same. This font, the above two Gospellers condemned to the hammer; but failing to break it to pieces, they caused it to be brought under the yew tree, where it was used as a trough to water the parsonage horses and cattle in. And this old font served the purposes of a trough until the Restoration.'*

After the Restoration of King Charles II Puritanism underwent an eclipse. Two thousand Dissenting clergy were expelled from their parishes and forbidden to preach within a radius of five miles. It was made illegal to hold religious worship, either in public or private, unless such meetings took place under the auspices of the Anglican Church.

Among the ministers ejected in 1662 by the Act of Uniformity, were Henry Walter and Watkin Jones. They still continued preaching, but chiefly in private houses. Their flock had to meet in secret through fear of the law.

Statistics compiled in 1669 revealed the presence of two hundred Non-conformists in Mynyddislwyn and Bedwellty. There were five conventicles (or secret gatherings), of which one was Watkin Jones's home at Sychpant.

Another source tells us that in 1676 Mynyddislwyn contained 142 Anglicans, 3 Roman Catholics and 38 Nonconformists. (This was the parish of Mynyddisiwyn and not just the Mountain).

In 1675 a list was prepared of all the Nonconformist Churches in Wales. Particulars were inserted in the Broadmead Records, Bristol, from which the following extract is taken. It was one of three entries for Monmouthshire - *'The second gathered church that was in this county from the beginning, is that whereof Mr. Henry Walter is Pastor, who, by his ministry at Mynyddislwyn, was the instrument to call most of all of the original members thereof. He also did bring them to church order, and continues still their pastor. The members of the church be scattered about Mynyddislwyn, aforesaid, Newport and Blaenau Gwent. They are altogether of an Independent judgement, except some few Baptists that be of their church. But they are moderate and free in their communion'.*

By this time, the persecution had slackened. In 1672, Henry Walter received an official licence to preach and teach in his house near Newport. A licence was also granted to Watkin Jones, Sychpant.

The Independents of north-west Monmouthshire moved their headquarters to Penmaen where a chapel was built in 1694. Neither Henry Walter nor Watkin Jones lived to see that chapel erected.

New Bethel Chapel. A photograph taken before 1894. Before that year there existed in the south wall of the chapel a fireplace which was the only means of heating the building. In 1894 the fireplace was removed, and the chapel was warmed by lighted lamps. The chimney stack from that fireplace can be seen on the left of the roof - the south side. Another clue to the age of the photograph is that the memorial to James Thomas hasn't been erected, to the left corner of the photograph. In the foreground are the steps leading up to the front porch of the Islwyn Schoolroom.

New Bethel Sunday School Group 1947-48.
Standing - Lionel Davies, Roy Fox, Ronald Ford, Adrian King.
Seated - Malcolm Ford, Mr. Ken Lawrence, Robert Fox.

Children of the New Bethel Sunday School, photographed in 1949.

The New Bethel Sunday School group in the early 1950s. The class was taken by Mr. Lewis Lewis (front centre).

The Deacons of New Bethel, taken about 1949.
Back row - Hughie Hughes (Headmaster Pentwynmawr School), John Charles Lewis, Lewis Lewis (Baker), Mr. Jones (Policeman), Joe Chick, Ken Lawrence.
Front row - Ben Stacey, Bert Williams (Undertaker), Ceiriog Richards (Minister), Rosser Williams, Mr. Treasure.

The Deacons of New Bethel, taken in May 1958.
Back row - George Padfield, Gareth Griffiths, Mr. Bowen, John Lambert, Josh Davies.
Front row - Ken Lawrence, Hughie Hughes, Bert Williams, Rosser Williams, Lewis Lewis.

The opening of New Bethel Manse in 1949. The first occupants were the Minister, Mr. Ceiriog Richards (second left) and his wife (at the end, right). One of the chapel Deacons, Mr. Lewis Lewis, the baker from Windy Ridge, was ill in bed with a long illness. Mr. Bert Williams, undertaker of Newbridge, (father of Ellis), is seen talking into a microphone. The opening service was relayed to Mr. Lewis Lewis in his sick bed after consulting Dr. McKay, who arranged for a nurse to sit at his bedside during the relay.

289

When the New Bethel Manse was opened in 1949, this crowd from the congregation, plus visitors, gathered outside in the lane. At the top of the photograph can be seen the back of the Nailers Arms Inn.

Islwyn Schoolroom

Rosser Williams of Penrhiwffranc died in 1860. In his Will is the following bequest - *'I give, devise and bequeath unto the trustees of New Bethel Independent Chapel for the time being, and their successor trustees for ever, the new Schoolroom near the said Chapel, and the ground under the Stable, and the house in the yard, to be freely enjoyed by them and at their discretion for the use of the said Congregation for ever, subject to the payment of Ten shillings a year unto my executors'.*

This suggests that Rosser Williams built the Schoolroom, or paid for it to be built. Over the porch is a stone inscription which reads -
ISLWYN
School Erected
1847

At that time the Minister was Moses Ellis. The Schoolroom was built across the road from the Chapel. It was used both as a Sunday school and a day school.

In 1894 it underwent considerable alterations. It was extended twenty feet on the southern side. In addition the boilerhouse, conveniences and *'ante-room for ladies to wash up'* were added to the northern end, and the present entrance made, the main entrance facing the road being covered by a porch (presumably the inscribed stone over the porch was moved from the original door). At the same time the entire flooring of the Schoolroom was renewed, and the roof of the Chapel house next door, which was formerly roofed with heavy stone tiles, was slated. In 1928 when electric lighting was installed at the Chapel, it was also fitted in to the Schoolroom.

Part of the New Bethel congregation outside the Islwyn Schoolroom.

New Bethel Minister, Mr. Ceiriog Richards, and wife, surrounded by the congregation and Sunday School children, outside the south end wall of the Islwyn Schoolroom, before going inside for a tea party.

Members of New Bethel chapel inside the Islwyn Schoolroom having a farewell party for Rev. Robert Banham. The window to the left of the photograph, in the south end wall, is the window shown in the previous photograph.

James Thomas

James Thomas was born on the 16th. February 1817 at a farm known as Hen Fryn. His parents were Thomas John Thomas and Mary Thomas, who were tenant farmers and not at all well off. He was born into a Welsh speaking home. Young James was sent to work underground in a coal mine at the tender age of 6 years, which was the usual practice of those days, when the benefits of education were denied to the masses and within the reach of the wealthy only. He started work as a door boy, sitting in almost total darkness for at least 12 hours a day opening and closing the heavy air-doors underground each time a tram passed. He recorded that it was his custom to walk three miles to work each day, leaving home at four o'clock in the morning, returning at eight o'clock at night.

His experience in all the practical routine of colliery work, from the duties of door boy to those of coal hewer, made him in course of time a most useful man in the neighbourhood in which he worked.

His success in acquiring wealth was not due to mere luck. It was the result of hard work and perseverance. His chief characteristic early in life was his desire to 'get on' and to shoot ahead of those around him, both in reference to the work done and income earned. Although it seemed at the outset that his life was ever to be one of toil and hardship he persevered, and was never discouraged.

From 1840 to 1862 he occupied very prominent positions in connection with several collieries both in the Monmouthshire and Rhondda Valleys. But it was in 1850 that he first made his debut as a colliery owner. He then entered into partnership with others and purchased a small colliery at Troedyrhiw near Porth (Rhondda Valley). His success in connection with this undertaking stimulated him to extend his enterprise in other districts, and in the course of a few years he figured as an active joint owner of Tynewydd and Ynysfaio Collieries, which pits were successfully sunk under his direct supervision. Subsequently he turned his attention in the direction of Caerphilly where he opened Energlyn Colliery. He sold Energlyn, leaving it in 1874, and made the Rhondda the field of fresh enterprise, and was responsible for the sinking of Ynyshir and Standard Collieries. He reached the coal in those pits in May 1877, and then directed his attention to providing houses for his colliers, resulting in the birth of Ynyshir in the Rhondda.

James Thomas was the third colliery owner to tap the treasures of the Rhondda coalfield, following Walter Coffin of Dinas and Mr. Insole of Cymmer. Up to the day of his death he was the oldest South Wales Colliery owner living.

In his latter years he devoted much of his time to farming, and could reckon among holdings several extensive farms, among them being Tynewydd and Ynyshir in the Rhondda; Glyngwyn, Energlyn, Tir Gibbon, Tir Merchant, Tir Ewen, in the Caerphilly area; Cross Farm and Ty'n y Park at Llanedarne; Mill Ditch at Peterstone; and Carnix Farm in the Vale of Glamorgan; Pye Corner farm near Rogerstone; and Pantygwew (Mon.).

He was a non-smoker. He was Congregationalist in religion. He took little or no part in public life.

He had a son, Thomas James Thomas (who died 16 years before him) by whom he had a grandson, William J. Thomas (who became a colliery agent) and three granddaughters.

The marble monument to James Thomas. He is believed to be looking out over the area where he started work as a doorboy in a coal level.

He was survived by three daughters - one married Alderman W.H. Mathias of Porth; one married Mr. D. Jenkins, Contractor, Porth; and a third married Mr. Richard Packer, Accountant, Porth.

James Thomas died at his home at Cross Farm, Llanedarne, near St. Mellons on Monday 29th July, 1901, in his eighty-fifth year. He had been ill for four months suffering from pneumonia and bronchitis. He was laid to rest at New Bethel Chapel on a Saturday afternoon with his wife Elizabeth (who died 41 years before him, on 11th April 1860) and three infant children, James, aged 1 year 6 months, died Nov. 1850, Ruth, aged 10 months, died July 1858, and Ruth, aged 6 days, who died April 1860 (her mother died six days later).

The cortege, consisting of a hearse and nearly twenty mourning coaches, and as many vehicles, left Cross Farm, Llanedarne, at noon, and journeyed to Mynyddislwyn, via Caerphilly. At Maesycwmmer a curious incident occurred which caused some delay. A horse drawing one of the coaches became affected by the great heat. The driver noticed that there was something the matter with the animal and stopped the carriage, and immediately afterwards the animal dropped down in the road. It was not until its head had been bathed with cold water for some minutes that the horse revived sufficiently to continue the journey. At Pontllanfraith bottom Station (Tredegar Junction) the funeral was joined by 1,500 colliers employed at the Ynyshir and Tynewydd collieries, who had travelled over from the Rhondda by two special trains provided by Mr. Thomas's relatives. As the procession moved along the Welsh hymns *'Yn y dyfroedd mawr a'r tonau'* and *'Daeth yr awr im' ddianc adre'* were sung. Rev. D.C. Davies, Congregational minister, Ynyshir, officiated at the chapel, assisted by Rev. J. Morgan, Ynyshir, and Rev. J.B. Llewelyn, pastor of New Bethel.

At the end of the ceremony the workmen were supplied with tea and refreshments in two large marquees which had been erected in the field behind the Chapel Schoolroom.

Alongside his grave, in a most prominent position, is James Thomas's memorial. It was made from Italian marble. For many years after its erection a father and son would travel from Italy every seven years to clean it. They would take a week then return home.

His grandson was knighted for his deeds to charity. Sir William James Thomas married the matron of Cardiff Royal Infirmary, and was a benefactor to the hospital.

James Thomas's nephew, Edmund, lived at Gilwern House before retiring to Bath. Edmund's two daughters married the two sons of Trevor Griffiths, solicitor, clerk to the council, son of the Vicar of Mynyddislwyn.

Tynewydd Colliery Disaster

James Thomas was part owner and resident manager of Tynewydd Colliery at Troedyrhiw (Porth) in the Rhondda Valley, and it is worth a mention in this book. He was involved in the sinking of the colliery, which was 98 yards deep to a Bituminous seam of coal, and which was opened in 1852.

Tynewydd Colliery in 1877. On the hillside, to the right, can be seen James Thomas's house, Ty Newydd, the name that is on his Memorial at New Bethel.

Graphic, April 1877.

At work on 11th April 1877 a collier reported to the assistant surveyor that water was coming out of the coal into his stall, or place of work. It was known

296

that some distance ahead were the abandoned workings of an old colliery. The manager must have been informed, but the surveyor had assured him that there was a geological fault between the stall in question and the old workings, and could see no danger of water breaking through from those old workings.

The day shift had just finished work at 4 p.m. and the colliers made their way to pit bottom for the ride up the shaft. That was a slow process and involved waiting about, so some of the colliers remained at their place of work a few minutes longer.

But the surveyor's report to the manager about no danger of water breaking in was tragically wrong. The colliers still in the pit heard a mighty roar. They were in two groups of five men each and two groups of two men each, making a total of fourteen trapped underground by the in-rushing water.

Each group was in its own stall or workplace, and as the water rose towards them they had no way out. The advancing water compressed the air in each stall far above atmospheric pressure.

Extra pumps were brought to the pit top to help lower the water level in the pit, allowing rescue teams to enter.

One group of five men tapped the walls continually in the hope of being heard, which they were. A rescue party in an upper level roadway started digging a tunnel through the 36 feet wall of solid rock to get to the trapped men. But tragedy struck at the moment of freedom, because as the rescuers broke into the flooded stall, the compressed air was released with such force that one of the trapped men was sucked into the rescue hole, killing him instantly, while rocks were hurled at the rescuers, injuring them. But of those five men, four were rescued alive.

That same night another rescue team cut into another stall and found two men drowned, while another two were found dead at their workplace a few days later. That left five men missing.

Two days after the accident, two divers from London were sent for. They bravely advanced five hundred feet through the black murky waters towards the five trapped colliers but had to turn back because the way was blocked.

On 16th April teams of rescuers began the enormous task of cutting a rescue tunnel through the forty yards barrier of solid coal to reach the trapped men. They worked in four shifts of four men each working day and night. On 18th April the voice of one of the trapped men was heard calling. Bore holes were made to try to pass liquid food to the trapped men, and to gently release the air pressure from their stall. But the attempt failed. The holes had to be plugged because the noise of the escaping air was deafening. But that escaping air meant that the water level around the trapped men rose, and they were up to their waists in water with nowhere to go.

A discharge of gas in the tiny rescue tunnel meant the rescuers had to retreat. During that period of dreadful suspense, eight volunteers came forward, to make one final attempt at rescue. The compressed air escaped in gusts each causing an explosion louder than the report of a cannon. But on the tenth day after the disaster struck, the five men were rescued. One was a fourteen-year-old boy. Two of them crawled forward and 'When they saw James Thomas, the resident proprietor, *who is very popular with the men, they pressed forward and embraced him with a great fervour'* (Graphic, April 1877). They had not eaten or drank in all the time of their entombment.

An Inquest on the five dead was opened a few weeks later. Most of the evidence was given in Welsh. The verdict stated *'We are of the opinion that the death of the five men arose from the culpable neglect of the Manager in not complying with the rules, and we return a verdict of Manslaughter against him, but at the same time, we are of the opinion that the neglect arose from a mistake he made in expecting to find a fault before he came to water'.*

James Thomas, the Manager, was committed for Trial on a Coroner's Warrant. Bail was allowed in the sum of £200.

Until the Tynewydd Disaster, the Albert Medal, First and Second Class, had been given only for bravery in saving life at sea. Queen Victoria announced - *'The Albert Medal, hitherto only bestowed for gallantry in saving life at sea, shall be extended to similar actions on land, and that the first medals struck for this purpose shall be conferred on the heroic rescuers of the Welsh Miners'.*

The Albert Medal First Class was conferred on four of the rescuers, while the Second Class Medal was conferred on twenty of the rescuers, among whom was James Thomas the Manager. His name appeared in the list in the London Gazette of 7th August 1877. But on the 10th August the London Gazette announced that his name had been removed from that list. He was in the position of being put up for an Albert Medal for bravery at the same time that he was awaiting Trial for Manslaughter in the same affair. So James Thomas never got his medal.

He stood Trial at Swansea Assizes on 6th August. The trial lasted two days, and at the end the jury could not agree. There was a second trial, at Cardiff, on

Yew Tree Cottage, just to the south of New Bethel Chapel (not to be confused with Yew Tree Cottages beyond St. Tudor's Church).

9th April 1878. Many remarks were made in favour of Thomas, and at the end the judge pointed out the difference between gross neglect and an error of judgement. James Thomas was found not guilty.

Numbers 1 and 2 Yew Tree Cottages are just uphill (south) of New Bethel Chapel. They are joined in a back-to-back formation. The 1839 Tithe Apportionment Book lists only one cottage with garden, owned by Rosser Williams of Penrhiwffranc Farm, but leased to Thomas Thomas. The cottage nearest to St. Tudor's was the original one, with a hay barn attached, which has since, at an unknown date, been converted into a second cottage. The original cottage has a stone spiral stairs in the end wall nearest the road, while the other cottage had a ladder to reach upstairs.

The present owners, Mr. and Mrs. Carpenter, married in 1948 and moved in with her mother, Mrs. Lewis in the newer cottage. Prior to that event, the two cottages were home to three families, the Lewis family, Mr. and Mrs. Ashman and Mr. and Mrs. Little (Coal merchants). When Mr. Little died Mr. and Mrs. Ellie Edwards moved into the original cottage, and when they moved out Mr. and Mrs. Carpenter moved in, and still occupy it. Mother Mrs. Lewis lived next door, so effectively the two cottages became one big house.

When Mrs. Lewis died in Millennium year, at almost 102 years of age, she was the oldest person on the Mountain, and also the one who had lived there the longest.

Looking out over the Pontllanfraith area from New Bethel. Newbridge Road can be seen, and the curve of Elim Way.

Penrhiwffranc Farm

Probably built in the 1500s as the home of a rich man. As its name suggests, it was built at the top of the hill, on the track up from Cwm Nant Yr Odyn. But where does the 'Ffranc' in the name come from, suggesting a French link? Whoever built it probably benefited from the vast increase in the cost of wheat between 1500 and the early 1600s. Yet no wheat is grown nearby today.

The house was built of local Pennant sandstone, with massive oak beams inside, which survive today with their chamfered edges. The external walls are battered so that they are wider at their bases than at eaves level.

Since the 1960s there have been changes to the outside of the house. The massive central pot-bellied chimney (that was above the huge Inglenook fireplace) has been replaced by a much smaller brick built chimney. Above the windows are stone 'drips' which have been covered over with a rendering of mortar. The stone tile roof has been replaced with modern roofing tiles.

The photograph on the next page shows a chimney at the extreme western end of the roof. This no longer exists, nor indeed is there any trace of the fireplace that it served. It must have been for a fire in an upstairs bedroom, but the present owners have no recollection of it.

Evidence suggests that the house was originally a Longhouse with beasthouse at the downhill (western) end, of which no trace remains. The western end gable wall is thinner than the other outside walls, so when the house was built this wall could have been inside the house, separating the dairy from the beast house.

As mentioned, there was originally a central Inglenook fireplace, which has been covered over, but it is still there to be opened up again one day. In the thickness of this central spine wall would have been a spiral staircase up to the first floor. It is possible that some years after building the house, that a spiral stairs was not considered grand enough for the owner, so a much more imposing stairs was built, with a large stair wing protruding out of the north facing wall - an uncommon feature in our area. Was he trying to keep up with the Jones's, or rather the Morgan's at Penllwyn Fawr, within sight across the valley? Again, the walls of this stair wing are thinner than the main walls of the house, suggesting that it was built at a different time to the main house.

Downhill from the farmhouse is the Mynyddislwyn Seam of coal, which was worked at this place nearly two hundred years ago. (Read the chapter on Coal). One of the early coal owners in the area was Rosser Williams who died in 1860. His connection with Penrhiwffranc is explained earlier in this chapter.

On 30th August 1886 Edmund Thomas (nephew of James Thomas whose statue is at New Bethel) of Tyla Gwyn and John Thomas Davies purchased the Penrhiwffranc Estate from the Williams family for £2,450. The sale included -

A) Tenement called Tyr Cross Fach with garden, stable and barn called Sgubor Ganol, cowhouse and fields known as Caid Duon Bach and Gwain Fach, alongside the highway from Croespenmaen towards Mynyddislwyn Church.

Penrhiwffranc Farmhouse. Believed to be Thomas Williams (died 1913) and family. He was the father of the first Ellis Williams who lived at Cwm Dows, Newbridge. The photograph shows a number of interesting features. The chimney at the apex of the roof was removed long ago, and today there is no evidence inside the house of the fireplace served by that chimney. The huge pot-bellied chimney in the middle of the roof was replaced in the 1960s with a much smaller chimney. To the left of the photograph, on the north wall, can be seen part of the stair wing. To the right of the photograph is the 19th century extension. The three ladies and child are standing at the downhill end of the house on the spot where the attached beast-house was believed to have originally stood.

B) Cottages, gardens, stables, outbuildings and fields known as Tir William Lawrence, situate near Penrhiwffranc.

C) Tenement, beasthouse, stable, two barns, two gardens, sixteen fields, known as Cae yr Lwyn, Gwain yr Ddayn, Tir Wain Goch Fach, Cae Bach, Worlod Dan y Ty, Caer Coed Mawr, Caer Coed Bach, Perlyn Bach, Caer Pwll Wain, Oflan y Ty, Caer Skiber Errw, Garn Errw Fir, Cae Haner ar Bach, Cae Glaes Ycha, and Cae Glaes Ysha, containing twelve Welsh acres (now better known as the farmhouse of Penrhiwffranc, with barns, stables and outbuildings, containing 40 acres, 2 roods, 26 perches).

In the chapter on 'Coal' mention was made of this farm. In his sworn affidavit, David Davies stated that he opened the coal level in the field below the farm, but he did not give a date, unfortunately. The following agreement is the first proven date of coal being worked at Penrhiwffranc.

Penrhiwffranc Farmhouse, viewed from the north, as it appeared until the mid 1960s, with its imposing stair wing protruding.

A drawing by Jean Burland.

'*Memorandum of an Agreement made the 30th day of January 1818 between George Maule of Lincoln's Inn, Esquire, John Llewellin of Rumney Works, Gentleman, and Joseph Kaye of London, Esquire, Executors of the late Benjamin Hall, Esquire, of the one part, and Edmund Prosser of the parish of Monythusloine in the county of Monmouth, Farmer, of the other part. Whereas the said Edmund Prosser is possessed of a certain Copyhold Tenement and Lands, commonly called Penrhiwfranc, now in the occupation of the said Edmund Prosser, situate near Pennar, in the said parish of Monythusloine, part and parcel of the said Manor of Abercarne. And whereas there is coal under the said Tenement and Lands. And the Lord of the Manor as such is entitled to the minerals which the said Edmund Prosser doth hereby acknowledge. Now the said George Maule, John Llewellin and Joseph Kaye, in consideration of the Royalty or Galeage of 4 pence per ton, agree to lease and grant full leave, licence and authority to the said Edmund Prosser to work the vein of coal under the said Copyhold Tenement and Lands, now opened upon at Pennar, for the term of 21 years. And the said Edmund Prosser agrees to carry the said coal along the Lord of the Manor's Tramroad and pay the regular and accustomed tonnage and wharfing*'.

A few things should be explained in connection with the above Agreement. Benjamin Hall was the Lord of the Manor. He died a young man in 1817, leaving a fifteen-year-old son, Benjamin, as his heir. The heir could not come into his inheritance until his 21st birthday, in 1823. The Will of the deceased Benjamin Hall stated that until his son came of age, Abercarne Estate was left in Trust, in the care of three Trustees, named in the above Agreement.

The other thing to mention is the last sentence in the above Agreement, that coal from Penrhiwffranc was to be carried on Hall's Tramroad. This was the tramroad already mentioned in the 'Coal' chapter than ran as far as Pennar Colliery, alongside the Nailers public house. There now follows a document whereby that tramroad was to be extended to the coal level at Penrhiwffranc. It was dated October 1818.

'To the Proprietors of the Monmouthshire Canal, Gentlemen,

As the owners of Lands in the Trust under the Will of the late Benjamin Hall, Esquire, Deceased, containing veins of coal in the parish of Monythusloin, we deem it necessary that a Tram Waggon Road should be made from a certain colliery called the Church Farm, in the said parish of Monythusloin, to the Nine and a half Mile Post on the Crumlin line of Canal, being a distance of Three Miles and eight hundred and five yards from Point to Point, partly across the Highway leading from Monythusloin Church to Pentwynmawr, and through the lands of Margaret Lewis, widow, Edmund Prosser, William Jones, Henry Jones, William Jones, Richard Jenkins, late Henry Phillips, or Thomas Jones, Edmund Mathews, William Phillips, William Edmund, and the Devisees in Trust of the said late Benjamin Hall, Esquire, for the purpose of conveying the coal to the Canal from under the said Church Farm (being the property of the late Benjamin Hall, Esquire), we have desired a plan of the Road to be laid before you, and if you would not undertake it yourselves, shall be obliged by an early answer that we may proceed on it without loss of time.

I have the honour to be Sirs,

Your very obedient Servant

John Llewellin, for George Maule
Joseph Kaye, and Self Devisees of
The late Benjamin Hall, Esquire'.

The above application was needed because as the tramroad was to be extended beyond Pennar, it constituted a new tramroad, and as such the Canal Company had to give permission for it to join the Canal. It joined the canal at Abercarne and the coal was then loaded on to canal barges to be taken to Newport where it would have been loaded on to larger boats to be sailed up or down the Bristol Channel. It was known as the Pennar Branch Tramroad.

The tramroad was listed on the 1839 Tithe Apportionment Book, drawn on a map of 1843 by John Prujean, and on the 1846 Tithe Map, and on the 1879 O.S. map, all going to the coal level below Penrhiwffranc. Prujean's map has the name 'Church Farm Colliery' at the end of the tramroad. Looking at the location of the coal level, a short distance underground and the coal would have been worked from under Church Farm land. The owner of the surface land owned the coal directly underneath, so it probably makes sense to call the level by that name.

In 1831, a newspaper advert tells us that Churchland Colliery was for sale. It seems highly probable that this was the same coal level, or colliery, as that just mentioned.

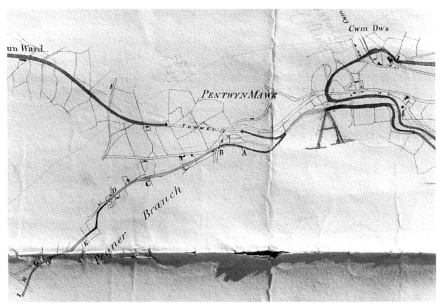

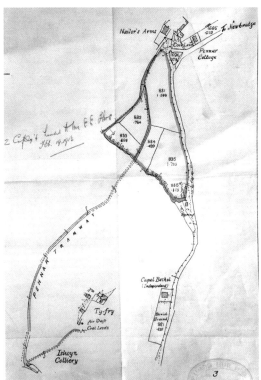

A different map to the previous one, but continuing where that particular map left off.

304

'MONMOUTHSHIRE TO BE SOLD BY AUCTION
On Monday the 11th of April, 1831, and following day, by order of the Assignees of Mr.
Richard Jenkins, a Bankrupt, on the Premises near Pennar, in the Parish of Monythusloyne.
The whole of the STOCK of the CHURCHLAND COLLIERY, consisting of 130
underground trams (in good repair), 9 old iron trams, 1 water tram, 14 tram shafts, 2 road
shafts, 15 bar hooks and 40 hitchings, 43 axles and 15 braces for ditto, 64 tram wheels, 8
tips and 1 fire lamp, 1 weighing machine, 1 large beam and scales, 1 small ditto, seven 112
lb. weights, one each 56, 28, 7, 4, 2, and 1 lb. weights, 250 colliers' mandrils, 30 bottom
mandrils, 50 sledges, 23 sets of blasting tools, a quantity of rock chisels, coal chisels,
wedges and rammers; 3 pair smith's bellows, 4 anvils, 1 vice, and a general assortment of
smith's tools; 50 yards of good rope, an excellent shaft engine and box; a small cart, Irish
car, ladder, and wheelbarrow; 2 large corn chests, 1 half bushel measure, 1 stable shovel,
and 7 pikes; a large baking table and flourbin; a good office desk and stool; and a quantity
of elm planks on shed. Also about 30 tons of loose tram plates, and about 100 tons in the
work, which will be offered for sale by the ton, either as they now lie, or will be delivered
outside, as may be agreed at the sale.
Mr. Hall, the lessor of the colliery, will agree to let the Coal now unworked, on
reasonable terms; and as the bankrupt has laid out a large sum of money in opening the
Colliery, no capital will be required to carry on the work beyond what may be necessary to
purchase the Stock, which may be viewed at any time previous to the day of the sale, on
application to the Auctioneer, Commercial Street, Newport'.
Towards the end of the nineteenth century the Pennar Branch tramroad was
extended beyond the Penrhiwffranc coal level to the boundary of Penrhiwffranc
land. That boundary is a small stream valley, Cwm Cydi, and a stone bridge was
built to carry the tramroad over the valley. The walls of the bridge still stand today.
Coal was then worked from under the fields approaching the Flannel Factory, and
continued to be worked, and carried along the tramroad, until the 1930s.

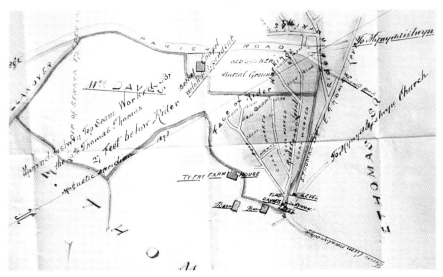

Coal working between Penrhiwffranc and Ty Fry Farms.

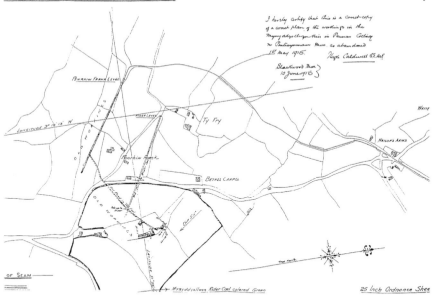

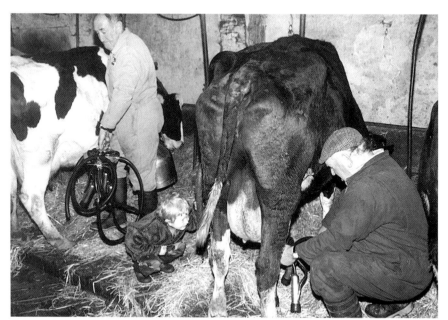

The sad evening of Monday 15th March 1999, with John and Ken Williams milking at Penrhiwffranc for the last time, assisted by the author's grandson Jac. Milk production ended that night, and they have since turned the farm over to fattening beef.

Downhill from Penrhiwffranc Farm lies Ty Fry Farm, another very old farm-house. It is almost in the shadow of New Bethel Chapel. In 1839 it was listed as owned by Henry Jones, leased out to George George. Its twenty-five fields and parcels of land added up to 44 acres, with its annual tithe rated at £2 8s 9d.

Ty Fry Farm seen below New Bethel Graveyard.

Originally this was a small farmhouse set end-on into the hill, with its barns detached. It was not a longhouse. Similar small farmhouses in the area, and photographed in this book are Ynysddu Farm, Cilfynydd Farm, and the un-named farmhouse at West End, Abercarne, which burned down killing Mrs. Keeble.

The original Ty Fry had thick stone walls, with no stone walls inside. It could well have been one-roomed. An oak-panelled partition was added, probably in the 16th century, to divide the single room into two, to make a dairy at one end of the house. The bedroom was above the dairy. At an unknown date the bedroom area was extended to cover all of upstairs, which was reached by a stone spiral stairs.

Over the last few years much building work has been carried on at the old farmhouse. The oak panel survives, and the original up-hill pine end wall survives, but extensions almost surround the original house.

The James family moved here in 1935. Neil James moved out to nearby Ton y Moch, and his son Martin now farms the land.

The North-East Corner

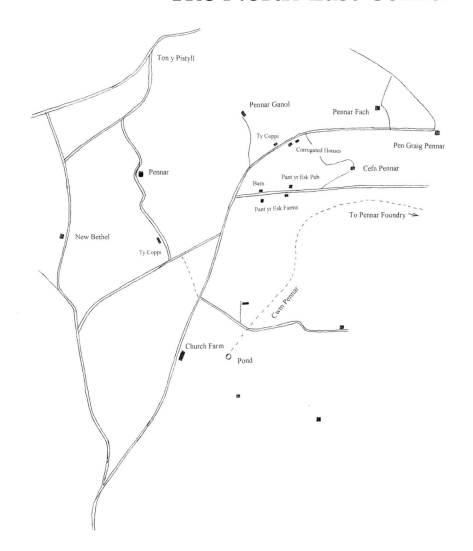

If the most common name on the western slope of Mynyddislwyn Mountain is Cae'r llwyn, then the north-east corner of the Mountain is dominated by the name Pennar. The stream flowing off the mountain past Pant yr Esk, the Nant Pennar, and Pennar Foundry down in the Ebbw Valley, have been mentioned in the earlier chapter on the Ebbw Valley. Pennar was the name given to five old farms, and there was also Pennar Cottage and Pennar Villa near the Nailers Pub, both mentioned earlier.

Of the farms, the largest is simply called Pennar. The Land Tax Assessment Register for 1805 lists Penner Farm, owned by William Phillips, valued at £3 17s 6d, with its Land Tax of 15s 6d. The Tithe Apportionment Book of 1839 lists Penar and Sychpant Farms together, owned and occupied by Ann Phillips, with a joint acreage of 132 acres, and a Tithe rated at £8 5s 11d. Possibly Ann Phillips inherited the farm from her father William.

But to confuse things, also listed in 1805 is Penner Tithe Farm, owned by Rev. Charles Gore (mentioned earlier in this book under Tithes), valued at £4 10s, with a Land Tax of 18 shillings. Also included is Cae Penner, owned and occupied by William Jones, valued at 5 shillings with a Land Tax of one shilling, and Tir Penner, occupied by Elias Edwards, value £1 5s 0d with a Land Tax of 5 shillings. But to which of the Pennar Farms did these belong?

Pennar Farm.

For many years this farm was owned by the Edmunds family, but it has now left their ownership. In recent years the old farm buildings have been tastefully converted into living accommodation for members of the present farmer's family.

This north east corner of The Mountain has always been dominated by farming. The years 1880-1900 were years of depression in agriculture and the 1880s was a decade of difficulty. Prices slumped as a result of cheap imports from America and Australia. (The area was now feeling the full impact of the Repeal of the Corn Laws of 1846, which removed protection for the farmer and began Britains dependence upon the import of cheap wheat and other such cereals). Local grain prices reached rock bottom, as did milk, if it could be sold at all.

That was a time of severe weather conditions, with heavy snowfalls each spring and deeply frozen grounds, which added to the difficulties in farming, with a series of bad harvests. That led to an agricultural depression.

Tom Edmunds and family at Pennar Farm in the 1920s. He was the eldest son of Thomas and Catherine Edmunds of Pant Glas Farm, mentioned at the beginning of this book.

Tom Edmunds.

Lord Tredegar, one of the major landowners on The Mountain, remitted a quarter of rents due to him, but many farms changed hands at that time.

Continuing up the road past Pennar Farm, it is now almost impossible to trace the ruins of Ty Coppi Cottage on the right hand side, (one of three by that name on The Mountain). It was part of Benjamin Hall's Abercarne Estate, occupied in 1839 by John Giles. An 1847 document concerning Hall's Estate lists its area as 32 perches with an annual rent payable to Hall of £3 10s. The original spiral stone stairs was in the end wall, leading directly into a bedroom. You walked through that room into the second bedroom.

Early in the twentieth century the Roberts family brought up thirteen children in that little cottage. At that time it was one house, but was partitioned off in the 1930s to form two, with an extra stairs added. The Roberts family continued to live in the bottom cottage, while a number of families lived in the top one. In the Second World War, Derek Ashby was an evacuee. He married Mrs. Ashby, and they lived in the top house, with his pigeon loft in the garden. Another family to live in the top house were the Savica's.

The well in the back garden was dug by the Roberts family. Prior to that event, water had to be carried by the family from the well at Pennar Farm, using two buckets over a yoke.

It can be remembered how the cottages had two bucket toilets, one up the garden, and one at the end of the house. Each had a long bench seat with a large hole and a small hole. Adults sat over the large hole while the children used the small one.

The cottages eventually had a demolition order served on them and they were pulled down in the late 1960s.

Louisa Roberts standing at the gate of Ty Coppi Cottage.

Just above Ty Coppi, the road met Lover's Lane at a T junction. Turning to the left, and left again, leads to the Pant Yr Esk area (originally Pant y Hesg - Hollow or Valley of Rushes). Yet strangely, the stream that runs down this valley is Nant Pennar.

Pant yr Esk Farm is two farms, Upper and Lower Pant yr Esk, very close together. Upper Pant yr Esk is one of the oldest buildings on The Mountain and was mentioned in the Land Tax Assessment Register of 1805 with a value of £1 10s and a Land Tax of 6 shillings. The Owner then was William Edmunds. The 1829 Register shows the same sums of money, so there was no inflation in those days. The 1839 Tithe Apportionment Book lists the Upper Farm as being owned by William Edmunds, at just over 27 acres, with its Tithe rated at £1 11s 4d. That same William Edmunds was the landlord of the Greyhound Inn, Pontllanfraith, and was mentioned in the earlier chapter on Coal, when he signed an agreement with Benjamin Hall in 1811 to work coal on this land. Across the road from the Upper Farmhouse is a barn alongside the road, with windows in it. The 1839 Tithe Apportionment Book lists that building as a house and garden. The Lower Farm was not shown on the Tithe Map, so it was built after 1846. Today, the Lower Farm is the working farm, with the Upper a house only.

Pant yr Esk.

Evidence of coal working can still be seen today, with a number of black waste tips. Also into the side of the Cwm Pennar valley, behind the farm, is the stone arched entrance to a coal level, which is today overgrown with brambles etc. That coal level worked into the 1920s, and the stone arch was probably the one opened in 1811.

In a document dated July 1857, William Edmunds' widow, Sarah, was entering an agreement with Benjamin Hall for the working of the coal at Pant yr Esk, and the area was called Caia Glyshon.

Thomas Watters, the first minister at New Bethel, lived at Pant yr Esk, where he kept the small farm, and ran a day school to supplement his income.

Down hill from the farm was the Pant yr Esk pub. It was mentioned as a pub on the 1871 census, occupied by Ebenezer Jones, Publican and Coal Tipper. The pub closed in 1988. In the ladies' toilet was a large slab of stone, put there before the toilet existed. When funeral processions passed this way, going up to St. Tudor's, the bearers would have needed a well earned rest, and some refreshment. The coffin was laid to rest on that stone slab while the bearers retired into the pub. Sadly, the slab of stone no longer exists. Painted on the roof of the pub was 'Phillips Ales' which many can remember, while the pub name was on the east wall visible on the pull up from Abercarn.

Mr. and Mrs. Roberts behind the bar of the Pant yr Esk pub in the 1980s.

A little way down the hill from the pub was The Donkey Hut alongside the road. As the name suggests, it was the stable for the donkey that worked in the coal level at the turn of the century, a hundred years ago.

A little further down the hill, a track leads off to the left, leading to Cefn Pennar Farm. A previous owner did some research into its history. The farm started its life as a little shepherd's cottage. Evidence of a small building can be

313

seen in the wall around the yard in front of the present farmhouse. The layout of buildings is unusual on The Mountain. The barn is in front of the house, and attached, and not at the side as in a typical Long House. Inside the barn, the floor is in two levels, and on the wall attached to the house, is a large fireplace with an enormous chimney. If it was in use when the barn was used as a barn it must have posed a huge fire risk. Could it be that the barn was turned over for farm labourers accommodation? Today the farm is a private house.

Cefn Pennar Farm.

Cefn Pennar was the dairy farm for the village of Abercarn at one time. A field to the west of the buildings was known as Well Field. In the top corner was a well. Water was drawn up the well and poured into a wooden sluice that ran down to the farm buildings, so in a way they had cold running water at the farm in times past.

Of particular interest is a stone wall alongside the farm, containing many holes. Stone slabs form the backs to the holes. They were rabbit hutches, when, in past times, rabbits would have been reared to provide fresh meat in the winter months.

Going back up the hill past Pant yr Esk, we continue with a right turn along the road. Pennar Ganol Farm is reached down a little lane. In the early twentieth century it was known as Mule Farm, because packs of mules were kept here, to be used to haul timber from the nearby forestry. It was a small Longhouse, divided into three sections. The top, uphill, part, was the stable. In the middle was the living accommodation for the farmer, and the lower, downhill, section, was the barn or beasthouse.

Pennar Ganol.

After re-tracing our steps away from Pennar Ganol lane, the road leads down past another old cottage called Ty Coppi, the third by that name mentioned in this book. This single house was originally two little farm workers' cottages, dating from the early 1700s. It still retains some of the features of two cottages, such as two spiral stairs and two fire places, each in the end walls. Its other feature is the bulge in the southern end wall, which allowed a bread oven to be built alongside the fireplace. There is little evidence of the oven in the northern wall. Renovation work over the years has all but destroyed it. The house has distinctive gables in the front roof line, making it almost identical in design to Penheol Cae'r Llwyn (Three Cocks), mentioned earlier.

The Land Tax Register of 1805 lists Tir y Gopi, value 5 shillings, Land Tax 1 shilling. The 1839 Tithe Apportionment Book lists it as Cefn Penar, owned by Benjamin Hall, with three fields, at just over 3 acres, with a Tithe rated at 4s 1d. The early O.S. map lists it as Ty Coedcae. All very confusing.

Almost opposite Ty Coppi is the site of two little single storey bungalows, built from corrugated sheeting. They were of early twentieth century origin. Nearest to Ty Coppi was Rose Monte, and next to that was Sunny Cote. Both were pulled down in the late 1990s to be replaced by two new houses. The story goes that many years ago, Rose Monte was used as a summer holiday retreat by Mr. Wallis Jones, the owner of furniture and carpet shops at Abercarn and Newbridge. A third corrugated metal bungalow stood immediately next to Ty Coppi Cottage, and was known as Ty Coppi Bungalow. This has also been replaced by a modern house on the site.

Ty Coppi Cottage, showing the back of the bread oven. Beyond the cottage, to the right of the photograph, can be seen the new house, built on the site of Ty Coppi Bungalow.

The corrugated sheeting Rose Monte and Sunny Cote.

Continuing along the road, the next little area was called Gwaun y Gaseg many years ago. A rough track on the left leads down to the very ruinous Pennar Fach Farm. This was built end-on to the sloping hillside, and the farmhouse and barn separated by the yard. The barn was divided into two parts, to give a cowshed and a barn under one roof. The barn end had a loft for the storage of hay.

The house itself has a few interesting design features. As the photograph below shows, there was an original lean-to room on the downhill end. The downstairs of the house was divided into two rooms by a stud and wattle partition, and not by a stone wall. In the wooden windows can be seen the remains of two diamond mullions, put there to deflect the wind at the time when it was not intended to have glass in the windows. A window to let light into the stairs also has the remains of diamond mullions. These are probably the only mullions known to the survive today on The Mountain.

The 1839 Tithe Apportionment Book tells us that Pennar Fach was owned by William Edmunds of The Greyhound, Pontllanfraith. It is listed as a Cottage, with no land, so paid no Tithe. So sometime before 1839, the fields that must have belonged to the farm had been sold off. It was last occupied in 1960 by William Pritchard and family.

The ruins of Pennar Fach Farm, last occupied in the 1960s.

The rough track leading down to the farm continues, and went past Ty Gwyn Farm, overlooking Newbridge, with a branch off the track leading down to Pen Rhiw Bica. The track itself is an ancient one, as shown by the number of very large beech trees which were laid to form a hedge generations ago.

Retracing our steps to the road, and turning left, we reach Pen Graig Pennar, which has been known as Pennar Graig on some maps. Confusingly, the Tithe Apportionment Book and the Tithe Map both incorrectly named this farm as Pennar Fach. It was owned by Benjamin Hall, at 26 acres, 3 roods and 39 perches with its tithe rated at £1 17s 10d pence. An 1847 document concerning Hall's Abercarne Estate names this farm as Penrhiw Penner, with an annual rent of £21 5s 0d payable to Hall. Until very recently this farm was still part of Llanover Estate, originally Abercarne Estate.

At first glance this looks like an old Longhouse, but looks can be deceptive. The uphill barn was originally separated from the square farmhouse, and at an unknown date, an extension to the house was built, joining the house to the barn. So today three buildings are joined as one. Down hill is a small building, too small to have been a barn. Was it a milking parlour for one or two cows? Was it a stable? The uphill end wall of the barn was built into the hillside giving easy access from outside to a small door into the hay loft above the barn.

As mentioned, the original farmhouse was a small square structure standing on its own. In this form it is possible that this was one of the oldest farmhouses on The Mountain, with the downstairs used for animals, and the upstairs used as living accommodation. In the cold winters small numbers of animals would have been stabled, rather than been loose in a field, and the heat rising from them would have been most welcome above. Heat meant survival to the family above, and was more important than the rising smells.

The road to this farm continues as a very rough track zig-zagging its way down the hillside to West-End, Abercarn, and crossed the River Ebbw by an old bridge. A map enclosed in a document concerning Abercarne Estate, dated 1807, shows this track crossing the river, with the words 'From Bedwellty' alongside. It was undoubtedly an old Parish Road, and would have been linked to other roads beyond Bedwellty Church. It is known that in the mid 1700s iron ore from the Heads of the Valleys area was carried to Abercarne Ironworks, probably in panniers on the backs of animals. Also in the 1780s, pig iron was carried from Hirwaun ironworks to Abercarne. So this rough old track could have seen much traffic over two hundred years ago.

If such traffic existed, as the author believes, it could account for the building of the uphill barn to provide shelter and food for both man and beast as these journeys passed.

Pen Graig Pennar Farm. The original farmhouse is in the foreground, with the detached barn in the distance. The part of the house in between did not originally exist.

Another view of Pen Graig Pennar, from the opposite direction to the previous photograph.

Towards the Church

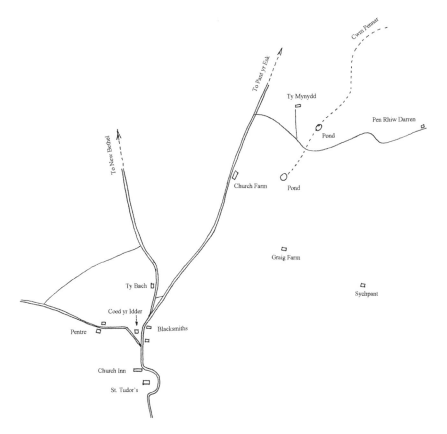

Taking up where previous chapters left off we now continue our journey towards St. Tudor's Church.

Having left the New Bethel area, on the right hand side is to be seen a detached house called Ty Siriol. This was originally a cottage very much smaller, called Ty Bach.

The little cottage had only one door, a front door facing south, towards St. Tudor's. Inside was a stone spiral stairs. At one time the cottage was called Coed Yr Idder Cottage, which must have been confusing, as the next cottage towards the Church has the same name.

The 1839 Tithe Apportionment Book lists it as Cottage and garden, measuring 32 perches, with no Tithe payment. It was owned by Benjamin Hall and leased to Thomas Elias.

By the 1930s it was the home of the Pritchard family, and by then it had acquired 12½ acres of land which was farmed. Three of the Pritchard daughters have written their wartime memoirs, which are at the end of this book.

Ty Bach, with pink washed walls, photographed after 1930, at which date the roof had been raised to increase space upstairs.

William George Pritchard outside his home at Ty Bach.

In September 1958 Mr. and Mrs. Ivor Fox and family moved in. Mrs. Rina Fox and her sister Rae were the two daughters of Lizzy Ann Thomas who was painted by Obediah Hodges (a few pages forward).

Behind Ty Bach, there was a small colliery, known as Tom Jones's Pit last going off. When it was sunk is unknown. It can be remembered how the single shaft was timber-lined, with a ladder for the colliers to climb down. On top was a small wooden headgear holding the sheave (wheel) and the rope was operated by a hand cranked winch. Coal came up in a large bucket. The document below tells us that the owner Tom Jones, was also the owner of The Church Inn nearby. With three fires in the pub, he would have needed a fair amount of his own coal on a cold winter's night.

Just past Ty Bach is a fork in the road leading past Church Farm to the area covered in the previous chapter. After that fork, on the left hand side, is the Blacksmith's public house. It closed in 1994 and is now a private house. The 1839 Tithe Apportionment Book tells us that it was a Public House, Yard and Garden measuring 18 perches, occupied by Thomas Elias. But the building is older than that, as a date stone of 1769 reveals. At the turn of the last century, it was the home of the Hicks family.

The Pritchard girls and friends Hay Making at Ty Bach in 1942.

The Hicks family outside the back door to the Blacksmith's in the late 1880s. Mr. Hicks was the publican. One of his daughters was Lizzy Ann, shown on the painting on page 325.

Just beyond the pub, down in a dip in the road, there was once a little cottage, also occupied in 1839 by Thomas Elias. That was believed to have been a Blacksmith's Shop, which gave its name to the pub, but nothing now survives. It would have been in the perfect position, alongside a stream (now dried up) whose water would have turned a small wheel to operate bellows to provide blast for the hearth.

The stone plaque outside the Blacksmith's.

Below: The Blacksmith's Arms' which ceased to be a public house in 1994, and is now a private dwelling.

Almost opposite the Blacksmiths pub is Coedyridder Cottage. A date on the name plaque gives the year 1689. That date is authenticated on an oak beam inside. The stone walls were laid dry with the minimum of clay pointing, having been built on the solid sandstone bed-rock.

The ground floor plan is a hall plus a divided inner room, but the dividing wall is now only a mark on the joist beams. The north room was probably the dairy. The hall has a wide fireplace with cupboard recesses on either side, and a stone spiral stairs. The beam with the date 1689 and ten initials, was originally the head-beam of the room-dividing wooden partition. The beam is square in section, of a newer style than the other chamfered beams in the house, suggesting that this beam, and the partition, is a later addition. That means that the cottage could well be older than the date shown. Upstairs, one original cruck-truss oak timber beam remains.

Coedyridder, painted by Obediah Hodges in 1909.

In the above painting, the lady in the foreground was Mrs. Lizzy Ann Thomas, who lived there with her family. When she got married she moved the short distance from the Blacksmith's pub where she had lived with her parents, Mr. and Mrs. Hicks. She told the story to her grandson, Granville Fox, that on the day Obediah was painting, she looked out and saw him with his easel. Being inquisitive, she wanted to know what he was doing. But being too shy, she needed an excuse. She picked up a churn and crossed the road to where he stood, besides the spout that supplied water for the house. On seeing her approach, he asked her to pose for a few minutes.

At the front gate can be seen two of her children. The lady at the side gate is unknown.

Much later in time, the cottage was known as Harry Allen's Cottage. He lived there with his sister. He was the Roadman for the Mountain, maintaining drainage ditches etc. besides the roads.

The 1839 Tithe Apportionment Book lists it as an un-named Cottage and Garden, with five fields. It covered 13 acres and 16 perches, with its Tithe rated at 8s 11d. An 1847 document concerning Benjamin Hall's Abercarne Estate named it Coedcae Rider, occupied by Thomas Elias (who occupied the Blacksmith's), who paid an annual rent of £9 to Hall.

The carvings on an inside oak beam at Coedyridder, as yet undeciphered.

Mrs. Lizzy Ann Thomas in later life.

In front of Coedyridder, the road turns sharply down hill towards Ty Pentre Farm. At the time of the 1839 Tithe Apportionment Book, the farm of that name was to the north side of the road, which is today a private house. It was owned and occupied by William Thomas, and its five fields covered a little over 12 acres, with its Tithe rated at 6s 1d.

Rev. Michael Jones was born in that house in 1934, the son of a farmer, but left at an early age. He was ordained as a deacon in Monmouth in 1958, and became a priest the following year. He was a curate in Newport, then Penhow, and vicar at Magor. He went to Australia, then to Kuwait in the Gulf. In 1990 he was seized as a human shield, with his wife Jean. They were held at gun point for four months by Saddam Hussein's troops, in squalid conditions at a power plant and arms factory in a bid to stop NATO planes from bombing them. But they survived.

To the south side of the road is the present Pentre Farm, which was unnamed in 1839. Then, it was owned and occupied by Philip Phillips. Its 46 acres were Tithe rated at £2 14s 2d. This same Philip Phillips was listed as occupying Yew Tree Cottages on the hill above, besides Twyn Tudor.

However, the original farm was in the hollow alongside the road, probably a Longhouse. That old farmhouse became an outbuilding and cattle shed when the present house was built. Until recently the old building had an oak beam, into which were carved 'C R 11 1672 X X 111'. That must have been carved by a Royalist sympathiser a few years after the Civil War ended, because it translates as Carolus Rex (Charles II), then the date, which was in the middle of his reign (1660-1685). The XX 111 was 23 years. The date of 1672 was 23 years after the execution of Charles's father, King Charles I in 1649. Sadly, that oak beam no longer exists. The date of 1672 was either the year in which the old farmhouse was built, or the year in which it changed hands, and the new occupant carved the date of his moving in. But with the restoration of the Monarchy in 1660, after Oliver Cromwell's days, it was safe to declare yourself a Royalist.

Returning to the top road, we will delay our visit to the church until completing the journey around the north-east corner of the Mountain, that we left unfinished in the last chapter.

Travelling towards St. Tudor's from the Pant yr Esk area, Pen Rhiw Darren Lane leads off to the left. Off that road, a lane leads to Ty Mynydd, the Mountain House.

Ty Mynyd was a Long-House. Downstairs it was divided into four areas, running from front to back of the building. At the up-hill end was the dairy, with a door leading into the living room. Below that was the through passageway, and below that, occupying the end of the building, was the beast-house. The photograph of the house shows a window at the up-hill end. That would have originally been a door, easily reached from the outside bank, used to load hay or cereals into the loft, where it was stored above the beast house at the other end of the building. Also in the photo can be seen two porches. The smaller one, nearest the camera, covers the original doorway to the through passage. In that passageway is one of the gems left remaining on The Mountain. It is a handsome doorway of Elizabethan style, surrounded by the white-washed wall.

That doorway, of solid oak, has a four-centred chamfered head. Such shaped heads are from the Early Renaissance period in Gwent. As in other parts of the county, there was only one such doorway in the house, and could have been added some years after the house was built. So this doorway is from a few years either side of 1600, but the house could well be earlier.

Ty Mynydd.

Ty Mynydd's solid oak Elizabethan doorway with its chamfered four-centre arch.

Where work has been done on the outside of the house in recent years, the removal of mortar off the walls has revealed that the walls are of dry-stone construction, and very thick. Over the windows the oak lintels survive. Inside, the oak beams are exposed, running the full width of the house from front to back.

Ledges on the chimney enabled the occupants of old to stand while lowering a bushy branch to clean out the soot. He stood in safety out in the fresh air, while the parlour had a fair covering of soot.

The 1839 Tithe Apportionment Book lists it as House Garden and Occupation Road, of 2 roods, with no fields and no Tithe rating. It was part of Benjamin Hall's Abercarne Estate, but occupied by Thomas Howells. So as early as that date it had lost its fields, and was no longer a farm.

Continuing along Pen Rhiw Darren Lane, our journey goes past Jan and Henry Chivers' Bryn Teg Bungalow, originally a small stone-built house built in 1880. It was altered in 1947, and in 1977 it was greatly enlarged to give its present appearance.

The road continues and now ends at the farm which gave its name to the lane, Pen Rhiw Darren. Originally, the road zig-zagged down the steep hillside towards Abercarn, but that hillside is now covered in forestry which has destroyed such a track. However, on leaving the forestry, the approach to the farm is via imposing stone walls which could well have held a gate or gates in the past.

The 1805 Land Tax Assessment Register lists it as owned by The Hon. Charles Morgan (Tredegar Estate), valued at £3 10s 9d with a Land Tax of 14s 1½d, occupied by Jenkin Jones. The 1839 Tithe Apportionment Book lists it occupied by Thomas Jones, the farm covering over 91 acres, with its Tithe rated at £2 12s 2d.

Nant Pennar is the stream running through Pen Rhiw Darren fields from a pond behind Church Farm (mentioned in the Ebbw Valley chapter as having been built to provide water for the Pennar Foundry in Abercarne). Close to Ty Mynydd Farm that stream has been formed into a pond, retained by original stone walls, with later bricks on top. The Tithe Map tells us that at that point was a cottage and garden. This leads to one of two theories. Was the cottage pulled down, leaving only lower walls, and the stream diverted into it to form a pond? Or did the stream originally go through the cottage because it was built as a mill ? Farms on this part of The Mountain needed to have grain ground into flour, or even grist ground for the animals. It was a long journey to one of the surrounding mills at Abercarne, Newbridge, Brynnar, or Gelligroes. But this is guesswork by the author. However, it is known that the pond was used as a sheep wash in more recent times.

Returning by the same road, almost opposite the entrance to Ty Mynydd is a track leading off to the south. Crossing fields will lead you down hill to a barn and then Sychpant Farm, overlooking Cwmcarn and the Ebbw Valley. The barn, which is now in severe ruin, was the place where Prayer Meetings were held in secret over two hundred years ago, before New Bethel Chapel was built in 1758. At the Chapel's two-hundredth celebrations in 1958, the congregation gathered at this old barn, as shown in the photograph on the following page.

Today, Sychpant is a mere ruin, but those ruins show what an impressive building the old farmhouse must have been. The 1805 Land Tax Assessment Register list it as owned by Isaac Jones, but occupied by John Williams. It was valued at 15d 8s with a Land Tax of 3s 1¹/₂d. The 1839 Tithe Apportionment Book lists Sychpant and Penar together, owned and occupied by Ann Phillips. Sychpant then had an Occupation Road and twelve fields or parcels of land.

New Bethel Chapel's 200th celebrations were held in 1958, and the congregations gathered at the old barn near Sychpant.

In the first part of the twentieth century Sychpant was the home of Mrs. Annie Thomas and family. By a second marriage she became Mrs. George Wood. The family lived at Sychpant Farm, Pentre Farm, Coedyridder Cottage and Glan y Nant (Cwmnantyrodyn). One of Mrs. Thomas's daughters, Emily, married Mr. George Hughes, and kept a shop opposite Pontllanfraith Top Station for many years. Many are the times that the author visited there.

The next occupants at Sychpant were the Allen family, with son and daughter. They moved into Graig Farm, then son Harry Allen and his sister moved to Coedyridder Cottage.

The next occupants at Sychpant were the Symmons family, who arrived via Cilfynydd Farm. In turn, they eventually moved to Graig Farm.

Sychpant Farm was last occupied about 1950.

Uphill from Sychpant, and half way to Church Farm, is the ruin of Graig Farm. It was not shown on the 1846 Tithe Map, but was on the 1880 O.S. map, so it was built some time between those dates. Upstairs were two bedrooms. When the Symmons family lived there, those bedrooms were for the ten children. There was one bedroom downstairs for Mr. and Mrs. Symmons, and they also had two lodgers. One of those ten children was Mrs. Lewis who settled at Yew Tree Cottage (near New Bethel) after her marriage.

The families of Mrs. Annie Thomas, and her second husband Mr. George Wood, at Sychpant Farm. Back row - Ethel Thomas (married John Thorne, Toneiddon Farm), Cecil Wood, Emily Thomas (married George Hughes). Seated - Dolly Wood, Annie Thomas (Wood), George Wood, Gladys Wood. The two boys are Arthur and Trevor Wood.

Mr. and Mrs. Symmons were followed as tenants of Graig Farm by their son Frank, who lived there with his wife and three daughters, until they moved out in the early 1950s. The last occupants at Graig Farm were Frank Symmons's niece Margaret and her husband Paddy in the early 1960s.

Graig Farm.

Mr. and Mrs. Edward and Clarice Symmons making hay at Graig Farm.

Mr. and Mrs. Edward and Clarice Symmons with baby Doris at Graig Farm.

At Graig Farm. Mrs. Clarice Symmons, Mrs. Elsie Ball and Mrs. Carter.

An old photograph that had written on the back 'On Mynyddislwyn'. Some reader must recognise the house and the family!

Leaving Graig Farm behind, a short walk using a public footpath and a few stiles will lead a walker to Church Farm. Until a few years ago, such a walk went past a low circular stone wall. That was the top of an air shaft, or ventilation shaft, connected to underground coal workings (see Penrhiwffranc). But it has now been filled in.

Church Farm had another connection with coal mining. When the deep collieries in the valley bottoms began giving summer holidays to colliers in the 1930s, the pits closed for two weeks each year. In that closure period, the many pit ponies underground were brought to the surface for their summer holiday. The ponies from Celynen South were walked up The Mountain and turned out in the fields of Church Farm. That must have been a sight to behold as they enjoyed their only taste of freedom for a whole year.

The name Church Farm is intriguing because way past living memory it has had no connection with St. Tudor's Church. But as we read at the beginning of this book, the whole Mountain had been a Grange for Llantarnam Abbey, with the monks living and farming on Mynyddislwyn Mountain to provide food for the Abbey. Was Church Farm one of their directly run farms where the monks lived and worked? If so, the buildings that we see today have been re-built since those far off medieval days, but the name has survived.

The front of Church Farm.

The first positive proof of Church Farm's existence to be found by the author is in the 1805 Land Tax Assessment Register. It was then part of Abercarne Estate, owned at that time by Samuel Glover, who was also Lord of the Manor of Abercarne. Its value was recorded as £4 15s 6d with its Land Tax set at 19s 1d.

In 1808 Benjamin Hall had acquired both the Abercarne Estate and the Lordship of the Manor of Abercarne. In March 1810 Hall's agent, John Llewellin, wrote to him *'Knight called on me about the Church Farm, and said he would give £55 - £60 for the whole if he should have it for 14 years. I informed him that when I had consulted you he should have an answer, and I told him it was my opinion it ought to be let for that term at £100 per annum, particularly as you intended building a new barn upon it'.*

The above letter shows that Church Farm was not for sale but was to be rented out or leased for a short term of years.

The 1839 Tithe Apportionment Book shows it being owned by Hall and leased to Thomas Howells. It covered 274 acres, which included the nine fields previously belonging to Ty Mynydd, now part of Church Farm. Its annual Tithe payment was rated at £9 3s 5d.

An 1847 Abercarne Estate document (in author's collection) lists Thomas Howells still leasing, and paying an annual rent to Hall of £95 19s 6d, a sum not far removed from John Llewellin's estimate of 1810.

Two architectural features at Church Farm are worth a mention. Inside the farmhouse are enormous stone stairs, easily the largest on The Mountain. The other is the roof. Both the house and carriage barn adjoining do not have roof timbers, they have cast iron trusses. These are not totally unique because the author knows of a similar roof at Tredegar and at Aberdare, but such a roof is certainly very rare. On the following page the first photograph shows the carriage barn without its roof tiles. Everything in that photograph is either cast or wrought iron. The numerous rods of wrought iron were for the purpose of hanging the stone roof tiles with wooden pegs. The second photograph shows a small detail of the same building after a new roof (timbers and felt) had been added in the early 1990s, but leaving the original cast iron frames in place. The solitary rod shown in the photo was a tie-bar to space the 'A' frames correctly and to hold them upright during construction. The numerous notches cast into the outside of the frames were to hold the wrought iron rods that took the weight of the stone tiles and onto which the wooden pegs hung. As originally built, there was no timber and no felt in this roof.

So how old is the iron roof? A clue could be in a letter written by Benjamin Hall in March 1812, in which he wrote *'I think I shall be able to do something considerable in introducing Iron Roofs into barracks for colliers'.* Further on in the letter is *'Weight and price of each - Door Frames and Window Frames'.* These were also to be of cast iron, but unfortunately the location is unknown. They were probably destined for Abercarne, but as colliers were widespread at that date, Hall could have been planning for anywhere in the locality.

The above reference is not to Church Farm, but it is included because it shows that Benjamin Hall, the owner of Abercarne Estate, of which Church Farm was a part, was at the cutting edge of modern technological ideas at that time. If he was planning to introduce Iron Roofs in colliers' houses, then it is logical that at about the same time he could have introduced them to other buildings on his estate.

At the date in question, Abercarne had a large Ironworks, with Forges, Foundry, Tilting and Turning Mill, Osmond Forge etc. and would have been

335

capable of casting the roof frames for Church Farm, and working the wrought iron rods. The Ironworks was on Hall's land, but leased out, so it seems highly probable that Church Farm's Iron Roof was made at Abercarne.

If the roof was even older, then Hall's predecessor as owner of Abercarne Estate was Samuel Glover, and he owned and managed the Iron Works at Abercarne, so if the roof was made in Glover's time, it would certainly have been made in his own works.

An inventory of part of Abercarne Estate in 1845 lists 'Iron Houses', proving that Hall's son, also Benjamin, did have buildings with iron parts.

We have now completed our journey around Mynyddislwyn Mountain, and a healthy walk from Church Farm leads to St. Tudor's Church, where our journey started. But there is one last building to mention, and last but not least. That is the Church Inn, today the only public house on The Mountain. In common with many other local parish churches, St. Tudor's has a public house as its nearest neighbour. Maybe people of old considered that getting married or burying the dead needed strong refreshment close at hand.

Although the public house is a very old building, the earliest proven record is the 1839 Tithe Apportionment Book, listing it as part of Sir Charles Morgan's Tredegar Estate, leased to Lewis Edmunds, but being exempt from a Tithe payment. What is today the car park was listed as being two gardens attached to the pub.

Under an Indenture of Settlement, dated 1st July 1896, Lord Tredegar empowered his two Trustees, Sir George Ferdinand Forestier Walker, and Henry Edzell Morgan Lindsay (his sons in law) to sell or dispose of any part of the Tredegar Estate as they saw fit. No doubt, any part not making enough money for the Estate! On 26th November 1920 they sold Church Inn to The Western

Valleys Brewery, Crumlin, (D.F. Pritchard) for £1,300. Edgar E. Jones was the tenant at the time of the purchase. Over the years, D.F. Pritchard Breweries became part of Rhymney Breweries, and in 1966 Rhymney sold the freehold to George Little, making it a freehouse. At that time Mr. and Mrs. Little lived upstairs, above the pub, while downstairs was completely different to today's layout. The pub was a series of little rooms and many doors. At one end (nearest to the kitchen) was the lounge for the Little family, out of bounds to the customers. The pub had three open fireplaces.

The present publican, Mrs. Dorinda Jones, with her husband Brian, bought the pub in the late 1970s and have since made many alterations, both inside and out. Gone are the three fireplaces, the lounge, partitions and doors, to leave us with the long open-plan design we see today. Also, the former bedrooms upstairs have gone to make way for a large room, which has many uses. First and foremost it is the restaurant, but has been used for fund-raising concerts, whist drives, and a Church hall.

Outside alteration can be imagined from the drawing below. About 1990 the three chimneys were removed from the roof, while gable windows were added to the roof. The window in the end wall was replaced by a door to provide outside access to the upstairs lounge, and the old mounting block made way for stone steps to that door. It is worth mentioning that at the extreme left of the sketch is the corner of the graveyard wall. Tucked into the corner of that wall was the small beer-garden of the pub.

Church Inn, before alterations in the 1990s.
A Jean Burland drawing.

338

The drawing shows an old building opposite the front door of the pub. That building has now been extended and converted into the publican's house. It was known as 'The Long Room', and was part of the Coach House of Church Inn. The ground floor consisted of stables, tack room, a storage area and a room for a carriage. The upstairs was reached by an outside stone stairs (shown on the drawing), and was one long room running the length of the building. There were two windows in the front wall, looking towards the pub. There were two fireplaces in the room, one at each end.

Towards the end of its working life, the Long Room was furnished with benches down both walls and tables each side, with a row of chairs to the centre, making it difficult to walk down the room when all the chairs were in use.

St. Tudor's Church used the Long Room for many functions. When there was a big service in the church, the robing of the clergy and choir took place in there. When there was a Confirmation Service the people being confirmed would go to the Long Room to have their veils put on. The choir would also robe there and then proceed to the church via the lych gate. If the church had a dinner or large party it would be held in the Long Room, while fund-raising events for the church were also held there.

Whist drives were held there on a Wednesday evening going back to the 1920s. They stopped after the Second World War to re-start about 1950, but finally stopped when the building went into disrepair. It can be remembered that when the fires were lit on a windy night, anyone opening the door caused the smoke to turn and fill the room so badly that people sitting down could hardly see one another.

A painting of the Long Room, dated 1953, shows some of the stone roof tiles missing, but the building continued to be used until the late 1950s, when it was abandoned. When the present publican bought the pub and Long Room in the late 1970s the chimneys had collapsed, due to years of neglect. As already mentioned, today it has been converted into the publican's home.

The Church Inn gets a mention in a book of Gwent Folklore by Alan Roderick. *'During Whitsun week Mynyddislwyn, Bedwellty and other parts of north-west Gwent held annual "Lamb Ale" competitions, when women were asked to chase after and catch a fat lamb using only their teeth. To make things that little bit more difficult for the women, their hands were bound behind their backs. It was forbidden to chase after pet lambs and it was not always the fittest or fastest women who got their lambs. Some of the women made up for lack of pace by an ability to coax the lambs not to run away from them. The victorious contestant, the woman who held the lamb between her teeth, was named "Lady of the Lamb" for the following year and presided over the feast following the chase, at the Church Inn, where her health was drunk in "Lamb Ale"'.*

*A part of the audience at a Music-hall charity event held upstairs at The Church Inn,
one of many similar events, to raise money for Felindre Hospital.*

*Hubert Morgan performing the honours for Jim Bowers, June Howells and John Purnell
in the lounge at the Church Inn.*

Agricultural Society

The earliest records of the Mynyddisiwyn Agricultural Society date from April 1875 but their origins lie at an earlier date. On 22nd March 1870 there was a Prize Ploughing and Fencing Match for the parishes of Mynyddislwyn, Bedwellty, Aberystruth and Llanhilleth, held near Aberbeeg. The 'Star of Gwent' reported the event -

'Ploughing - *for ploughing half an acre of land in the best and most workmanlike manner within 4½ hours with a pair of horses without a driver. Swing ploughs only to be used without flags, the furrows not exceeding eight inches wide and five inches deep.*

Hedging and ditching - *for hedging and ditching two perches (14 yards) in the best and most workmanlike manner within five hours'.*

Lieut. Temple Stroud of the Blackwood Volunteers (a local colliery manager) was the first President of the organisation.

In March 1871 the 'Monmouthshire Merlin' reported *'First meeting of the Ploughing and Hedging Society for the parishes of Aberystruth, Bedwellty, Mynyddislwyn and Llanhilleth. A Fencing Match at Argoed'.*

The above event attracted the attendance of about 1,000 persons. In the evening the Society held a dinner, chaired by Lieut. Temple Stroud.

In March 1872 the 'South Wales Daily News' reported *'Mynyddislwyn and Bedwellty Ploughing Match... Matches of this description are becoming annual gatherings among the Agricultural Class, This year the match took place on Tuesday 26th. March on land belonging to Twyn Gwyn Farm'.* The three classes for ploughing and one for hedging were limited to the parishes of Mynyddislwyn and Bedwellty.

In 1873 it was decided to hold the Ploughing and Hedging Match as part of a great Agricultural Show to be held at Penllwyn Fawr. It was in effect the first Bedwellty Show. Excursion trains were run from surrounding areas bringing in several thousand spectators to the two Pontllanfraith railway stations.

The 1874 event was held at Gwaelodywaun Farm near Bedwellty Church. The 'South Wales Daily News' gave advance notice *'Forthcoming Show and Ploughing Match... This grand event which comes off on Thursday next on land near the old parish Church bids fair to be one of importance and the members of the Mynyddislwyn and Bedwellty Agricultural Society are deserving of very great credit for the efforts they have put forward year after year to encourage farming pursuits'.*

With events moving more towards a Bedwellty Show, the original idea was reformed as a result of a meeting at the Bird in Hand pub (Pontllanfraith) in April 1875, when the Mynyddislwyn and Bedwellty Agricultural Society was established. Its main aim was ploughing and hedging competitions, and the first Match was 9th March 1876, and since then all matches have been held in March. From this date and for the next 78 years the Presidency of the Society was held by the Morgan family of Tredegar House, by the First Viscount Tredegar, the Second Viscount Tredegar and the Hon. John Morgan.

In the 1877 Match Lady Llanover (who through her late husband owned much land in the area) gave a special prize for 'The Best Yoke of Oxen; to plough on the spot'.

The next few years were difficult times for farmers, with an agricultural depression brought about by a number of bad harvests caused by severe weather conditions with heavy falls of snow each spring and frozen ground, and also by a slump in corn prices as a result of cheap imports from America and Australia. No Matches were held in the years 1886, '87 and '88, and after Matches in 1889 and '90 there were again none in 1891, '92 and '93 because of heavy snowfalls. But from 1894 onwards there was a match each year, except during the First World War years.

Many remembered how the U Boat campaign of the First World War had nearly starved Britain into submission, so at the start of the Second World War it was realised that much grassland would have to be ploughed to increase the supply of home grown food. It was decided to continue with the Mynyddislwyn Society's Ploughing Matches in view of the urgency of increased food production at home even though this area was mainly pastoral. The proceeds of such Matches was donated to a War Charity.

It was in 1942 that the first class for tractors was held, and a new era began within the Society. In 1943 women entered competition for the first time in the Society's history, when Land Girls of the Women's Land Army competed against one another. They competed again in 1944 and 1945, after which date their organisation was disbanded.

The post war years saw the gradual decline of horse ploughing and the change to the tractor. But until the day of the last Match it was good to see a horse team making an appearance - a memory of bygone days.

On the 8th March 1972 the Society held its Centenary Match, but sadly the Match of 1995, held at Church Farm, was to be the last ever of the Mynyddislwyn Agricultural Society.

Although the Centenary Match of the Agricultural Society was held in 1972, there had been years when no Match was held. A special Brass was cast to mark the occasion of the one hundredth Match which was held at Church Farm in 1985.

Mynyddislwyn Agricultural Association,
(EST. 1875).

PRESIDENT — — Rt -Hon. VISCOUNT TREDEGAR.

45th Annual Match

CHURCH FARM, Mynyddislwyn, Nr. Pontllanfraith,

On WEDNESDAY, MARCH 6th, 1929.

FIRST PRIZE

Class   No.

MYNDDISLWYN AGRICULTURAL SOCIETY
(Established 1875)
President: RT.-HON. VISCOUNT TREDEGAR, F.R.S.A., F.I.L.

65TH ANNUAL MATCH

Penrhiwfranc Uchaf and Church Farm, Mynyddislwyn,

On WEDNESDAY, MARCH 9th, 1949

SECOND PRIZE

SPECIAL CLASS.

Class   No.

MYNYDDISLWYN AGRICULTURAL SOCIETY (1872)

The Society is affiliated to the British Ploughing Association

89th ANNUAL
Horse & Tractor Ploughing
Hedging & Ditching Matches

WEDNESDAY, 20th MARCH, 1974

at GWERNA GANOL FARM, MAESYCWMMER, MON.

(off Maesycwmmer—Bedwas Parish Road)

by kind permission of John Jones, Esq.

President—Col. M. JONES, O.B.E., T.D., D.L.

Vice-Presidents :

Sir. Julian S. Hodge, Col. K. D. Treasure, C.B., C.B.E.
Mrs. J. F. Laramy, J. D. Jones, Esq., R. T. Jones, Esq.
B.A., John Lewis, Esq. R. H. Edwards, Esq., J.P., C. P.,
Woodiwiss, Esq., Leslie Davies, Esq., A. R. Gibbs, Esq.
J.P. Illtyd David, Esq., D. O. Packer, Esq., L. Stephens
Esq., Edgar Jones, Esq., Ben Harris Esq., Edgar Evans
Esq., Peter J. Davies, Esq., Richard H. Williams, Esq.,
T. Lyn Rees, Esq., W. T. James, Esq.

Chairman—Fredrick Williams, Esq., Pentwyn Farm.

Vice-Chairman—B. H. Davies, Esq., Gelligynes Farm.

Treasurer—E. B. Edwards, Esq., Pant Farm.

Secretary—Ivor R. Edwards, Esq., Cwmdu Farm,
Maesycwmmer, Hengoed, Glam, CF8 7SN.

Telephone : Hengoed 813224.

D. Matthews & Son (Printers) Ltd. Tel.: Blackwood 3178

A fine team of horses which competed at the Centenary Match at Church Farm in 1972.

344

A glimpse of the past as these horses competed at the Centenary Match at Church Farm in 1972.

Ken Williams, now of Penrhiwffranc, but then of Cwm Brynar Farm, competing in the Youth's Section of the Ditching and Hedging Match in the late 1950s. He was pleaching a well balanced hedge to make it stock-proof.

Ken Williams, a little older and wiser, competes at the 1972 Centenary Match.

Bert Slatcher and Bob Robinson at one of the Society's Matches.

Edmunds

Throughout this book mention has been made of the Edmunds family, one of many families who have had connections with The Mountain over many years, and possibly centuries. While researching this book, the author made contact with members of the Edmunds family who are trying to trace their roots. By pure coincidence, one group of the family are from Australia, and another group are from America. Each knew nothing of the other group, and of that group's searches. But both groups must have a common ancestor from Mynyddislwyn Mountain.

Towards the end of the nineteenth century a certain Walter Edmunds, of Australia, who had family roots at Mynyddislwyn, was planning to get married, and evidently his intended bride's family wanted to know more about his background, so he got in touch with his father, Charles, also in Australia, whose reply to him has survived.

7th November, 1888.
New Norfolk.

My dear son Walter,

Your last letter afforded me a great pleasure. I had a strong belief in Providence that such self-devotion as yours in supporting your father's family would not go un-rewarded. I assume from the knowledge of your character that the young lady's parent knows the circumstances and it meets with his approbation - just the very being I would have counselled you to select. I believe the same young lady called here to see me many months ago, but failed as I had gone to divine service that afternoon. With regard to your request that I would furnish you with an account of my home in England and connections etc. I will do so.

To begin with my father's side. Your great grandfather was possessed of great herds of horses and cattle, which were driven by his herdsmen from one great fair to another - a mart in those days, upwards of one hundred years ago - for the sale and purchase of livestock by which transactions he accumulated considerable wealth, and finally settled in South Wales, purchasing the estate upon which the family have ever since resided. The estate is situate in the parish of Myhyddyalwyn in Monmouthshire. I cannot give you the pronunciation of the 'latter word', it came up to the church walls enclosing the church yard and church.

It would have been considered sacrilegious in those days to bury your dead unless in close proximity to the church, or indeed with regard to the old or better class, or in all events the wealthier class, to be interred within the walls of the church itself. There was a large family vault inside the church, but an alteration in the laws took place, and when your grandfather died he was buried close to the entrance of the church porch as he could not be placed in the family vault. The family homestead was about a mile from the church and extended some distance beyond - how much I cannot say - but I think I would be within compass to state that the property composed and area of about 1^1/$_2$ square miles (1^1/$_2$ miles square).

There was another small estate comprising eighty acres only belonging to your grandfather, and since became very valuable from the discovery of a rich coal seam on the property, of considerable extent. This last information was given to me by a relative in Hobart, a Mr. Jnc. Thomas, a surveyor who was at one time employed by the Tasmanian Government to survey the district of Scotisdale, Ringaroome, etc. and considered a remarkably clever man, and would have attained a good position in this colony only for his terrible indulgence at times in strong drink.

I remember well myself when a boy that my uncle used to send a cart with men and bring home a cart load of coal in the evening from his eighty acres plot of my father's. Upon the death of your great grandfather, the estate fell to the eldest son John. The live and dead stock of the farm, or the value thereof, was the second son's share. My uncle John paid his brother the value, and the youngest son, my father, was left the hard cash in hand, which must have been something handsome as it enabled him to open and stock a large store in the neighbouring mining district where he had the supplying with all classes of goods, groceries, wearing apparel, etc. to the company and miners, numbering a few thousand persons. The men were paid monthly, the account of stores being sent into the company's office also monthly.

The respective sums owing by each miner was deducted from the amount earned by him, and handed over to my father. The store flourished well and my father was in a fair way of making a handsome fortune, when most unexpectedly the whole affair was brought to ruin and my father was beggared, by the villainy of the manager who was a connection by marriage of the family. I must now go back a little and state some incidents that occurred some years before.

There were two young women, daughters of a Mr. Phillips, owner of a fine estate called Chapel Farm. They were left orphans and co-heiresses of the estate. My uncle John married one of them and a man named Llewelyn married the other, and they were to pay a rental for the half of the estate to the other sister, my uncle's now wife.

In the course of years after having borne my uncle five sons, his wife died, leaving her half of the estate by Will to her eldest son Edmund, my uncle being left sole guardian. Now the half of the estate belonging to my uncle's wife contained a forest of splendid oak trees besides the cultivated portion, and I believe the same on the other half. It eventually transpired that this man Llewelyn had been cutting down and selling some of the most valuable trees on the half estate not his, and it was some considerable time before it came to my uncle's knowledge, but when it did he saw for himself and instituted an action against the trespasser and got damages against him, if my memory serves me correctly, of about four thousand dollars, which sum was placed out at interest for his son. Now I resume my pen. I must refer to another incident in the life of my uncle John after his wife's death. A gentleman farmer from the fertile plains of England visited that part of the country contiguous to my uncle's estate and purchased a number of farms half surrounding my uncle's property, and commenced cutting down the high quick set hedges dividing the several farms into cosy well sheltered fields, that perhaps a century or more of experience had dictated to shelter the cattle and also the growing crops from the inclemency of the climate, a very different climate evidently to what he had been accustomed to, throwing a number of fields into one with divisions of open iron fences, handsome gates to enter the different fields, painted white fences and all, which certainly looked very handsome. My uncle, thinking it was the idea, followed suit, not to be outdone

I suppose, against the advice of his old friends of the neighbourhood, practical farmers, and to his sad experience he had ultimately to restore the old fashioned high hedges which took some years to attain to the required degree of shelter, etc. This experiment on the part of Mr. Parkes, the gentleman before alluded to, ruined himself and he left that part of the country a sadder and wiser man. This foolish experiment of my uncle's involved him in difficulties so that the old family property had to be mortgaged to an userer, not often the most merciful of men!

However, when my cousin Edmund came into his property (mother's property), what with the accumulated rent of his half and the amount of damages obtained as mentioned previously, the first thing that he did was to redeem the old family homestead and property and he went himself to reside upon his own property, the 'Chapel Farm'.

Since then of course he must have come into the old family estate, for I suppose long ere this my uncle must have passed away, so that my cousin must be enormously wealthy.

Now I must tell you what a Mr. Thomas told me in this country many years ago, that on the Chapel Farm a very rich seam of bituminous coal was discovered, and a company was formed to work it, yielding my uncle one thousand five hundred dollars a year royalty, and since presumably my uncle's death reverted to him my cousin. This is all I think it necessary to tell you of your father's family on the male side, except perhaps I may incidentally mention that they all belonged to the Church of England, and it was customary for all the surrounding farmers of the same persuasion to meet on certain nights at my uncle's for an all round prayer meeting. I and my brothers were present at some of them, when on a holiday visit, my uncle's premises being the most commodious for that purpose.

I may now tell you all I remember or know about my mother's side. Your great grand father on this side by what I could glean, was a fancy cabinet maker, an inlayer of different coloured woods of a highly artistic character. I have seen some of these remarkably rich cabinets in gentlemen's houses, some of them probably may have been his work. The last time my mother saw her father was when he was just 99 years old. When entering her mother's home she enquired for her father and was told he was in his little workshop engaged on a lady's workbox or something of that sort at which he had amused himself for upwards of two years. He had discontinued business for over forty years, so I presume he must have acquired some wealth to live on. I never saw the old gentleman myself, but I remember after his death my grand mother came on horseback over thirty miles to see her daughter, my mother. I recollect well when she reined up the horse close to some stone steps and a platform on the top purposely for ladies to dismount, that she (my grandmother) sprang out of the saddle with all the smartness of a young person. She must have been then getting on for eighty years of age.

All I know about my mother's family is this - there were four sisters, my mother who had a yearly income for life, and the others had sums of money left them, one married a Mr. Evans, a builder, the others, one married a Mr. Jenkyns, Headmaster of a large school near Merthyr Tydfil, a scholar and author, he wrote a work on the antiquities of Wales, which he had collated from old manuscripts at the different castles, etc. which caused a considerable amount of interest at the time amongst scholars interested in such a subject. I may also mention ad interim, that on my father's side a second cousin, a Mr. Stevens, wrote a book on the harmony of scripture and geology which was noised

349

about a great deal - he was a preacher - then there was a Mr. Davies who was reputed skilful, a second cousin and a brother of his a large linen draper and another of the name of Edmunds, owner of a large hotel and private house under the same roof, who never allowed any of his children to enter the hotel, had a separate entrance. I remember he had a number of beautiful, very beautiful fair haired daughters whom he brought up and educated as young ladies. They had a brother, a remarkably handsome fellow, a druggist.

Now to begin again about my mother's family. One married to Mr. Evans, one to a Mr. Jenkyns, and one to a Mr. Turner. I know not what he had been, but what I now remember of his appearance, I should think something of the quill driving fraternity. He married my aunt Hannah. They kept a large hotel, half way halting place for commercial travellers, tourists, etc. between Newport and the Welsh Hills. As a curiosity, I will give you the different heights in stature of your grand mother's sisters and herself Mrs. Evans stood 5 feet 7 inches

Mrs. Turner stood 5 feet 9 inches
Mrs. Jenkyns stood 6 feet
Mr.? a little one stood 5 feet.

All my male cousins were fully 6 feet and over. On my father's side - one uncle 6 feet 4 inches, the others near 6 feet.

My uncle Turner dying left all, hotel and everything, to my aunt. There were five children, three boys and two girls (at that time they were young men and women). After some time a Mr. George, owner of a large farm in the neighbourhood and also steward for the large Estate of Llanover, the country residence of Sir Benjamin Hall, for which I believe he had a good salary, independent of working his own farm, he made overtures to my aunt for marriage (he being a widower, she consented), and he being a very honourable and of course a man well in, insisted that my aunt should sell everything she possessed and make it over to the children before she entered her new house, so they came in for something decent besides a home for them all there.

About my early days - it can be summed up in a few words. My father died before I was eight years old and some time after, mother married, worse luck, and we three boys packed off to boarding school until I was between 13 and 14 years of age. Afterwards I was apprenticed to a trade. I wanted to be an artist and mother set her face against it. I was two years and a half with this man, his father dying being the owner of a large foundry. Upon his father's death he gave up his painting business and took charge of the foundry, and I was released.

I then went straight to London, went home again, and returned to London again, and from London I came out to these colonies and ultimately here.

Try and get me out of this place by all means. You know not how much I suffer here mentally and otherwise.

With love to all my dear children, including yourself, Clara and her husband.

I am,
Your ever affectionate father,
Charles Edmunds.

Mother you know always lived independently upon her income paid out of Llanover Estate half yearly'.

Charles Edmunds did not arrive in Australia in 1844 of his own free will. His trial papers survive at the Public Record Office, London, and they tell us that he *'Was indicted for feloniously assaulting Matilda Potter, and attempting to discharge at her a pistol loaded with gun-powder and a leaden bullet, with intent to murder her. Second count, stating his intent to be to do her some grievous bodily harm'*.

Charles Edmunds, author of the letter, photographed in Australia in 1873. He never returned home.

Matilda Potter was a widow, living with her mother who kept a coffee shop in Southwark, London. Charles Edmunds had been a lodger there in 1843, but after he left there, he continued to visit to see Matilda. But she did not approve. He visited again, and after an argument she heard the snap of a pistol, and turned to find it within a few inches of her ear. He was apprehended by some gentlemen in the coffee shop until the police arrived. Luckily for Matilda, the cap had not exploded. A witness stated that the nipple was too large, that the cap was perfect, and that there was detonating powder in it. The policeman stated that the touch-hole was clogged up.

Twenty-four-year-old Charles Edmunds was found guilty and Transported for Fifteen Years. But a petition was got up in March 1844, signed by a long list of Newport towns-people, including the Mayor, a number of Magistrates, and many traders. That petition reads *'To the Right Hon. Sir James Graham, Her Majesty's Secretary of State for the Home Department.*

Right Hon. Sir,

The undersigned, your memorialists, respectfully beg permission to lay before you the following statement and petition.

Charles Edmunds, a young man native of this county, now at Newgate under sentence of Transportation for fifteen years, for shooting at Matilda Potter, is the son of respectable parents, and has always until the perpetration of this offence, maintained a character free from criminal practices.

Your memorialists humbly beg you to take this circumstance into consideration, and coupling it with the fact that the deed was committed at a moment of passionate excitement caused by the young woman's refusal to receive his addresses, they beseach you with great deference to recommend to her Majesty a mitagation of the Sentence of the said Charles Edmunds'.

But the petition did no good, and away he went, never to see Mynyddislwyn again.

Charles must have been a 'somebody' to be the subject of that petition, or maybe his father was. The son of a landless farm labourer would not have had that attention from such a list of signatories.

In October 1865 his son Walter George Edmunds was born, in the District of Kyneton, Tasmania. Charles was then 45 years of age, married to 25 year old Ellen, formerly Miss Lewis. By the marriage they already had baby Clara, aged 2½ years old, (mentioned in the last line of the letter). By a previous marriage, Charles had children Margaret, aged 17; Charles, aged 15; Lavinia, aged 13, and Emma Louise aged 9 years.

So it appears that when Charles had served his time, he did not return home. At the date of this letter, November 1888, Walter was 23 years old and planning his own marriage.

In the letter it is possible that Charles has exaggerated a bit in order to create a good impression with his son's future in-laws. However, parts of it can be authenticated.

Early in the letter Charles mentions Mr. Jnc. Thomas, a relative that he met in Hobart. That was John Thomas, the third child of Morgan and Mary Thomas of Ynysddu. John was the younger brother of William Thomas (Islwyn the poet). Islwyn's own family tree mentions brother John being a Surveyor in Tasmania.

In the letter is reference to Mr. Phillips of Chapel Farm and his two daughters. On the inside wall of Saint Tudor's is a memorial plaque to the Phillips family of Chapel Farm. Daniel Phillips died in 1820. He has a mention elsewhere in this book for selling land in 1810 to Benjamin Hall on which Hall built the houses of The Spiteful. The same plaque mentions his daughter Mary and her husband Edmund Llewelyn. An adjoining memorial plaque names the other daughter Margaret, and her husband John Edmunds of Pant Glas Farm.

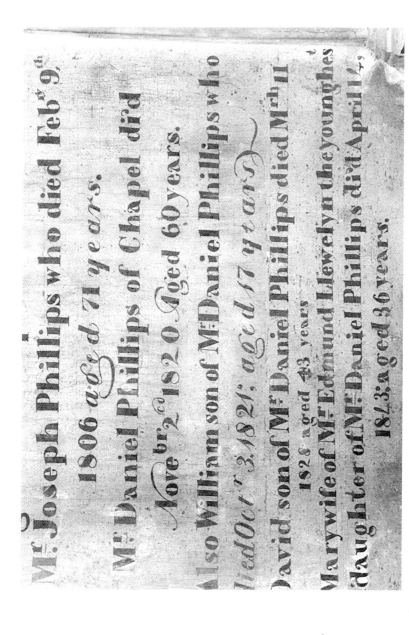

Mr. Joseph Phillips who died Feb.ry 9th 1806 aged 71 years.

Mr. Daniel Phillips of Chapel di'd Novr 2 1820 Aged 60 years.

Also William son of Mr Daniel Phillips who died Octr 3 1821; aged 17 years

David son of Mr. Daniel Phillips died Mch 11 1828 aged 43 years

Mary wife of Mr. Edmund Llewelyn the youngest daughter of Mr. Daniel Phillips di'd April 14, 1843; aged 36 years.

Part of a memorial plaque inside St. Tudor's Church, in memory of the Phillips family of Chapel Farm. Daniel Phillips, died 1820, sold land on which Benjamin Hall built The Spiteful. At the bottom of the memorial is mentioned Daniel's daughter Mary, wife of Edmund Llewelyn. This couple are mentioned in Charles Edmunds's letter.

353

TO THE MEMORY OF

MARGARET
WIFE OF JOHN WATTERS of Pantglase in this Parish
WHO DIED NOVEMBER 6ᵀᴴ 1774 AGED 49 YEARS.

ALSO THE ABOVE JOHN WATTERS
WHO DIED DECEMBER 27ᵀᴴ 1790, AGED 69 YEARS.

ALSO ELIZABETH WIFE OF THOMAS EDMUNDS,
OF THE ABOVE NAMED PLACE AND YOUNGEST DAUGHTER OF THE
ABOVE JOHN WATTERS WHO DIED NOVEMBER 28ᵀᴴ 1806, AGED 59 YEARS.

ALSO THE ABOVE THOMAS EDMUNDS WHO
DIED NOVEMBER 14ᵀᴴ 1808, AGED 44 YEARS.

ALSO TO THE MEMORY OF MARGARET WIFE OF JOHN EDMUNDS OF
OF THE ABOVE NAMED PLACE AND ELDEST DAUGHTER OF
Mᴿ DANIEL PHILLIPS OF CHAPEL FARM IN THIS PARISH WHO DIED
JULY 6ᵀᴴ 1826, AGED 24 YEARS.

A L S O
OF THE ABOVE JOHN EDMUNDS WHO DIED
MAY THE 27ᵀᴴ 1866, AGED 77
YEARS

Another memorial plaque inside St. Tudor's Church, showing a link between the Watters and Edmunds families of Mynyddislwyn. Towards the bottom of the plaque is mentioned Margaret and John Edmunds, mentioned in Charles Edmunds' letter. Margaret was the sister of Mary Llewelyn, mentioned in the previous photograph.

This memorial stone in St. Tudor's church names Margaret wife of John Edmunds. Margaret was the daughter of Daniel Phillips of Chapel Farm, and the couple are mentioned in Charles' letter. This John Edmunds, Charles' uncle, was the son of Thomas Edmunds, making Thomas the grandfather of Charles who Wrote the letter. But we still don't know Charles' father's name. This stone leaves no doubt that Pant Glas was Charles's paternal family home.

These people are also mentioned in a document of 1829 that is in the author's possession -

'WHEREAS Daniel Phillips, late of the Chapel, in the parish of Monythusloin in the County of Monmouth, Gentleman, deceased, and by his last Will and Testament bearing date on or about the Eleventh day of October One thousand eight hundred and twenty, and executed and attested in the manner prescribed by Law for devising Freehold Estates, gave and devised, subject to the payment of his Debts and Funeral Expenses ALL that Freehold Messuage, Tenement, Farm and Lands called the Chapel, wherein he then resided, situate in the said parish of Monythusloin, unto his wife Mary Phillips for and during the term of her Widowhood, and from and after her intermarriage or decease, which should first happen, he gave and devised the same unto his two Brothers, William Phillips and John Phillips, their Heirs and Assigns, upon the trusts and to and for the uses and intents and purposes therein and hereinafter mentioned (that is to say) TO the use of his Son David Phillips for his Life, with remainders to his first and other sons, and in default of such issue, To all and every the Daughter and Daughters of the said David Phillips, as Tenants in common, and in default of such issue TO THE USE AND BEHOOF of the said Testator's own right Heirs and Assigns for ever. AND WHEREAS the said David Phillips died in or about the second day of March One thousand eight hundred and twenty eight, unmarried and without having had issue, whereupon the said Messuage, Farm and Lands descended between his two Sisters, Margaret the wife of John Edmunds, and Mary the wife of Edmund Llewellyn, subject to the Estate of their Mother, the said Mary Phillips therein during her Widowhood. AND WHEREAS the said Margaret Edmunds has departed this life leaving her husband, the said John Edmunds, and an infant Son her surviving... '

Charles's Aunt Hannah re-married to a Mr George 'owner of a large farm in the neighbourhood and also steward for the large Estate of Llanover'. Such a person was Edmund George who farmed the 101 acres of The Pant. He was the Woodward to Abercarne Estate (before it became incorporated into the Llanover Estate). This same Edmund George was one of many who gave evidence on behalf of Benjamin Hall in the court case against Sir Henry Protheroe over the building of the houses at Spiteful in 1810. The first part of Edmund George's sworn affidavit reads 'Edmund George of the Parish of Monythusloin in the County of Monmouth, Yeoman, maketh oath and saith that he lived as Woodward about twenty years with the late Samuel Glover, Esquire, and perfectly knows every part of the Abercarne Estate now in the possession of the said Defendant (Benjamin Hall)... '

In another part of the letter Charles mentions his mother's sisters, one of whom married a man 'of the name of Edmunds, owner of a large hotel and private house under the same roof'. Unfortunately neither Mr. Edmund's Christian name nor hotel name are mentioned, but he could have been William Edmunds, the owner of the Greyhound Hotel at Pontllanfraith (just outside this book's area). His wife was Sarah. William has been mentioned in this book as owning Ty Gwyn and Pant yr Esk Farms.

They had a son Edmund Edmunds. After the Chartist uprising and march on Newport in November 1839, the leaders were caught and stood trial for Treason. Others of lesser importance also stood trial. One such man was Edmund

Edmunds of the Greyhound. He had two different offences against him. He was charged with allowing a room at the Greyhound to be used as a Chartist's Lodge. His mother swore an affidavit in which she said -

'Has seen Frost at the Lodge once and Vincent twice... There were a good many Chartists in the Lodge on that Saturday night... There was so much noise in the house that Witness could not hear the noise outside. The people left the House about 7 o'clock and said they were going to Newport'.

A second charge against him was that he was armed and at the front of the marching Chartists as they approached Newport. In a sworn affidavit, Israel Furmen of Gelligroes said -

'I know Edmund Edmunds of the Greyhound. He was there, he was armed. I can't say whether he had a musket or a sword, I cannot say. He was in the front with Mr. Frost... He was along with the rest of the Commanders in the front. The mob halted by the Waterloo (Pub) the Prisoner (Edmunds) with them. There Prisoner cry'd out "All you with muskets come forward in front and the pikemen next and you as have clubs and bludgeons stop in the rear"'.

So Edmund Edmunds could well have been Charles's cousin. With a skeleton like that in the cupboard there is no way that Walter's intended wife and in-laws would have been impressed, so it is understandable that Charles chose not to mention it in his letter.

Finally, his home on Mynyddislwyn is not named, but with land bordering up to the Church, it was undoubtedly Pant Glas Farm.

Faith Coller, formerly Edmunds, is an artist living in London. She has worked with the Australian branch of her family to try to unravel the mystery of who Charles Edmunds was. Following a visit to Mynyddislwyn she wrote the following.

'In his letter to his son Walter, written in 1888, our great grandfather Charles Edmunds gives us quite a lot of information about the family, but tantalisingly omits such items as his mother's maiden name, and the names of his brothers. What we do know of him is that he was one of three sons - he does not mention any sisters. His father died young when Charles was not quite eight years old. His father was the youngest of three brothers, one of whom was called John, whose wife's maiden name was Phillips. They had a son Edmund. (This was the Chapel Farm connection).

Charles says that there was a family vault in the church but that because of a new law, for legal reasons, his father was buried outside the church, not far from the south door.

When I visited the area I went straight to Mynyddislwyn. There is a church with a square tower and a pub next to it. I found exactly where Charles described, a gravestone, flat on the ground, with the wording -

To the Memory of Thomas Edmunds of this Parish
Died September 19th 1828, aged 35 years.

All you that by me pass along
Pray think how soon my life has gone
God does not always warning give
Therefore be careful how you live.

It then gives the names of a William Edmunds and his wife Mary, buried there at a later date. Presumably, any relatives buried before Thomas were buried in the vault inside the church.

When I examined the Parish Records I found the record of the burial of Thomas Edmunds of Ynysddu, on 26th September 1828, aged 35. Reckoning that he was born about 1793, I found a Thomas, son of Thomas Edmunds, baptised 20th September 1792. There was no other Thomas near that date, so this one must have died just before his 36th birthday. I think that there is no doubt that we have found Charles's father. A few years previously, in 1788, a John, son of Thomas Edmunds, was baptised on 20th June. Unfortunately, there is no record of another son, and Charles said that his father was the youngest of three brothers.

Going back further, there was a Thomas who could have fathered these two. He was Thomas, son of John Edmonds alias Dywedydd, baptised 1749. The same father had another son Thomas, baptised 1747. Presumably the latter died an infant. John Edmond of Dywedydd was buried 23rd Feb. 1756, with his wife Mary buried 1st June 1752.

Do not be put off by the spelling of the name. Almost without exception the spelling is Edmond or Edmund in the 1700s, sometimes with the two spellings on one document e.g. the vicar wrote Edmond and the bridegroom wrote Edmund. Early 1800s we start to get Edmunds consistently.

I examined the baptism records 1743-1853 and found no mention of a Charles Edmunds, but did not look after the marriage records after 1815, so at some later date I may yet find Thomas' marriage around 1819-20, as Charles was born around 1821, if he was nearly eight when his father died. (The same date fits in with Charles's trial, being a 24 year old in 1844)'.

Another branch of the Edmunds family, from America, have been trying to trace their roots. On a visit to Mynyddislwyn early in the year 2001 they passed on some letters that had been written by Edmund Edmunds of this area, in 1904, to his cousin in America, containing very interesting facts about the Edmunds family. It would be lovely to prove that the people mentioned below were related to Charles Edmunds. The first letter reads -

Machen,
near Newport,
10th April, 1904

Dear Cousin,

Your very kind and interesting letter, duly to hand, and am pleased to find you still alive and well after all these years since last we met in 1878. I, and my father before me, had a strong love for Aunt Mary, your mother, especially myself, having passed much of my young days with her on the farm near here. I remember well the day she left with Aunt and Uncle Lewis from Newport in a ship loaded with the Rhymney Iron Company, under whom my father served. That was in 1848. What changes since, and all are dead. I note your remarks about Aunt Viah. She has gone now, I know. When she left home in 1835, it was an Uncle and Aunt William and, I think, Catherine Rowlands. Anyway, this Miss Rowlands married one of the Edmunds' of Ty Gwyn (the home of my people for centuries and close where I now live). The descendants of this Rowlands are now in Ohio. I am astonished but pleased that your father and step-mother are still alive. Your father must be over 80 years old. Give them both my love, and tell your father the Crumlin railroad bridge still stands as good as ever.

I will now say a little about myself, so that when anything should happen to me (the oldest male of my name and family) you and your children can let your thoughts bring you over here, if you cannot come in body, and know that I rest with my fathers in the old churchyard of Mynyddislwyn, where my people, with few exceptions, have gathered for centuries.

Two hundred, one hundred and fifty, one hundred years ago, the Edmunds, barring the Lord of the Manor, were the principal landowners in the parish of Mynyddislwyn (around where we were born), and all underlying minerals to the extent of three million tons of coal to every acre, and my people owned roughly 1500 acres, with the home steads. My great-grandfather's first wife was a lady named James, daughter of a good Mynyddislwyn family of position. The marriage took place about 1786. My grandfather was the only issue to live. Unfortunately, his mother died in 1796, and his father got entangled with one of the servants of Ty Gwyn, and after a host of illegitimate children, he married her shortly before he died in 1815, more for his soul's sake than for the hussy he made his second wife. The redeeming point of his life was this he kept the property intact, and a fine one it is today, with the coals being worked. At his death, this woman, who hated my grandfather, he being heir to the property if she had never got my great-grandfather in her meshes, did all she could to undo the work of centuries, in litigation and riotous living with her children, and unfortunately grandfather was no better, though married. Anyhow, between them all, in 1839, the lawyers let the hounds loose for the last time. The old homestead with the lands and minerals went for a song, and my grandfather, a beggar except what he was heir to after his mother Margaret James of Pen-y-Fan, but which was no good to him then because it was all minerals not then worked, and not wanted then as they are now. Could he have done anything with it, I would not have this tale to tell. In 1806 Watkin James sold his Pen-y Fan homestead of 165 acres for £2,000, but reserved the mineral rights for himself and heirs. All the James's are dead and I am the nearest to them living. My grandfather, father and myself knew of the reservation of all minerals in 1806, but what was the good of them unworked? So grandfather died penniless in 1849, my father, the eldest son, in 1861, his only brother, Edmund, having died in 1851. About twelve years ago, deep collieries having been opened, with more coal wanted. The 165 acres had changed hands four times since my people in 1806, but thanks to our law, the reservation had to be respected for a hundred years. I was going to sea at that time, but they soon found me out, and wanted to lease a portion of the coals. It was an uphill job to satisfy the law. The principal point was pedigree, but otherwise I had no opposition. I saw the lawyers would never get through, so resolved to abandon the sea, and stop on land, and push it to a successful issue, which I did in 1896, since which time I have leased nearly all the minerals, but little of them are yet worked, and it will take 40 years to work them all out, long after I am gone. I had to trace a legitimate pedigree from 1718 down to myself, my brother and my two cousins, Henry and Edmund Edmunds, alone share with me. Had it been Freehold, I would have taken all, as it is in law, but I share with the sons of grandfather's sons. By the time (in 40 years hence, say) all minerals are worked out at the rate of Royalties to us, the affair will return us about a million pounds. Neither my brother, my cousins nor myself will live to see derived the full benefits, but the males of Edmunds living will. I draw at present roughly £4,000 to £5,000 annually from it. As *already stated, it is only a little of the wreck that that woman and grandfather Edmunds left to his two sons. My cousins in America knew nothing of it until I advised them, and had it not been for me, neither my brother nor they would have had a copper. They were in America and I did all the work. It very nearly finished me. The worry was too much, and I am not the same man since. My cousins however have treated me right, since, and feel very grateful. I had my eldest cousin from Ohio here lately. He returned about a month ago. He is not married. The youngest I have never seen. He is married and has a family of daughters and no son. I now conclude with best love to you, dear Mary, from my wife, who is fairly well, from my children and self to you all. I may come to see you once again ere I die. I should much like to, but am now 61 years old. Reply for certain as soon as you can. I remain,*

Your loving cousin,
Edmund Edmunds

In December 1904 he wrote again.

Pontllanfraith,
Mynyddislwyn.
13th December, 1904.

'A History (in brief) And The Pedigree Of The Edmunds' of Ty Gwyn In The Parish Of Mynyddislwyn In The County Of Monmouthshire, South Wales.

Since my promise to you to furnish the pedigree of my family and your mother's (my Aunt), I have again inspected the Rolls of our Manor commencing in 1610, also the register of our old parish church of Mynyddislwyn, commencing at 1630. I find by the former the Edmunds were at Ty Gwyn from the earliest date, living on their own lands, and by the latter I find marriages, births and deaths, with burials equally so. It is therefore a matter of opinion at what early date in the history of our parish the first of my family, and your mother's, settled at Ty Gwyn, but sufficient for me and mine to know they resided for centuries on their own lands, and of which Ty Gwyn was the homestead.

The earliest document I possess is dated 1742, a sheepskin, and calling a Court Baron on behalf of the Lord of the Manor, one Henry de Burgh, and held at Newbridge.

In this document appears the name of my Great-Great-Grandfather Henry Edmunds (1), one of the Homagers of Ty Gwyn. I have failed to know who was his wife owing to the faded condition of the Register. At that date the whole of the property was held by him (some 1,500 acres), he being an only son.

That Henry Edmunds had a daughter, born 1742, who died in infancy. In 1744 another daughter was born, named Margaret, who lived, and married Edward Hyatt, Curate of Mynyddislwyn. That Edward Hyatt was a member of an old family of the adjoining parish of Bedwas, lived to be a vicar, died and was buried at Bedwas. His wife outlived him, to die at Pontypool at an advanced age, childless.

In 1748 a son was born named Henry Edmunds (2). That was my Great Grandfather.

In 1752 another son was born, and named Edmund Edmunds, the last child to be born to them.

The forenamed Henry Edmunds (2), my Great-Grandfather, married in 1778 Margaret James, the eldest daughter of Mr. Watkin James of Pen-y-Fan Isaf, in the parish of

Mynyddislwyn, a gentleman of good family, and living on his own lands. His wife Mary was the daughter of Squire Williams of Maesruddud, and at present one of the wealthiest families of the adjoining parish of Bedwellty.

This Henry Edmunds (2), my Great-Grandfather, being the eldest son, retained more of the estate than his brother Edmund. In 1780 he had a daughter, Viah, who died unmarried in 1806. She was buried with her mother (Margaret, nee James) who died in 1796, inside our old parish church at Mynyddislwyn.

In 1787 a son was born (my Grandfather) and names Henry Edmunds (3), he being the only son and last child by the first wife.

During his life and up to his death, the entire estate of 1,500 acres, with mineral rights, were owned by my Great-Great-Grandfather (Henry 1) he being the only son, but with the coming by him of two sons, my Great-Grandfather, Henry (2), being the eldest, retained all the lands to the north of the road leading from Newbridge to Pontllanfraith, with the youngest son, Edmund, taking all lands to the south of said road. Edmund married about 1779 a wealthy woman of an old Caerleon family named Williams, and founded a younger branch of my family, living firstly at Abercarne Uchaf, and latterly at a country seat then held by Benjamin Hall (Lord Llanover). This property Edmund sold to the then Lord of the Manor, Samuel Glover. He then went to his other property at Ty Gwyn. He left one son and one daughter, and departed this life having been drowned at Abercarne. He was buried with his wife and eldest son Edmund (died in infancy in 1780) inside our parish church of Mynyddislwyn. I may add of this younger branch of the family, that it has nearly died out now, the only one now surviving being my mother-in-law, Mrs. Jacob James, now 80 years of age.

I now again take to pedigree. After my Great-Grandmother's death, unfortunately for all the Edmunds' since and in particular myself, as the eldest now living, my Great Grandfather Henry (2) succumbed to the evil influences of a servant woman named Joan Evans, by whom he had several illegitimate children. However, I presume he had trouble with his conscience, and not caring to leave this world living in adultery, unfortunately for us all, he married her in 1804, after which he had two sons born in wedlock. He left a will, which was proved 'invalid', and died in December 1815, aged 69 years, to be buried at Beulah Baptist Chapel (the first of his race not buried at the old church).

I now deal with my Grandfather, Henry (3), the only child by his father's lawful first wife. Grandfather was unfortunately a wayward and riotous man from his youth to his end. He married, in 1810, Cecelia Oldfield of Abercarne, by whom he had five daughters and two sons, your mother being one daughter, and my father Henry (4) being the eldest son. Grandfather died in 1849, aged 61 years, and was buried at the feet of his father in the Beulah Chapel. Grandmother died a few years later in 1853 and was buried with him.

Those left to perpetuate the name are all of the older branch, namely myself as the oldest, my brother Henry (5), and my uncle Edmund's sons in Ohio, Henry (6) and Edmund. I have two sons. My cousins in Ohio, Henry, is a bachelor, while Edmund is married, but with no son. Therefore it lays with myself and my brother to keep the old name going.

Edmund Edmunds

Another letter, written at Pontllanfraith, is not dated.

A Commentary, Handed Down, Of My Great-Grandfather, Also One On What Has Been Handed Down, And What I Know By Personal Knowledge Of My Great Grandfather And My Father.

Firstly, my Great-Grandfather; he appears to have been a steady man for one of his time and position, but of a fiery temperament that would brook no interference. He married a good woman, who died at an early age, but not before the evil influences of one of the servant maids over my Great-Grandfather made itself felt, sufficient to embitter her life, and lay the foundation of subsequent ruin of my family. When he died in 1815, intestate, he thereby left all his copyhold lands to my Grandfather and the two sons born in wedlock by the servant, and all freehold lands to my Grandfather, according to the law of the Manor of Abercarne. My Grandfather was then married, residing at his own place, named Bryn Gwyn (above Newbridge), and that woman got to law. Her plea was that she had nothing to live on. Grandfather had no doubt looked on her as an interloper (and rightly too) and possibly had to feel the effects of her undue influence over his parents' lives. Anyhow, she claimed dower. Grandfather resisted, and at the same time led a riotous life, not caring how things went, as long as he had his cash, and she with her family, some 5 or 6 girls and 3 boys, not caring likewise. Besides being now fairly in the grip of the lawyers, who no doubt saw that they had fools to deal with, and the sooner the better they were deprived of their estates. A mortgage of £1,000 was rose on Ty Gwyn, which was all wasted. Ty'r Brachty estate was sold; Pen y Fan Fach sold; Cefn Coch sold; Troed y Rhiw (Freehold) sold. During all Grandfather led a careless life, the woman and her crowd doing likewise, and to crown all, the blaguard lawyers of that day, Mostyn and McDonald, did their best likewise. Meanwhile, the Manor of Abercarne had changed hands, from Samuel Glover to Benjamin Hall, who no doubt plucked such fools as my people, and the time came for the mortgager of the £1,000 on Ty Gwyn to die, as well as the wretched servant girl that was by now an old woman. The name of the mortgager was Lawrence Foord. He died in 1835, about the same time as the old Joan. He left his estate to his son. In the meantime and during all those years, our Grandfather (Henry 3) did nothing but squander his patrimony, until there was no more to squander. From my own documents, the son of this Foord called in the mortgage in 1836, possibly due to the interest not being paid. His demand not being complied with, a sale was effected after a couple of years of difficulty to find a purchaser, Grandfather and the two sons by the second marriage refusing to sign a surrender. At last, in 1839, the High Court, through the two lawyers already named, sold the property, under pressure, along with Bryn Gwyn (where my father and your mother were born), and Ty Brachty, in all about 120 acres, and unfortunately the mineral rights also, for £1,475 to a fellow named John Llewellin, Estate Agent to the Lord of the Manor Benjamin Hall, and it is in his family to this day.

My Great-Grandfather laid the foundation of the family ruin through his reckless intrigue with the wretched woman, and my Grandfather, a worthless, gay, reckless character from his youth to his grave, along with her, consumed it. The work of centuries wrecked in a lifetime. I feel it the most, firstly because I know most about the family history, and secondly because I am the eldest now living, and thirdly because I am now living on the ground and under the shadow, practically, of the old parish church, and by my surroundings am put constantly in mind of the wreck, as enunciated.

As to Grandfather, Henry Edmunds (3) better known as Harry Emwnt-fach, I recollect him well, as he used to come to see us at Newport. He generally remained two or three days, and would leave in the evening, be on the road all night as a rule, and half tipsy getting home, but that was his mode all his life. I presume my father had no influence over him in his old age. After he sold Bryn Gwyn, he lived for a short time in Newbridge, and Aunt Mary with them, after which my father bought the cottage called Ysgubor Goch for them all to live in. My father kept them and buried them. Grandfather died in 1849 aged 61, and Granny in 1853. If I mistake not, you were born in that cottage. I know your mother left there to come to Newport with your father, on their way to America, and instead of following my father's instructions to lock up the house and bring the key to my father in Newport, my Aunt, (your mother) gave the same to Jacob James (who later became my father-in-law) who was then living at Ty Gwyn, close by, in the promise of giving the key to my father when they met. My father had not being enrolled as owner, which I presume Jacob James knew, and James refused to give up the key. The consequence was that my father lost possession, and remained unfriendly with James until his (my father's) death. A further consequence of your mother's act was that my father had made provision for me to inherit it, but I never did.

As to my father (Henry 4) and his life. He was born in 1818 at Bryn Gwyn and had to leave his home aged about 15, partly because of his father's reckless life, and found a home with his mother's twin brother Anthony Oldfield in Newport. He was, I am pleased to say, quite an opposite man from his father. A man with strong Welsh religious views and upright to his fellow men. A fiery temper was about his only weak point, and perhaps too free with his money. He took service under the old Rhymney Iron Company, first in a very minor position, but soon rose to be next to the Agent, on a good salary, a position he held to within a short time of his death in November 1861, aged 43 years. His death being sudden was brought about by excitement at the municipal election of that night.

My mother's maiden name was Mary Stevens, a native of Newport. Her parents were Welsh, natives of Crickhowell. She made a careful industrious wife and a good mother to us children, and myself in particular. She remained my father's widow for 41 years and died in 1901 at the age of 81. Out of her eight children, two boys and four girls survive.

There is something in blood and pedigree which only those can feel that can form a chain of legitimate record for births, marriages and deaths, such as this. An old family living from father to son down through centuries on their own lands, never going beyond their own parish for their wives or graves, doing the same son after son. Then in a cursed and evil hour, the woman steps in with her wiles, influences the man to the ruin of his prosperity. Such has been the fate of the Edmunds family.

Edmund Edmunds
Pontllanfraith
Mynyddislwyn.

The final letter to return home was written by Edmund from Pontllanfraith to his cousin in Lockport, New York.

'Dear Cousin,
    I now enclose you a form of pedigree along with other information, all concerning those of my race who are long since gone.

You will see by the history that I have nothing to thank my Grandfather for, he having done all he could to ruin the whole patrimony belonging to his family. The minerals I hold with my brother and cousins, and which he would have wasted if he could, did not come to us as heirs-at-law after six long years of legal and sometimes doubtful fighting, from any of the Edmunds property, but from a Great-Great Grandfather on the maternal side, Mr. Watkin James of Pen y Fan Isaf. That property was sold in 1806, but the surface only, comprising 150 acres, all mineral rights being reserved for himself and heirs.

This family, two sons and three daughters, (the two former as bad as Grandfather), all died without issue, except the oldest girl who was my Grandfather's mother (Margaret James). It is therefore for want of issue on the James' part that we have come in as next male kin of Watkin James for the property, according to real estate law, and besides which the custom of our Manor of Abercarne. Had it been freehold instead of Copyhold, I would inherit the whole. As it is, the difference between copyhold and freehold is so small, I am not sure along with circumstances extant, whether I am not the sole heir, but rather anything but litigation. If you win you lose. The lawyers see to that. Had he done what Watkin James did and reserved the mineral rights, things would not be so bad. Even he wasted the surface, but no, he sold his soul to follow his worthless life, and not caring one iota what became of his children, much less himself. I think I have told you pretty well all I have to and hope it will interest you all.

I only moved here the end of October last from Machen. The house I now live in belonged some 60 or 80 years ago to a relative of my family, Henry James by name. He died years ago and it now belongs to the heir-at-law.

I should like now to end my days here under the shadow of the old church, where I shall one day be, but would like to visit the States before I go.

With kind regards to all. I remain,
Edmund Edmunds'.

Edmund Edmunds's letters leave many unanswered questions. He did not name the sons of the servant maid Joan Evans, either the illigitimate ones or the two legitimate ones after her marriage to Henry Edmunds (2). Presumably they all had the Edmunds surname. In 1839 Ty Gwyn was lost to the Edmunds family. However, the Tithe Apportionment Book tells us that in 1839 Ty Gwyn was owned by William Edmunds of the Greyhound public house, Pontllanfraith (whose son Edmund Edmunds was connected with the Chartists). That document must be accepted as correct. If the Tithe enumerator made his list early in the year, and Ty Gwyn was lost later in the same year, both statements would be correct.

William Edmunds *could* have been the eldest of the servant maid's sons. In the letter from Australia this author has speculated that Charles Edmunds could have been related to the above named William (a cousin), thereby linking two branches of the Edmunds family in Australia and America. But it will be for others to prove.

It is proposed by the members of the Sunday School, and Congregation of Mynyddislwyn Church, to make a present of suitable Books to Mr. Edmund Edmunds, Superintendent of the above School, and Churchwarden of the said Parish, as a slight acknowledgment of his unwearied services and self-denying efforts, in the above two Capacities; as well as in appreciation of his readiness at all times to do every thing in his power, to promote the Cause of Education, and every other good work in the Parish. With this view the above friends respectfully solicit the kind Contributions of those who are disposed to further a meritorious Cause.

Paid	£	s	d	Paid	£	s	d
Reverend I. Griffiths	0	5	0	Mrs Lewis (Newbridge)	0	1	0
,, I. Jones	0	2	6	John Howells Church	0	1	0
,, & E. John	0	1	0	Mary Radgen	0	1	0
,, A. Rowlands	0	1	0	John Rees	0	1	0
I Lewis Schoolmaster	0	2	6	Joseph Rees	0	1	0
Aneurin Elias	0	2	6	Noah Elias	0	1	0
Peter Jones Commercial	0	2	6	Anne Elias	0	0	6
Joseph Workman	0	2	6	Anne Williams	0	1	0
Mr. Jones Post Office	0	2	6	Lemuel Lewis	0	0	6
William Elias Troedyrhiw	0	2	6	John Thomas	0	0	6
Miss Howells Factory	0	2	6	William Howells	0	0	6
Henry Harries	0	2	0	Thomas Howells	0	0	6
Miss Jenkins	0	1	6	Anne Campbell	0	0	6
Michael Richards	0	1	6	William Jones	0	0	6
Phillip Rees	0	1	0	Meriam Davies	0	0	6
William Jones	0	1	0	Watkin Lewis	0	0	6
Henry Morgan	0	1	0	Margaret Thomas	0	0	6
Miss Margaret Jenkins	0	1	0	Mary Jones	0	0	6
Mrs. Davies	0	1	0	Margaret Richards	0	0	6
Mary Lewis	0	1	0	Thomas Lewis	0	0	3
A Friend	0	1	0	A Friend			
William Edmunds	0	1	0	Margaret Howells	0	0	6
George Elias	0	1	0	Total amount	2	16	7

Page from Edmunds family bible which lists the contributors to a collection at Mynyddislwyn Church.

Wartime Memories

Memories of Mrs. Holly John nee Pritchard

I remember the War as being something nasty that was happening elsewhere away from Mynyddislwyn. There was only one occasion when I felt the 'real war' came near to us. It was one evening as I was getting ready for bed and my mother was looking out of the bedroom window. She seemed very upset and didn't want me to look, but I was just able to see flares and flashes in the sky behind the Blacksmith's Arms and the Church beyond. This was most likely to have been one of the heavy bombing raids on Bristol.

I knew of two army camps at Mynyddislwyn during the War. The first that I remember was on the Lemage, where the new graveyard is now. One Sunday afternoon there had been a fair covering of snow. We were in Sunday School when we heard that there was to be a snowball fight afterwards. On our way home, waiting for us behind the wall, was the army cook. He was wearing a white jacket and chef's hat that seemed to blend in with the snow. He must have had plenty of time on his hands because he had made a pile of snowballs that he lobbed at us with much excitement.

The second camp that I remember was in the field next to Church Farm. This is where they had a searchlight. They must have held some sort of public event because I can remember being there one evening with my parents and a large gathering of other people. Amidst all the activity I could see beams of light criss-crossing in the sky. In the gloomy distance there was a soldier, seated and swivelling around, on what seemed to be Frank Symons's (Graig Farm) hay-cutting machine, but with the long barrel of a gun attached.

One of my favourite places to play was the piece of open ground between our house (Ty Bach, now Ty Siriol) and the Blacksmith's Arms. I spent many a happy hour picking whinberries that grew next to the long wall near the Church, and gathering blackberries from the various patches. There was also one special spot where sweet wild raspberries grew. At the end, next to the Blacksmith's Arms garden wall, was a large patch of scrubby rose bushes, where I helped my sister Rosemary gather rose-hips to take to school as part of a nationwide effort to make rose-hip syrup.

In readiness for the expected invasion, several old coal trams had been placed around on this bit of land. I thought that they were great fun to play on. There were also several rolls of barbed wire by a tram where the road narrowed to go to Church Farm. In the event of an invasion, the trams and barbed wire would have been used to barricade the road, in the hope that it would impede the enemy.

Motorists did not use their headlights during the black-out, so to help them see the edge of the road, white washed stones lined the verge by our hayfield.

No one had television during the War (we did not have electricity until the 1950s). We did have a wireless powered by a battery and an accumulator. The accumulator had to be charged up from time to time by Mr. Moore of Gelligroes Mill. The wireless was used very sparingly so that we did not run out of 'juice'.

The most popular programme was The News, and when we heard the 'pips' we had to be quiet as my father told us to 'shush'. I can still see him sitting near the wireless, listening intently, and looking grim if the news was bad. He had served in France with the Royal Engineers during the First World War, so knew only too well what it would have been like. One programme that we all enjoyed listening to was Tommy Hanley in ITMA.

One of the happiest of occasions that I can remember was the Victory Tea that took place in the Church Vestry. Lots of people were there (some I had never met before), and everyone seemed very happy.

- - - - -

Memories of Mrs. Rosemary Scull nee Pritchard.
One of my memories of war-time is of seeing groups of our soldiers marching smartly, all in step, past our house (Ty Bach).

The American soldiers had a camp at Penllwyn, across the valley, and I can remember seeing a group of them on a route march, but they were far more casual and just seemed to amble along. Nevertheless, the American uniforms looked far smarter that the course material of our soldiers' uniforms.

Often, over the channel from Newport, silver grey barrage balloons hovered, and some nights we could hear the sound of flack. The engine noise of German aeroplanes made a different sound to our aircraft. I remember feeling terrified when I heard the drone of a German plane and would run with head pounding to try and hide in the nearest hedge.

- - - - -

Memories of Mrs. Margaret Fritz nee Pritchard.
I will always remember where I was when I heard that War had been declared. I had attended the 11 o'clock service at Mynyddislwyn Parish Church with my sister Rosemary, and we were on our way home, walking down the Church hill, and coming up to Harry Allen's cottage (Coed yr Idder), when we met Megan Suter coming the other way. She said excitedly to us 'War is declared, and my Gran is crying'. Little did I think then, at age 14, what a big change this was to make to my life.

It was feared that the Germans would use gas attacks on the people, so we were all measured for gas masks. When the gas masks were issued to us we had to carry them to school every day. We were fortunate that we didn't have to use them. I attended Greenfield Central School in Newbridge, and all the school children were assigned to the neighbourhood houses. If an air-raid warning sounded while we were at school, we would have to take our gas masks and run to the house to which we had been assigned. After the 'all clear' siren, we would walk back to our classroom at school.

At night we would cover our windows with dark material so that no light would show through to give aid to the enemy planes. 'Put up the blackouts' my mother would say, when we lit our oil lamps in the evening. The air-raid wardens would patrol the area and let us know if any light could be seen from the windows. Living so far out in the country, at Ty Bach, we were grateful that we did not have any bombings near us. However, we did hear the enemy planes flying over and hear the air raid sirens, and it was very, very frightening to me, especially at night.

In due course we were issued with ration books as some food stuffs were rationed, butter, cheese, sugar, meat and sweets. My father always kept a garden of potatoes and other vegetables, and we kept some chickens, so we always had enough to eat. My mother made the tastiest dinners. I still remember the delicious aroma of her stew when we would come in from school, and we could hardly wait for my father to come home from work so that we could all enjoy it.

The big excitement for Mynyddislwyn was the installation of a searchlight battery on one of the fields of Mr. Jones, Church Farm, by the British Army. It created an immense interest amongst the people who would gather in the field to look at it. Later on though, it became 'off limits'.

Mynyddislwyn Church holds many memories for me. For a couple of years Dorothy Miles and myself pumped the Church organ (which was a pipe organ in those days) for Katie James, our organist. I remember that the Church bells were not allowed to ring during the War. They could only be rung in the event of an enemy invasion. We missed hearing them ringing on a Sunday as we hurried to church services.

But my special memory of Mynyddislwyn Church was my wedding to American Serviceman Walter Fritz, whom I'd met while working as a typist at the American Army Headquarters, in Newport. My father gave me away and my two sisters, Rosemary and Holly, were my bridesmaids. Canon B. Jones-Evans officiated. I remember the pretty white roses that I had placed on the altar were from the flower garden of Harry Allen. Afterwards friends and family all enjoyed a lovely reception which my mother had prepared for us, in the Church Vestry.

I will always remember Mynyddislwyn with the greatest affection. We were far removed from the bombings and horrors that so many places experienced during the War. I will always remember the little things - the scent of new mown hay, listening for a cuckoo in the spring, picking water violets and forget-me-nots in our fields, and seeing the fantastic view from our little cottage.

Mynyddislwyn was the best place to be - even in World War II.

Foot note. Mrs Fritz has lived in America for over fifty years.

- - - - -

Memories of Mrs. Myfannwy Carpenter.

About the War, there isn't much that I can say as I was working long hours and spent little time at home. In the early part of the War I worked as a nurse at Llanfrechfa Grange Maternity Hospital, then later as a cashier with the British Alumunium Company, where I stayed until after my marriage and the birth of my baby boy.

The soldiers were first based at the Old Factory, opposite the pond that fed the old Woollen Factory. Then they moved to the Lemage above St. Tudor's Church, and afterwards on to Church Farm where they stayed all the time the War was on. Every Friday mother made a large loaf cake for them, which they said they enjoyed. Also on Friday, after dinner, they went down to Nine Mile Point Colliery to bath at the pit-head baths. Mother used to have two of them every Sunday, when they had 24 hours leave, to spend the day with us just for a little break. That was when we lived at Old Factory Cottage. Mother also had three evacuees, two boys and a girl, who still keep in touch.

- - - - -

Memories of Mr. Roy Fox.
My grandparents on my father's side came to live on the Mynyddislwyn Mountain (overlooking Newbridge) about 1912. After a few changes of address, we moved to Ton y Moch in 1939.

My grandfather trained sheep dogs and sold them on Mynyddislwyn Mountain. My father assisted his father in the moving of sheep from the Mountain to the Market at Pontllanfraith (where there is now a small garage on The Tramroad, opposite the Greyhound Pub), and thence to the sidings at Pontllanfraith Low Level railway station.

During the War my father was in the Home Guard. I remember firing practice in Cwmnantyrodyn Quarry. During the War I remember the troops at Church Farm and a search light sited near the parish Church. I also recall going into school late on Tuesday mornings after fetching fresh eggs for the headmaster from Graig Farm (behind Church Farm), a trip of some $2^1/_2$ miles before school.

One Saturday morning in 1941 I was with my father and brother on the way to grandfather's to 'kill the pig', when we heard of the death of my grandfather. Father sent us home, and the pig had a reprieve, for a very short time, because of the Killing Licence, with its strict terms and limits, and its enforcement by the police, and not least the cost of a new licence.

I recall the snow and ice of 1947. My father had horses, and during that time they were used for transporting anything and everything, including a specially adapted sleigh to move 140 lb. bags of flour from the main road to Windyridge Bakery.

- - - - -

This seems the appropriate part of the book to include a mention of the Land Girls, some of whom were stationed on the Mountain. Soldiers, sailors and airmen may have risked their lives for their country in the War but behind them was an army of volunteers who helped to keep us fed. Nationwide, more than 80,000 women volunteered to work as farm labourers during the War, and at the end of the conflict they were producing more than 70% of the food in Britain, and keeping bread off the rationing list.

Work on the farm was hard and it was not unusual for girls to begin work at 4 a.m and be in bed by 9-30 p.m. Work would start before breakfast and often involved getting the cows in from the fields for milking.

Birds of Mynyddislwyn

by J.M. Steer

Mynyddislwyn Mountain and its surrounding parish provides a home to over 60 different species of resident and visiting birds. Its attractiveness lies in the rich variety of habitats of deciduous and evergreen woodland in combination with pasture, ponds and heath. Most of the familiar bird families as we know them have been established for over three million years and much of their evolution has been closely linked to our own. In comparison the last millennium is short on the evolutionary time scale. However, population density, changing farming practices, and, particularly over the last two hundred years or so, industrialisation, have all greatly affected the local environment and the birds in it.

The present day landscape on The Mountain is dominated by hill farming. Sheep and cattle graze and fertilise the ground as they go about their daily business, the result of which creates a patchwork of rich organic ground. Pastureland such as this provides an important habitat for a variety of birds capitalising on the insects, beetles, parasites and seeds to be found here.

Daily visitors include the Lesser Black Backed and Herring Gulls which flight from their coastal roosts in the morning, returning late in the evening. These birds have adapted to this inland habitat to use the valuable food source, sharing it with resident Pied Wagtails and Meadow Pipits. The latter spends the summer breeding in pairs but during the winter can be seen at night in small communal roosts on the ground. Another bird frequently seen on the pasture fields is the Buzzard, feeding off carrion and worms, which forms the bulk of its diet, or soaring high on the thermals which carry it effortlessly. By far the most common residents to The Mountain are the crow family. Magpies, Jays and Carrion Crows can be seen and heard all year round, while the Jackdaws are in their greatest numbers during the summer.

Dotted around The Mountain are a number of deciduous woods rich in caterpillars, flies and other invertebrates. It is here that the Great Spotted Woodpecker, with its striking red topped head, and the laughing call of the Green Woodpecker, can be seen and heard. These birds exploit the bark-creeping saprophytic bugs using an enormously long tongue. Other birds to exploit this habitat include the camouflaged Treecreeper, with its narrow, slightly curved beak, and the Nuthatch, with its short well built beak, to exploit the less accessible places in the trees' armour. All have individual tools for their jobs, but each needs to be alert for the ghostly Sparrowhawk, which patrols in silence for the unaware. An ambush predator, this bird is discrete in its presence, often unnoticed by the casual observer, it is only betrayed by the scolding songbirds it pursues for food. The other hunter, which has become much more popular in recent years, is the Peregrine Falcon, which enjoys a number of isolated quarry faces on The Mountain.

Although modern farming does not encourage the Barn Owl, these majestic birds are still to be seen on The Mountain, along with other smaller species of Owl. At one time every farm building had its triangular hole in the end wall, to encourage the Barn Owl to rid that building of rats and mice.

In addition to the visiting choirs at St. Tudor's Church, The Mountain is guest to a number of impressive bird vocalists. A welcome resident to the area is the Skylark, inhabiting the rough grassland of Mynydd y Lan and the scattered gorse across the top. This bird is in national decline. A small but sprightly bird, it is a pleasure to watch it spring with a distinguishing voluminous call and flight which takes the bird vertically to a small speck in the sky before plumetting back to the ground, singing all the way.

One of the more unusual sounds belongs to the Lapwing, a handsome and conspicuous bird, with a particularly individual wandering cry. Although groups of between 20 and 30 gather on occasions, there are normally no more than one or two during the winter. Known as 'the farmer's friend' because of its pest-eating diet, this bird is in some decline, and many will remember larger numbers breeding in past years.

The Curlew represents the soloist of the choir with its distinctive plaintiff cry, ending in an exciting babbling chorus. Its song is as noticeable as its long curved bill, designed for probing the soft foreshore mud for invertebrates and small molluscs. It is the abundant insect life required for its young which brings it from the Bristol Channel to breed on The Mountain in April.

In addition to many resident birds on The Mountain there are a good number which visit for shorter periods. The most notable long distance migrants are the Swallows, Swifts and House Martins. Many of these travel from the far south of Africa, over 2,000 miles away, to take advantage of conditions for breeding. Arriving in April or May these birds breed hurriedly to coincide with the abundance of summer food supply.

Other summer visitors include the Willow Warbler, Blackcap and Chiffchaf, along with the Redstart, a striking bird whose diminutive presence but cheerful song is a pleasure to hear. The Wheatear is another visitor from Africa, with its striking white rump and plumage, attracted to The Mountain by the network of stone walls that it uses for a nest site. The Cuckoo's famous call has been heard less in recent years but glimpses can be found on Mynydd y Lan seeking out the nest of a suitable foster parent.

Winter also has its share of visitors fleeing the colder climate of northern Europe, such as the Fieldfare and Redwing, both members of the Thrush family. Commonly seen in November in large groups, these birds enjoy the fruits of the holly and ivy. However, as winter food diminishes on The Mountain, so too do the birds. Two more secretive visitors are the Snipe and Woodcock. Present in small numbers, the Woodcock take advantage of the worm-rich pastures at night, and the large areas of forestry where they can rest in peace during the day. Migrating from the Scandinavian countries, these birds generally arrive in two waves in October and November, usually coinciding with a full moon.

Ducks and Herons have exploited the demise of the valleys' heavy industries, breeding on the Sirhowy and Ebbw rivers which were once so heavily polluted.

Like a barometer, their numbers have increased steadily over recent years with improved conditions, and both are attracted to the numerous mountain ponds and pools. Herons are communal breeders and have established themselves a small colony at nearby Crosskeys. Birds from that colony travel alone to use our quiet ponds, feeding on small fish, insects, water snails, frog-spawn, tadpoles and even frogs.

Mallard also use the ponds, particularly during the winter, flighting in to feed at dusk and off at dawn to large areas of water to rest. The small, secretive and colourful Teal also use these sources of water, many of which have migrated from Russia, the Baltic Sea and eastern Europe to spend the winter in our part of the world. When you consider the distances that these birds travel you realise what Mynyddislwyn Mountain has to offer.

Acknowledgements

National Assembly of Wales Air Photography Department.
National Library of Wales.
National Museum of Wales.
Newport Reference Library.
Public Record Office.
Mr. Rimmer and Staff at County Record Office.
Royal Commission of Historical and Ancient Monuments.
Welsh Rural Life Museum, Saint Fagans.

Throughout this book I have quoted from the 1839 Tithe Apportionment Book, the 1846 Tithe Map, and the little booklet about the childhood memories of Mrs. Ann Meyrick. I have also quoted from Bradney's Hundred of Newport, The History of Mynyddislwyn Agricultural Society, New Bethel by Gareth Griffiths and John Lambert, and Stone and Steam in the Black Mountains.

The following have provided information or photographs in compiling this book and the author is extremely grateful for their assistance.

Michael Blackmore	Alan Booth	Donald Brean
Jean Burland	Ralph Caple	Mrs. M. Carpenter
Jan and Henry Chivers	Faith Coller	Robert Collins
Col. Cook	Barbara Davies	Granville Davies
Lionel Davies	Peter Downing	Tony Edwards
C. Fish	Granville Fox	Roy Fox
Mrs. J. Francis	Foster Frowen	Jan and Chris Galloway
Ann and Selwyn Gardiner	Margaret Gorman	Mrs. H. Greenslade
Dr. Madeline Grey	G. Harry	Dr. Glyn Harris
Janet Hazell	Dr. John James	Neil James
Ann Jardine	Betty Jenkins	Dorinda Jones
Drusilla Jones	Mike Jones	John Lewis
Lionel Milsom	Bert Morgan	Betty Morgan
Ted Morgan	Vince Morris	Mr. and Mrs. Payne
Herb Powell	Terry Powell	Rita and John Purnell
Glyn Roberts	Margaret Roberts	John Roberts
Beryl Rumble	Alan Sharpe	Rose Skull and sisters
J.M. Steer	David Taylor	Mr. and Mrs. D. Thomas
Margaret Thomas	John Venn	Graham Waters
Mrs. Cissie Way	Alan Webb	Iris West
Ena Williams	Joan and John Williams	Odette and Ken Williams

Special and sincere gratitude is due to those who have made financial contributions towards the publication of this book. Without their most generous support it would not have been produced and the author's appreciation is absolute.

Particular thanks are also extended to the small committee for its involvement from the very beginning. Again, without the members' prolonged efforts in raising the necessary funds, a book there would not be!

A SELECTION OF OTHER TITLES OF THE SURROUNDING AREA
AVAILABLE FROM OLD BAKEHOUSE PUBLICATIONS

0 9512181 6 6	Blackwood Yesterday, Book 1	Ewart Smith
1 874538 65 4	Blackwood Yesterday, Book 2	Ewart Smith
1 874538 76 X	Blackwood Yesterday, Book 3	Ewart Smith
1 874538 29 8	Blackwood Yesterday, Book 4	Ewart Smith
0 9512181 4 X	A Look at Old Tredegar, Vol. 1	Philip Prosser
1 874538 81 6	A Look at Old Tredegar, Vol. 2	Philip Prosser
1 874538 01 8	Collieries of the Sirhowy Valley	Rayner Rosser
1 874538 40 9	Portrait of Rhymney, Vol. 1	Marion Evans
1 874538 70 0	Portrait of Rhymney, Vol. 2	Marion Evans
1 874538 41 7	Portrait of Rhymney, Vol. 3	Marion Evans
1 874538 02 6	Portrait of Rhymney, Vol. 4	Marion Evans
1 874538 11 5	A History of Fochriw, Vol. 1	Peter Price
1 874538 56 5	A History of Fochriw, Vol. 2	Peter Price
0 9512181 5 8	Old Aberbeeg & Llanhilleth, Vol. 1	Bill Pritchard
1 874538 35 2	Old Aberbeeg & Llanhilleth, Vol. 2	Bill Pritchard
1 874538 97 2	Look Back at Old Aberbeeg & Llanhilleth	Thomas & Morris
1 874538 37 9	Look Back at Old Abertillery, Vol. 1	Thomas & Morris
1 874538 31 X	Bargoed & Gilfach, Vol. 1	Paul James
1 874538 07 7	Bargoed & Gilfach, Vol. 2	Paul James
1 874538 64 6	Bargoed & Gilfach, Vol. 3	Paul James
0 9512181 7 4	The Black Domain	Ralph Thomas
1 874538 66 2	A Picture Book of Cwm, Vol. 1	Margaret Blackwell
1 874538 92 1	A Picture Book of Cwm, Vol. 2	Margaret Blackwell
1 874538 06 9	The Flavour of Islwyn Remembered	Kay Jenkins
1 874538 85 9	Folklore of Blaenau Gwent	BGBC Planning Dept.
1 874538 12 3	Glimpses of Gwent, Book 1	Gareth John
1 874538 34 4	Glimpses of Gwent, Book 2	Gareth John
1 874538 79 4	Old Gelligaer	Griffiths & Herold
0 9512181 9 0	Hills of Fire and Iron	Peter Morgan Jones
1 874538 91 3	Place Names of Eastern Gwent	Osborne & Hobbs
1 874538 59 X	Place Names of Western Gwent	Osborne & Hobbs
1 874538 86 7	Pictorial Memories of Old Pontypool, Vol. 1	Bryan Roden
1 874538 04 2	Pictorial Memories of Old Pontypool, Vol. 2	Bryan Roden
1 874538 80 8	Trinant in Photographs	Clive Daniels
1 874538 69 7	Senghenydd	J. Basil Phillips
1 874538 39 5	Old Ystrad Mynach in Photographs, Vol. 1	Griffiths & Herold
1 874538 57 3	Old Abercarn Urban District	David Taylor
1 874538 17 4	The Aneurin Bevan Inheritance	Gareth Jones
1 874538 46 8	History of Webbs Brewery Aberbeeg	Ray Morris